Beyond Cheering and Bashing

Beyond Cheering and Bashing: New Perspectives on The Closing of the American Mind

Edited by
William K. Buckley
and
James Seaton

Bowling Green State University Popular Press
Bowling Green, Ohio 43403

Contents

Introduction
On Horace Mann, Jay Gatsby and Allan Bloom

The Closing of the American Mind may no longer be on the bestseller lists, but the debate over the central issue confronted in *Closing*—the role of the university and the liberal arts in the United States—has become increasingly urgent and contentious. Now that the uproar over the work itself has died down, it is possible to consider Allan Bloom's contribution to the overall debate from a broader perspective. Accordingly, the goal of this collection is not to record another series of yeas and nays on Bloom, but rather to consider what one may learn about the dilemmas confronting American culture through a consideration of both *The Closing of the American Mind* and the debate it has aroused. Our contributors differ among themselves as to the validity of both the diagnoses and the solutions Bloom offers, yet they refuse to engage in "Bloom-bashing" or hero-worship. (The goal of this volume is to place the debate over *Closing* within a larger context than a book review format allows.)

We will not summarize the views of the individual essays here, nor count up the "pro" or "anti" contributions. We will, instead, point out some of the connections between one essay that does not deal directly with *The Closing of the American Mind* (Christopher Lasch's "The Great Experiment: Where Did It Go Wrong?") and the issues raised by *Closing*. Lasch's study provides the sort of historical perspective that has rarely informed the controversy over Bloom. If, as Christopher Lasch argues, American public education is in large part the result of generations of reformers, of whom Horace Mann was one of the first and most influential, the philosophy of reform must be held at least partially responsible for "the wreckage of the school system in America" (1). Bloom's ideas, then, cannot be dismissed simply because they contradict contemporary versions of the "liberal humanitarianism" (8) professed by Horace Mann and the other reformers.

Bloom's book repays study as a work of literature. *The Closing of the American Mind* may not be a novel, as Robert Wolff suggested with malice aforethought, but the book can be read as a "confession," governed, in Northrop Frye's words, "by a creative, and therefore fictional, impulse to select only those events and experiences in the writer's life that go to build up an integrated pattern" (307). To consider *Closing* as literature need not be an exercise in deconstruction nor a polite way of avoiding the book's ideas. The emotional impact of *Closing* on both admirers and bashers does suggest that the book is more than the sum of its opinions; it is, perhaps, a "confession," whose main character evokes an intensity of response beyond the protagonists of most novels. It may be, indeed, that an understanding of both the narrator of *Closing* as a dramatic voice, and the resonance of that voice in our society, may be best

1

achieved by a comparison of Bloom's work to one of the great American novels. For the Allan Bloom portrayed in *Closing* bears a striking resemblance to the eponymous protagonist of F. Scott Fitzgerald's *The Great Gatsby*.

One way to gain some perspective on the issues raised by Bloom's subtitle—"higher education has failed democracy and impoverished the souls of today's students"—is to take a new look at the philosophy of the founder of the American public school system, Horace Mann. Mann argued for an educational system that would serve as an agency of democratization. He succeeded in getting his ideas adopted throughout the nation—and yet, notes Christopher Lasch, that very success raises fundamental questions about the ideas themselves, since the school system which Horace Mann influenced so pervasively seems today to have largely failed in its mission, not only as a stimulus to democracy but also as a transmitter of basic skills and information. This failure prompts Lasch to pose a question that is central to *The Closing of the American Mind* as well: "...whether liberal humanitarianism provides the best recipe for a democratic society" (8). Bloom is content to argue that the *ethos* that informs the university, and particularly the elite, research university, should function as a kind of conservative counterweight to the democratic impulses of the larger society, about which, it seems, a philosopher can do little or nothing. Bloom is not so concerned with reforming society as he is with ensuring that some public space is preserved within which "the philosophers" can teach and think. Lasch, on the other hand, goes even further, suggesting that the governing spirit of the entire public school system must be challenged. The preservation and invigoration of republican institutions requires, Lasch seems to be saying, an end to the hegemony of liberal humanitarianism—which need not entail, it is important to note, the end of either liberalism or humanitarianism.

Lasch suggests that Mann's ideas about the treatment of war, religion and politics in the classroom reveal the limitations of the "liberal humanitarian" view. Lasch offers his criticisms on behalf of democratic principles themselves, not because of any sympathy for a more stratified society or any nostalgia for a simpler past. In doing so Lasch differentiates liberalism from both democracy and the "republican tradition," thus implicitly differing with those who conflate the philosophy of liberal humanitarianism with democracy itself. Like Mann, Lasch aims for schooling that would enable students to become citizens of a republic rather than mere subjects of a state. The useful subject need not learn anything beyond the skills of a trade, while the citizen of a republic must be ready to judge and debate the public issues confronting society as a whole.

Lasch notes that Horace Mann, in common with most progressive thinkers, abhorred not only war but also its accompanying attitudes. Arguing that education should not rouse "the dissocial emotions" (9) connected with war, Mann ignored the ways in which the attitudes associated with war and military life are not "dissocial" at all. Although Mann called himself a republican, his views reveal the decline of a "republican tradition" which had emphasized the "connection between martial virtue and citizenship" (9). Lasch points out that any society requires citizens with "courage, patience and fortitude" (11), and democracies especially need citizens willing to make personal sacrifices—for the public good. The "virtue" which Mann praises as simply the opposite of "vice" has neither public importance nor any association with activity and power. Mann and his fellow reformers, with their emphasis on private morality, lose sight of the assertive, public-spirited virtue which distinguishes the republican citizen from the subject of a monarchy.

Lasch argues further that Mann's fear of warlike emotions led him to press for an educational system where the emotions of politics and religion would also be muted, thereby allowing citizens to live together in harmony. Mann believed, as Lasch puts it, that "Nothing of educational value...could issue from the clash of opinions, the noise and heat of political and religious debate" (22). Mann's ideal world "was a world in which everyone agreed, a heavenly city where the angels sang in unison" (19). It is this utopian ideal, with all its undeniable appeal, that arouses Lasch's strongest criticisms. Mann was suspicious of war because it is the most destructive form of conflict, but he was also afraid of the passions raised by political disagreement and the sectarianism of religion as well. The earthly version of his "heavenly city" is a society where people go about their business without bothering or even disagreeing with one another. Mann ignored the possibility that such harmony occurs only when citizens have nothing very important about which to disagree. The citizens of his ideal polity would not be zealots, but they would likewise have no particular "love of liberty" (21), as Orestes Brownson noted, nor of anything else.

Today, according to Allan Bloom, American students are taught that there are finally no matters really worth fighting about or even arguing about. All choices are equally "valid," since all can be reduced to questions of personal preference. The notorious "openness" of the American mind is achieved only by "closing" itself to the possibility that any principles are truly important, any cause worth dying for, any love worth a lifetime commitment. When Bloom criticizes those Americans who "...cannot believe that any really intelligent and good person does not at bottom share the Will Rogers *Weltanschauung,* 'I never met a man I didn't like' " (225), he is not criticizing American *naivete* or benevolence so much as the comfortable assumption that there are no differences worth arguing about. What's a difference of opinion among friends? Bloom is not so much interested in spreading his own philosophy as he is in creating an atmosphere in which it is possible to live the "serious life," a life in which one must indeed make choices, but in which there is no guarantee that all the choices are the right ones:

A serious life means being fully aware of the alternatives, thinking about them with all the intensity one brings to bear on life-and-death questions, in full recognition that every choice is a great risk with necessary consequences that are hard to bear. (227)

Contemporary American culture, on the other hand, encourages "choice" but implies the triviality of the decisions we are called to make by telling us that all choices are equally valid:

America has no-fault automobile accidents, no-fault divorces, and it is moving with the aid of modern philosophy toward no-fault choices. (228)

A world in which everyone agrees—Mann's "perfect world"—may be "a heavenly city where the angels sing in unison" (19), but its twentieth century embodiment is also a world where nobody listens because nothing really matters. Bloom cautions that a culture which deprives philosophy, politics and literature of their intensity thereby ensures the appeal of "charismatic" figures whose intensities derive from other, more questionable sources. In contemporary America, for example, many people "who are good democratic liberals, lovers of peace and gentleness" all too easily allow themselves to be "...struck dumb with admiration for individuals threatening or using the most terrible violence for the slightest and tawdriest reasons," since the resort to violence seems a proof of "real commitment, which they themselves lack" (221).

Horace Mann wanted to create a system of public education that would nourish a democratic polity. He perceived the dangers to democracy in political and religious sectarianism, and he succeeded in creating a public school system which functioned as the so-called "melting-pot," countering ethnic and religious divisions—at least where legalized segregation did not foreclose that possibility. On the other hand, Lasch notes that our public school system cannot be called a success even by Mann's own standards: "We have incorporated into our schools the worst of Mann and somehow managed to lose sight of the best" (23). Teaching is still regarded as a less than "honorable calling," academic standards have declined rather than risen, and schools succeed neither in teaching "purely academic subjects" (23) nor in instilling the "character traits" (24) Mann thought would compensate for any "loss of intellectual rigor" (23).

If Christopher Lasch is right in thinking that the time is right to ask whether the governing philosophy of American education has not been "insufficiently liberal and humanitarian but whether liberal humanitarianism provides the best recipe for a democratic society" (8), then perhaps it is time to read *The Closing of the American Mind* with careful attention, rather than denouncing it out of hand as "insufficiently liberal and humanitarian." Bloom argues that in the interests of democracy itself, it is the university's mission to resist the dominant *ethos* of democratic society:

It is necessary that there be an unpopular institution in our midst that sets clarity above well-being or compassion, that resists our powerful urges and temptations, that is free of all snobbism but has standards. (252)

Since, as Tocqueville correctly perceived, the "great democratic danger...is enslavement to public opinion" (246), the university must, for the good of the larger society, articulate principles to which defenders of the unpopular or the unfashionable can appeal. In a society ruled by tradition, it would be the task of the university to defend the new by appealing to critical reason. But

in a democracy it [the university] risks less by opposing the emergent, the changing and the ephemeral than by embracing them, because the society is already open to them, without monitoring what it accepts or sufficiently respecting the old. There the university risks less by having intransigently high standards than by trying to be too inclusive, because the society tends to blur standards in the name of equality. (253)

Thus Bloom agrees with many of his left opponents in arguing that the university should encourage a critical perspective toward contemporary society, agrees indeed that such encouragement is the first duty of the university. But is it possible to institutionalize a spirit of criticism? Christopher Lasch's presentation of nineteenth century progressivism suggests how easily the mission of enlightenment can be transmuted into a drive to conformity. Just as Horace Mann's reasonable antipathy to war led to a more questionable fear of the divisive powers of literature, religion and politics in the public schools, so present-day progressives move from an uncontroversial rejection of racism to an embrace of "diversity" as an all-sufficing formula for "togetherness." When "diversity" becomes an official slogan, all too often an atmosphere is created in which "privileging" agreements or works on the basis of the criteria of disciplines such as philosophy, history and literary study becomes a suspect activity, evidence of a lack of political correctness. Proponents of "diversity" thus become agents of a new conformity, sniffing out morally objectionable attitudes among those who insist on making distinctions on intellectual rather than ideological grounds. Bloom would argue that such campus radicals are not so much critics of contemporary society as followers of its most pervasive trends or even fashions. Whatever side one takes in this debate, Christopher Lasch's critique of Horace Mann suggests that the issues raised by *The Closing of the American Mind* have an importance beyond the "twenty or thirty best universities" (22) about whose students Bloom claims acquaintance. If education in a democracy needs to be guided by principles other than those of "liberal humanitarianism," then *The Closing of the American Mind* is a good place to start looking for alternatives. Bloom has been accused of a great many things, but nobody yet has called him a "liberal humanitarian."

In the "Foreword" to *Closing* Saul Bellow found that Bloom was "willing to take the risks more frequently taken by writers," daring to discuss the "truest truths" in a "profoundly personal" way (12). The "republic of letters" was once capacious enough to include history, biography, and philosophy, not to mention sermons and political oratory, as well as poetry, literature and drama. *The Closing of the American Mind* can be read as an intellectual autobiography, a "confession" in the tradition of *The Education of Henry Adams*, Thomas Mann's *Reflections of a Nonpolitical Man*, or the *Confessions* of Rousseau and St. Augustine.

Yet perhaps the drama of Bloom's work can best be captured by a comparison to an American novel, F. Scott Fitzgerald's *The Great Gatsby*. Like Bloom the protagonist is a Midwesterner who finds on the shores of the Great Lakes a world utterly unlike the rest of the Midwest. Like Bloom, James Gatz is more than willing to undertake the personal transformation which entrance to that world requires. James Gatz became Jay Gatsby as soon as he met the millionaire Dan Cody at Little Girl Bay off Lake Superior. Cody's yacht "represented all the beauty and glamour in the world" (100-101) to the young Midwesterner. Gatsby's enchantment with the possibilities represented by that yacht leads him to "the service of a vast, vulgar, and meretricious beauty" (99). This "service" ends, of course, in Gatsby's own disillusion and death. Nor has Gatsby harmed only himself: his association with Meyer Wolfsheim of the "Swastika Holding

Company'' (171) suggests that Gatsby was complicit in a variety of crimes, including murder, bootlegging and perhaps fixing the World Series. Nevertheless, knowing all this, Nick Carraway in his last words can shout "They're a rotten crowd... You're worth the whole damn bunch put together" (154). This is said in the heat of the moment, yet it is Nick's collected reflection that Gatsby possessed "some heightened sensitivity to the promises of life... an extraordinary gift for hope, a romantic readiness" which allows him to assert, thinking over the whole story, that "Gatsby turned out all right at the end" (2).

Of course *The Closing of the American Mind* does not suggest that Allan Bloom is intoxicated with wealth, but his first sight of the University of Chicago seems as determinative an event as Gatsby's sighting of Dan Cody's yacht:

When I was fifteen years old I saw the University of Chicago for the first time and somehow sensed that I had discovered my life. (243)

Just as the yacht stands for a world beyond North Dakota, a world beautiful and complete in itself, so the "fake Gothic buildings" of the University of Chicago are different from anything Bloom has seen before in a "Middle West... not known for the splendor of its houses of worship or its monuments of political glory" (243). For the first time, the fifteen-year-old Allan Bloom saw structures

...evidently dedicated to a higher purpose, not to necessity or utility, not merely to shelter or manufacture or trade, but to something that might be an end in itself. (243)

Unlike Gatsby, however, Allan Bloom was not so transfixed by his first vision of possibility that he became incapable of further discrimination. Gatsby remains "faithful to the end" to his first vision, the sort, says Fitzgerald, "that a seventeen-year-old boy would be likely to invent" (99). Bloom, on the other hand, comes to learn that the buildings "were fake, and that Gothic is not really my taste" (243). He tells himself that the university is "after all only a vehicle for contents in principle separable from it" (245). Still, he does not renounce his original discovery that possibilities unknown or obscure in the outside world reside in the university: "For me the promise of these buildings was fully kept" (244). Bloom retains, that is, despite his anger—which is all most of his critics have noticed—"an extraordinary gift for hope, a romantic readiness" to discover spiritual greatness, true philosophy, true friendship at the university—the same institution denominated already in the sixties as the "multiversity" by a pragmatic Clark Kerr.

Undoubtedly Bloom's exhilaration blinds him to much that others see. He refers quite straightforwardly to "the philosophers" who, ancient and modern, "were perfectly conscious of what separates them from all other men, and they knew that the gulf is unbridgeable" (290). Fitzgerald's famous comment about the rich in the opening of "The Rich Boy" is equally Bloom's thesis about "the philosophers": "They are different from you and me... They are different" (177). Jay Gatsby never wavered in his acceptance of that faith. F. Scott Fitzgerald, however, was quite capable of seeing through the aura of the "very rich", as "The Rich Boy" itself demonstrates. There is nothing in *The Closing of the*

American Mind that suggests that Bloom is capable of any comparable skepticism about "the philosophers."

And yet Bloom's wholehearted commitment to his vision of the philosophical life as the life most worth living, narrow and flawed though that vision may be, allows him to articulate insights that any less grandiose vision would not have allowed. It may not be true that

Men may live more truly and fully in reading Plato and Shakespeare than at any other time, because then they are participating in essential being and forgetting their accidental lives. (380)

"Essential being" may not be what one "participates" in when reading Shakespeare or even Plato. It seems likely, however, that one who accepts some version of this assertion is more likely to attain generosity of mind than those whose beliefs are bounded by the orthodoxies of the present, "politically correct" or not. Whatever Bloom's flaws, he has retained a sense of wonder and of possibility that go far to redeem the serious limitations of *The Closing of the American Mind* justifiably emphasized in many of the following essays. (The essays for this volume are printed by permission of their respective authors.)

Works Cited

Bellow, Saul. Foreword. *The Closing of the American Mind: How Higher Education Has Failed Democracy and Impoverished the Souls of Today's Students.* By Allan Bloom. New York: Simon and Schuster, 1987.

Bloom, Allan. *The Closing of the American Mind: How Higher Education Has Failed Democracy and Impoverished the Souls of Today's Students.* New York: Simon and Schuster, 1987.

Fitzgerald, F. Scott. *The Great Gatsby.* 1925. New York: Charles Scribner's Sons, 1953.

———. "The Rich Boy." *The Stories of F. Scott Fitzgerald.* ed. Malcolm Cowley. New York: Charles Scribner's Sons, 1951. 177-208.

Frye, Northrop. *Anatomy of Criticism: Four Essays.* Princeton: Princeton UP, 1957.

Lasch, Christopher. "The Great Experiment: Where Did It Go Wrong?" *Beyond Cheering and Bashing: New Perspectives on The Closing of the American Mind.* Ed. William K. Buckley and James Seaton. Bowling Green: BGSU Popular P, 1991.

William K. Buckley
James Seaton

The Great Experiment:
Where Did It Go Wrong?

Christopher Lasch

If we cast a cold eye over the wreckage of the school system in America, we may find it hard to avoid the impression that something went radically wrong at some point; and it is not surprising, therefore, that so many critics of the system have turned to the past in the hope of explaining just when things went wrong and how they might be set to rights. The critics of the fifties traced the trouble to progressive ideologies, which allegedly made things too easy for the child and drained the curriculum of its intellectual rigor. In the sixties, a wave of revisionist historians insisted that the school system had come to serve as a "sorting machine," in Joel Spring's phrase—a device for allocating social privileges that reinforced class divisions while ostensibly promoting equality. Some of these revisionists went so far as to argue that the common school system was distorted from the outset by the requirements of the emerging industrial order, which made it almost inevitable that the schools would be used not to train an alert, politically active body of citizens but to inculcate habits of punctuality and obedience.

There is a good deal to be learned from the debates that took place in the formative period of the school system, but an analysis of those debates will not support any such one-dimensional interpretation of the school's function as an agency of "social control." I do not see how anyone who reads the writings of Horace Mann, which did so much to justify a system of common schools and to persuade Americans to pay for it, can miss the moral fervor and democratic idealism that informed Mann's program. It is true that Mann resorted to a variety of arguments in favor of common schools, including the argument that they would teach steady habits of work. But he insisted that steady habits would benefit workers as well as employers, citing in favor of this contention the higher wages earned by those who enjoyed the advantages of a good education. He was careful to point out, moreover, that a positive assessment of the effects of schooling on men's "worldly fortunes or estates" was far from the "highest" argument in favor of education. Indeed it might "justly be regarded as the lowest." (V:81) More important arguments for education, in Mann's view, were the "diffusion of useful knowledge," the promotion of tolerance, the equalization of opportunity, the "augmentation of national resources," the eradication of poverty, the overcoming of "mental imbecility and torpor," the encouragement of light and learning in place of "superstition and ignorance," and the substitution of peaceful methods of governance for coercion and warfare. (IV:10; V:68, 81, 101, 109; VII:187) If Mann pretty clearly preferred the high ground of moral principle to the lower ground of industrial expediency, he could still appeal to prudential motives with a good conscience, since he did not perceive a contradiction between them. Comforts and conveniences were good things in themselves, even if there were loftier goods to strive for. His vision of "improvement" was broad enough to embrace material as well as moral progress; it was precisely their compatibility, indeed their inseparability, that distinguished Mann's version of the idea of progress from those that merely celebrated the wonders of modern science and technology.

As a child of the Enlightenment, Mann yielded to no one in his admiration for science and technology; but he was also a product of New England Puritanism, even though he came to reject Puritan theology. He was too keenly aware of the moral burden Americans inherited from their seventeenth-century ancestors to see a higher standard of living as an end in itself or to join those who equated the promise of American life with the opportunity to get rich quick. He did not look kindly on the project of getting enormously rich even in the long run. He deplored extremes of wealth and poverty—the "European theory" of social organization, as he called it—and upheld the "Massachusetts theory," which stressed "equality of condition" and "human welfare." (XII:55) It was to escape "extremes of high and low," Mann believed, that Americans had "fled" Europe in the first place; and the re-emergence of those extremes, in nineteenth-century New England, should have been a source of deepest shame to his countrymen. (VII:188, 191) When Mann dwelled on the accomplishments of his ancestors, it was with the intention of holding Americans to a higher standard of civic obligation than the standard prevailing in other countries. His frequent appeals to the "heroic period of our country's history" did not issue from a "boastful or vain-glorious spirit," he said. An appreciation of America's mission brought "more humiliation than pride." (VII:195) America should have "stood as a shining mark and exemplar before the world," instead of which it was lapsing into materialism and moral indifference. (VII:196)

It is quite pointless to ask whether reformers like Horace Mann were more interested in humanitarianism than in work discipline and "social control." A good deal of fruitless debate among historians has been devoted to this question. Mann was not a radical, and he was undeniably interested in social order, but that does not make him any less a humanitarian. He was genuinely moved by the spectacle of poverty and suffering, though he also feared that poverty and suffering would breed "agrarianism," as he and his contemporaries called it— the "revenge of poverty against wealth." (XII:60) When he preached the duty to "bring forward those unfortunate classes of the people, who, in the march of civilization, have been left in the rear," there is no reason to think that he was concerned only with the danger of social revolution. (XII:135) He defended property rights, to be sure, but he denied that property rights were "absolute and unqualified." (X:115) The earth was given to mankind "for the subsistence and benefit of the whole race," and the "rights of successive owners" were "limited by the rights of those who are entitled to the subsequent possession and use." (X:114-15) Every generation had an obligation to improve its inheritance and to pass it on to the next. "The successive generations of men, taken, collectively, constitute one great commonwealth." (X:127) The doctrine of absolute property rights, which denied the solidarity of mankind, was a morality for "hermits." (X:120) In Mann's view, the "successive holders" of property were "trustees, bound to the faithful execution of their trust, by the most sacred obligations." (X:127) If they defaulted on those obligations, they could expect "terrible retributions" in the form of "poverty and destitution," "violence and misrule," "licentiousness and debauchery," "political profligacy and legalized perfidy." (X:126) Here Mann was truly prophetic, in the strict sense of the term. He called his people to account, pointing out that they had inherited a demanding set of obligations to live up to and foretelling the "certain vengeance of Heaven" if they failed. (X:126) He was a prophet in the vulgar sense as well: his predictions have come true—his predictions of the specific evils that would assure "knowledge and virtue," the necessary foundations of a republican form of government. (XII:142) Who can look at America today without recognizing the accuracy of Mann's cautionary rhetoric, right down to the "legalized perfidy" of our political leaders? The only thing Mann failed to foresee was the drug epidemic, though that could be included, I suppose, under the heading of "licentiousness and debauchery."

Yet Mann's efforts on behalf of the common schools bore spectacular success, if we consider the long-term goals (and even the immediate goals) he was attempting to promote. His countrymen heeded his exhortations, after all. They built a system of common schools attended by all classes of society. They rejected the European model, which provided a liberal education for the children of privilege and vocational training for the masses. They abolished child labor and made school attendance compulsory, as Mann had urged. They enforced a strict separation between church and state, protecting the schools from sectarian influences. They recognized the need for professional training of teachers, and they set up a system of normal schools to bring about this result. They followed Mann's advice to provide instruction not only in academic subjects but in the "laws of health," vocal music, and other character-forming disciplines. (VI:61, 66) They even followed his advice to staff the schools largely with women, sharing his belief that women were more likely than men to govern their pupils by the gentle art of persuasion. They honored Mann himself, even during his lifetime, as the founding father of their schools. If Mann was a prophet in some respects, he was hardly a prophet without honor in his own country. He succeeded beyond the wildest dreams of most reformers; yet the result was the same as if he had failed.

Here is our puzzle, then: why did the success of Mann's program leave us with the social and political disasters he predicted, with uncanny accuracy, in the event of his failure? To put the question this way suggests that there was something inherently deficient in Mann's educational vision—that his program contained some fatal flaw in its very conception. But if this was the case, we are not likely to find the flaw by harping on "social control" or by rewriting the history of American reform as the "triumph of conservatism," as Gabriel Kolko put it in the title of his history of the progressive movement. This was the favorite strategy of revisionist historians in the sixties; but the strategy is played out. The history of reform—with its high sense of mission, its devotion to progress and improvement, its enthusiasm for economic growth and equal opportunity, its humanitarianism, its love of peace and its hatred of war, its confidence in the welfare state, and above all its zeal for education—was much more the history of liberalism than of anything recognizable as conservatism. If the reform movement gave us a society that bears little resemblance to what was promised, we have to ask, not whether the reform movement was insufficiently liberal and humanitarian but whether liberal humanitarianism provides the best recipe for a democratic society.

We get a little insight into Mann's limitations by considering his powerful aversion to war—superficially one of the more attractive elements of his outlook. Deeply committed to the proposition that a renunciation of war and warlike habits provided an infallible index of social progress, of the victory of civilization over barbarism, Mann complained that school and town libraries were full of history books glorifying war.

How little do these books contain, which is suitable for children!... Descriptions of battles, sackings of cities, and the captivity of nations, follow each other with the quickest movement, and in an endless succession. Almost the only glimpses, which we catch of the education of youth, present them, as engaged in martial sports, and the mimic feats of arms, preparatory to the grand tragedies of battle;—exercises and exhibitions, which, both in the performer and the spectator, cultivate all the dissocial emotions, and turn the whole current of the mental forces into the channel of destructiveness. (III:58)

Mann called himself a republican (in order to signify his opposition to monarchy), but he had no appreciation of the connection between martial virtue and citizenship, which had received so much attention in the republican tradition. Even Adam Smith, whose liberal economics dealt that tradition a crippling blow, regretted the loss of armed civic virtue. "A man, incapable either of defending or of revenging himself, evidently wants one of the most essential parts of the character of a man." It was a matter for regret, in Smith's view, that the "general security and happiness which prevail in ages of civility and politeness" gave so "little exercise to the contempt of danger, to patience in enduring labor, hunger, and pain." Given the growth of commerce, things could not be otherwise, according to Smith; but the disappearance of qualities so essential to manhood and therefore to citizenship was nevertheless a disturbing development. Politics and war, not commerce, served as the "great school of self-command." If commerce was now displacing "war and faction" as the chief business of mankind (to the point where the very term "business" soon became a synonym for commerce), the educational system would have to take up the slack, sustaining values that could no longer be acquired through participation in public events.

Horace Mann, like Smith, believed that formal education could take the place of other character-forming experiences, but he had a very different conception of the kind of character he wanted to form. He shared none of Smith's enthusiasm for war and none of his reservations about a society composed of peace-loving men and women going about their business and largely indifferent to public affairs. As we shall see, Mann's opinion of politics was no higher than his opinion of war. His educational program did not attempt to supply the courage, patience, and fortitude formerly supplied by "war and faction." It therefore did not occur to him that historical narratives, with their stirring accounts of exploits carried out in the line of military or political duty, might fire the imagination of the young and help to frame their own aspirations. Perhaps it would be more accurate to say that he distrusted *any* sort of appeal to the imagination. His educational philosophy was hostile to imagination as such.

He preferred fact to fiction, science to mythology. He complained that young people were given a "mass of fictions," when they needed "true stories" and "real examples of real men." (III:90-91) But his conception of the truths that could safely be entrusted to children turned out to be very limited indeed. History, he thought, "should be rewritten" so as to enable children to compare "the right with the wrong" and to give them "some option of admiring and emulating the former." (III:59-60) Mann's objections to the kind of history children were conventionally exposed to was not only that it acclaimed military exploits but that right and wrong were confusingly mixed up together—as they are always mixed up, of course, in the real world. It was just this element of moral ambiguity that Mann wanted to eliminate. "As much of History now stands, the examples of right and wrong...are...brought and shuffled together." (III:60) Educators had a duty to sort them out and to make it unambiguously clear to children which was which.

Mann's plea for historical realism betrayed not only an impoverished conception of reality but a distrust of pedagogically unmediated experience—attitudes that have continued to characterize educational thinking right down to the present day. Like many other educators, Mann wanted children to receive their impressions of the world from those who were professionally qualified to decide what it was proper for them to know, instead of picking up impressions haphazardly from narratives (both written and oral) not expressly designed for children. Anyone who has spent much time with children knows that they acquire much of their understanding of the adult world by listening to what adults do not necessarily want them to hear—by eavesdropping, in effect, and just by keeping their eyes and ears open. Information acquired in this way is more vivid and compelling than any other, since it enables children to put themselves imaginatively in the place of adults instead of being treated simply as objects of adult solicitude and didacticism. It was precisely this imaginative experience of the adult world, however—this unsupervised play of young imaginations—that Mann hoped to replace with formal instruction. Thus he objected to "novels and all that class of books," which offered "mere *amusement*, as contradistinguised from instruction in the practical concerns of life." His objection, to be sure, was directed mainly against "light reading," which allegedly distracted people from "reflection upon the great realities of experience"; but he did not specifically exempt more serious works of fiction, nor is there any indication, in the vast body of his educational writings, that he recognized the possibility that the "great realities of existence" are treated more fully in fiction and poetry than in any other kind of writing. (III:60)

The great weakness in Mann's educational philosophy was the assumption that education takes place only in schools. Perhaps it is unfair to say that Mann bequeathed this fatal assumption to subsequent generations of educators, as part of his intellectual legacy. An inability to see beyond the school, after all—a tendency to speak as if schooling and education are synonymous terms—should probably be regarded as an occupational hazard of professional educators, a form of blindness that is built into the job. Still, Mann was one of the first to give it official sanction. His thinking on this point was more striking in what it omitted than in what it said in so many words. It simply did not occur to him that activities like politics, war, and love—the staple themes of the books he deplored—were educative in their own right. He believed that partisan politics, in particular, were the bane of American life. In his Twelfth Report, he described the excitement surrounding the presidential election of 1848 in language that unmistakably conveyed the importance of politics as a form of popular education, only to condemn the campaign (in which he himself had won election to the House of Representatives) as a distraction from his more important work as an educator.

Agitation pervaded the country. There was no stagnant mind; there was no stagnant atmosphere... Wit, argument, eloquence, were in such demand, that they were sent for at the distance of a thousand miles—from one side of the Union to the other. The excitement reached the humblest walks of life. The mechanic in his shop made his hammer chime to the music of political rhymes; and the farmer, as he gathered in his harvest, watched the aspects of the political, more vigilantly than of the natural, sky. Meetings were every where held... The press showered its sheets over the land, thick as snow-flakes in a wintry storm. Public and private histories were ransacked, to find proofs of honor or proofs of dishonor; political economy was invoked; the sacred names of patriotism, philanthropy, duty to God, and duty to man, were on every tongue.

The campaign of 1848, as Mann described it, elicited an intensity of popular response that would be the envy of our own times, yet Mann could find in all this only "violence" and "din"—a "Saturnalia of license, evil speaking, and falsehood." He wished that the energy devoted to politics could be devoted instead to "getting children into the schools." (XII:25-26) Elsewhere in the same report he likened politics to a conflagration, a fire raging out of control, or again to a plague, an "infection" or "poison." (XII:87)

Reading these passages, one begins to see that Mann wanted to keep politics out of the school not only because he was afraid that his system would be torn apart by those who wished to use it for partisan purposes but because he distrusted political activity as such. It produced an "inflammation of the passions." (XII:26) It generated controversy—a necessary part of education, it might be argued, but in Mann's eyes a waste of time and energy. It divided men instead of bringing them together. For these reasons, Mann sought not only to insulate the school from political pressures but to keep political history out of the curriculum. The subject could not be ignored entirely; otherwise children would gain only "such knowledge as they may pick up from angry political discussions, or from party newspapers." But instruction in the "nature of a republican government" was to be conducted so as to emphasize only "those articles in the creed of republicanism, which are accepted by all, believed in by all, and which form the common basis of our political faith." Anything controversial was to be passed over in silence or, at best, with the admonition that "the schoolroom is neither the tribunal to adjudicate, nor the forum to discuss it." (XII:89)

Although it is somewhat tangential to my main point, it is worth pausing to see what Mann considered to be the common articles in the republican creed, the "elementary ideas" on which everyone could agree. (XII:89) The most important of these points, it appears, were the duty of citizens to appeal to the courts, if wronged, instead of taking the law into their own hands, and the duty to change the laws "by an appeal to the ballot, and not by rebellion."

(XII:85) Mann did not see that these "elementary ideas" were highly controversial in themselves or that others might quarrel with his underlying assumption that the main purpose of government was to keep order. But the substance of his political views is less germane to my purpose than his attempt to palm them off as universal principles. It is bad enough that he disguised the principles of the Whig party as principles common to all Americans and thus protected them from reasonable criticism. What is even worse is the way in which his bland tutelage deprived children of anything that might have appealed to the imagination or—to use his own term—the "passions." Political history, taught along the lines recommended by Mann, would be drained of controversy, sanitized, bowdlerized, and therefore drained of excitement. It would become mild, innocuous, and profoundly boring, trivialized by a suffocating didacticism. Mann's idea of political education was of a piece with his idea of moral education, on which he laid such heavy-handed emphasis in his opposition to merely intellectual training. Moral education, as he conceived it, consisted of inoculation against "social vices and crimes"—"gaming, intemperance, dissoluteness, falsehood, dishonesty, violence, and their kindred offenses." (XII:97) In the republican tradition—compared with which Mann's republicanism was no more than a distant echo—the concept of virtue referred to honor, ardor, superabundant energy, and the fullest use of one's powers. For Mann, virtue was only the pallid opposite of "vice." Virtue was "sobriety, frugality, probity"—qualities not likely to seize the imagination of the young. (XII:97)

The subject of morality brings us by a short step to religion, where we see Mann's limitations in their clearest form. Here again, I want to call into question the very aspects of Mann's thought that have usually been singled out for the highest praise. Even his detractors—those who see his philanthropy as a cover for social control—congratulate Mann on his foresight in protecting the schools from sectarian pressures. He was quite firm on the need to banish religious instruction based on the tenets of any particular denomination. In his lifetime, he was unfairly accused of banishing religious instruction altogether and thus undermining public morals. To these "grave charges" he replied, plausibly enough, that sectarianism could not be tolerated in schools that everyone was expected to attend—compelled to attend, if he were to have his way. (XII:103) But he also made it clear that a "rival system of 'Parochial' or 'Sectarian' schools" was not to be tolerated either. (XII:104) His program envisioned the public school system as a monopoly, in practice if not in law. It implied the marginalization if not the outright elimination of institutions that might compete with the common schools. His opposition to religious sectarianism did not stop with its exclusion from the public sector of education. He was against sectarianism as such, for the same reasons that made him take such a dim view of politics. Sectarianism, in his view, breathed the spirit of fanaticism and persecution. It gave rise to religious controversy, which was no more acceptable to Mann than political controversy. He spoke of both in images of fire. If the theological "heats and animosities engendered in families, and among neighbors, burst forth in a devouring fire" into school meetings, the "inflammable materials" would grow so intense that no one could "quench the flames," until the "zealots" themselves were "consumed in the conflagration they have kindled." (XII:129) It was not enough to keep the churches out of the public schools; it was necessary to keep them out of public life altogether, lest the "discordant" sounds of religious debate drown out the "one, indivisible, all-glorious system of Christianity" and bring about the "return of Babel." (XII:130) The perfect world, as it existed in Mann's head, was a world in which everyone agreed, a heavenly city where the angels sang in unison. He sadly admitted that "we can hardly conceive of a state of society upon earth so perfect as to exclude all differences of opinion"; but at least it was possible to relegate disagreements "about rights" and other important matters to the sidelines of social life—to bar them from the schools and, by implication, from the public sphere as a whole. (XII:96)

None of this meant that the schools should not teach religion; it meant only that they should teach the religion that was common to all, or at least to all Christians. The Bible should be read in school, on the assumption that it could "speak for itself," without commentaries that might give rise to disagreement. (XII:117) Here again, Mann's program invites a type of criticism that misses the point. His nondenominational instruction is open to the objection that it still excluded Jews, Mohammedans, Buddhists, and atheists. Ostensibly tolerant, it was actually repressive in equating religion narrowly with Christianity. This is a trivial objection. At the time Mann was writing, it still made sense to speak of the United States as a Christian nation; but the reasoning on which he justified a nondenominational form of Christianity could easily be extended to include other religions as well. The real objection is that the resulting mixture is so bland that it puts children to sleep instead of awakening feelings of awe and wonder. Orestes Brownson, the most perceptive of Mann's contemporary critics, pointed out in 1839 that Mann's system, by suppressing everything divisive in religion, would leave only an innocuous residue. "A faith, which embraces generalities only, is little better than no faith at all." Children brought up in a mild and nondenominational "Christianity ending in nothingness," in schools where "much will be taught in general, but nothing in particular," would be deprived of their birthright, as Brownson saw it. They would be taught "to respect and preserve what is"; they would be cautioned against the "licentiousness of the people, the turbulence and brutality of the mob"; but they would never learn a "love of liberty" under such a system.

Although Brownson did not share Mann's horror of dissension, he too deplored the widening gap between wealth and poverty, "the division of society into workingmen and idlers, employers, and operatives," in his words—a "learned class and an unlearned, a cultivated class and an uncultivated, a refined class and a vulgar." He too saw popular education as a means of overcoming these divisions. Unlike Mann, however, he understood that the real work of education did not take place in the schools at all. Anticipating John Dewey, Brownson pointed out that

our children are educated in the streets, by the influence of their associates, in the fields and on the hill sides, by the influences of surrounding scenery and overshadowing skies, in the bosom of the family, by the love and gentleness, or wrath and fretfulness of parents, by the passions or affections they see manifested, the conversations to which they listen, and above all by the general pursuits, habits, and moral tone of the community.

These considerations, together with Brownson's extensive discussion of the press and the lyceum, seemed to point to the conclusion that people were most likely to develop a love of liberty through exposure to wide-ranging public controversy, the "free action of mind on mind."

Wide-ranging public controversy, as we have seen, was just what Mann wanted to avoid. Nothing of educational value, in his view, could issue from the clash of opinions, the noise and heat of political and religious debate. Education could take place only in institutions deliberately contrived for that purpose, in which children were exposed only to knowledge professional educators considered appropriate. Some such assumption, I think, has been the guiding principle of American education ever since. Mann's reputation as the founding father of the public school is well deserved. His energy, his missionary enthusiasm, his powers of persuasion, and the strategic position he enjoyed as secretary of the Massachusetts Board of Education made it possible for him to leave a lasting mark on the educational enterprise. One might go so far as to say that the enterprise has never recovered from the mistakes and misconceptions built into it at the very outset. Not that Horace Mann would be pleased with our educational system as it exists today. On the contrary, he would be horrified. Nevertheless the horrors are at least indirectly a consequence of his own ideas, unleavened by the moral idealism with which they were once associated. We have incorporated into our schools the worst of Mann and somehow managed to lose sight of the best. We have professionalized teaching by setting up elaborate requirements for certification, but we have not succeeded in institutionalizing Mann's appreciation of teaching as an honorable calling. We have set up a far-ranging educational bureaucracy without raising academic standards or improving the quality of teaching. The bureaucratization of education has the opposite effect, undermining the teacher's autonomy, substituting the judgment of administrators for that of the teacher, and incidentally discouraging people with a gift for teaching from entering the profession at all. We have followed Mann's advice to de-emphasize purely academic subjects, but the resulting loss of intellectual rigor has not been balanced by an improvement in the school's capacity to nourish the character traits Mann considered so important—self-reliance, courteousness, and the capacity for deferred gratification. The periodic rediscovery that intellectual training has been sacrificed to "social skills" has led to a misplaced emphasis on the purely cognitive dimension of education, which lacks even Mann's redeeming awareness of its moral dimension. We share Mann's distrust of the imagination and his narrow conception of truth, insisting that the schools should stay away from myths and stories and legends and stick to sober facts; but the range of permissible facts is even more pathetically limited today than it was in Mann's day. History has given way to an infantilized version of sociology, in obedience to the misconceived principle that the quickest way to engage children's attention is to dwell on what is closest to home—their families, their neighborhoods, the local industries, the technologies on which they depend. A more sensible assumption would be that children need to learn about faraway places and olden times before they can make sense of their immediate surroundings. Since most children have no opportunity for extended travel, and since travel in our world is not very broadening anyway, the school can provide a substitute—but not if it clings to the notion that the only way to "motivate" them is to expose them to nothing not already familiar, nothing not immediately applicable to themselves.

Like Mann, we believe that schooling is a cure-all for everything that ails us. Mann and his contemporaries held that good schools could eradicate crime and juvenile delinquency, do away with poverty, make useful citizens out of "abandoned and outcast children," and serve as the "great equalizer" between the rich and poor. (XII:42, 59) They would have done better to start out with a more modest set of expectations. If there is one lesson we might have been expected to learn in the hundred and fifty years since Horace Mann took charge of the schools of Massachusetts, it is that the schools can't save society. Crime and poverty are still with us, and the gap between rich and poor continues to widen. Meanwhile, our children, even as young adults, don't know how to read and write. Maybe the time has come—if it hasn't already passed—to start all over again.

Works Cited

Jonathan Messerli, *Horace Mann* (New York: Alfred A. Knopf, 1972), is the standard biography. Discussions of Mann's educational ideas and program appear in Merle Curti, *The Social Ideas of American Educators* (New York: Scribner's, 1935); Rush Welter, *Popular Education and Democratic Thought in America* (New York: Columbia UP, 1962); David Tyack and Elizabeth Hansot, *Managers of Virtue: Public School Leadership in America, 1820-1980* (New York: Basic Books, 1982); Maxine Green, *The Public School and the Private Vision* (New York: Random House, 1965); Carl F. Kaestle, *Pillars of the Republic: Common Schools and American Society, 1780-1860* (New York: Hill and Wang, 1983); R. Freeman Butts, *Public Education in the United States* (New York: Holt, Rinehart, and Winston, 1978); and many other books on American education. See also Maris A. Vinovskis, "Horace Mann on the Economic Productivity of Education," *New England Quarterly* 43 (1970): 550-71; Barbara Finkelstein, "Perfecting Childhood: Horace Mann and the Origins of Public Education in the United States," *Biography* 13:1 (1990): 6-20; and Lawrence Cremin's introduction to his collection of Mann's writings, *The Republic and the School: Horace Mann on the Education of Free Men* (New York: Teachers College P, 1959).

The historical scholarship of the fifties, which deplored the influence of progressive dogma on American education, is best exemplified by Arthur Bestor, *The Restoration of Learning* (New York: Alfred A. Knopf, 1955). Revisionist works of the sixties and seventies, which saw the school system essentially as an agency for the imposition of industrial work-discipline, middle-class morals, and political conformity, include Raymond E. Callahan, *Education and the Cult of Efficiency* (Chicago: U of Chicago P, 1962); Michael J. Katz, *The Irony of Early School Reform* (Cambridge: Harvard UP, 1968), and *Class, Bureaucracy, and Schools* (New York: Praeger, 1971); Robert H. Wiebe, "The Social Functions of Public Education," *American Quarterly* 21 (1969): 147-64; Raymond A. Mohl, "Education as Social Control in New York City, 1784-1825," *New York History* 51 (1970): 219-37; Ivan Illich, *Deschooling Society* (New York: Harper & Row, 1971); Joel H. Spring, *Education and the Rise of the Corporate State* (Boston: Beacon P, 1972), and *The Sorting Machine* (New York: David McKay, 1976); Colin Greer, *The Great School Legend* (New York: Basic Books, 1972); and Clarence J. Karier, *The Individual, Society, and Education* (Urbana: U of Illinois P, 1986). Not all these studies deal specifically with Mann, and those that do by no means refuse to credit him with any good intentions at all. Taken together, however, they leave the impression that school reform, like other reform movements, owed less to humanitarian or democratic considerations than to a pervasive, almost obsessive concern with social order and industrial productivity. The stock reply to this kind of interpretation—that humanitarian considerations were more important after all—does nothing to challenge the existing terms of debate. For this type of argument, see Lawrence Frederick Kohl, "The Concept of Social Control and the History of Jacksonian America," *Journal of the Early Republic* 5 (1985): 21-34; David Rothman, "Social Control: The Uses and Abuses of the Concept in the History of Incarceration," *Rice University Studies* 67 (1981): 9-20; and Thomas L. Haskell, "Capitalism and the Origins of the Humanitarian Sensibility," *American Historical Review* 90 (1985): 339-61, 547-66.

All the quotations in this essay, except the ones from Adam Smith and Orestes Brownson, come from the long reports Mann submitted to the Massachusetts legislature as Secretary of the Board of Education. The page references cited in the text are from the *Annual Report of the Board of Education, together with the Annual Report of the Secretary of the Board*, Vol. 1-3 (Boston: Dutton and Wentworth, 1838-1848), in twelve volumes. Smith's reflections on the demoralizing effects of commerce appear in *The Wealth of Nations*, Book V, chapter 1 ("incapable either of defending or of revenging himself"), and *The Theory of Moral Sentiments*, D.D. Raphael and A.L. Macfie, eds. (Oxford: Clarendon P, 1976), pp. 146 ("great school of self-command"), 152-3 ("war and faction"), 205 ("general security and happiness"). Brownson's attack on Mann appeared in the *Boston Quarterly Review* 2 (1839); 394 ("educated in the streets"), 404 ("a faith, which embraces generalities only"; "much in general, nothing in particular"), 411 ("respect and preserve what is"; "licentiousness of the people"; "love of liberty"), 434 ("free action of mind on mind").

On Philosophy and History:
"The Truth—the Good, the Bad and the Ugly"

John K. Roth

On 7 July 1987, Lt. Col. Oliver L. North began his testimony in the Iran-*Contra* hearing by announcing that he would reveal "the truth—the good, the bad and the ugly." Far less in the spotlight, although not without his share of publicity, Allan Bloom concurrently advanced his insights on those same themes in a nationwide bestseller. The issues raised by Allan Bloom's *The Closing of the American Mind: How Higher Education Has Failed Democracy and Impoverished the Souls of Today's Students* lacked the media glitter of Colonel North's testimony. Those issues, however, are even more fundamental—especially where philosophy and history are concerned—than the vital questions about authority, the separation of powers, and constitutional government posed by "Irangate."

Throughout the hearings that riveted American attention in the summer of 1987 the basic problem was to find out who knew what and how. That inquiry placed a premium on establishing the truth. But much more was involved because, contrary to the old adage that "the facts speak for themselves," a sound grasp and appraisal of their meanings is not easily obtained. As philosophers and historians, our concern is to know and even to affect what others—our students in particular—ought to know. It may do us good therefore to raise some questions about "the truth—the good, the bad and the ugly" and their relation to philosophy and history, allowing Bloom to help focus the investigation.

"Was Socrates Right or Wrong?"

The historian Frederick Jackson Turner argued in an 1893 essay that the American frontier had already closed. Turner's appraisal in "The Significance of the Frontier in American History" included the thesis that frontier life had encouraged "intellectual traits of profound importance" (37). Among them, asserted Turner, were "scorn of older society, impatience of its restraints and its ideas, and indifference to its lessons" (38). Allan Bloom is silent about Turner; in fact, his book says relatively little about the modern discipline of history. Nevertheless, Bloom suggests that factors such as those identified by Turner help to explain why, less than a century later, the closing of the American mind is one of the sequels to the passing of the frontier.

If Ollie North made Americans worry about the health of our body politic, Allan Bloom draws attention to the state of democracy's soul. Among other things, Bloom contends, that task should return us to ancient Greece. Specifically, the American mind needs to encounter Socrates and inquire anew whether he was "right or wrong" (308). Although is it nearly obligatory to honor Socrates, Bloom doubts that many Americans do so well. Far from thinking Socrates was right, we tend not even to ask whether he might be, having already concluded that he was wrong. That result is one way to sum up the closing of the American mind.

Forces in American democracy, including its various frontier expressions, account for some of this closing. Bloom's list of culprits, however, is long, varied, and complex. The academy itself—along with rock music, psychoanalysis, feminism, and a host of other phenomena, many of them rooted in the sixties, a period Bloom deplores as "an unmitigated disaster" for the universities (320)— is also responsible for our predicament. Here I cannot explore the full range of ingredients that Bloom identifies; instead I will reflect briefly on two that are crucial for understanding his claim that Socrates stands at the crux of our problem.

Topping Bloom's list of pernicious influences is the conviction that "truth is relative" (25), in Bloom's view a dubious outlook which, however, functions as a "first principle" among today's students. The view that "truth is relative" may be seen as a consequence, however unintended, of a combination of the American faith in equal, inalienable rights and the historical experience of the frontier. It moves from the assumption that every person is entitled to an opinion to the claim that what counts as truth for anyone—at least where values, if not facts, are concerned—is more a matter of opinion than anything else. Part and parcel of this disposition are appeals to be "open" to the views of others, whatever they may be. Insofar as such "openness" rejects "the possibility of knowing good and bad," which Bloom finds typically to be the case, it is symptomatic of the closing that troubles him (40).

Abandoning "the quest for knowledge and certitude," relativism travels with indifference, which can make "surrender to whatever is most powerful, or worship of vulgar success, look principled" (41). Such "openness" is baneful. What we need instead, Bloom insists, is openness that sustains the possibility that truth's relativity is a half-truth at best. This openness to knowing would then have to inquire accordingly, lured by the awareness that there is more to truth than the perceptions of believers.

Bloom's indictment is that, far from being open to knowing, our American milieu is hostage to dogmatic relativism. The academy ought to liberate us from such prejudice. It does so best when it keeps "the permanent questions front and center" (252) and teaches us to read not through the spectacles of our own prejudices, but with the writer's original intentions as the first focal point. Instead, Bloom charges, the academy aids and abets our captivity and nowhere more effectively than in its tendency to embrace historicism, a second key that locks the American mind. Bloom defines historicism as "the view that all thought is essentially related to and cannot transcend its own time" (40). Its rule erodes the status of philosophy and history as objective searches for truth. Instead they fall prey to one or both of historicism's cousins: psychologism or reductionism that classifies them merely as ideological weapons in the service of social class and political-economic power.

As Bloom points out, however, no more than a thoroughgoing relativism can a thoroughgoing historicism logically sustain itself. If these corrosive articles of faith are to have their self-proclaimed authority, they depend on a non-relativistic, non-historicist, non-psychologistic, and non-reductionist foundation. Otherwise they rest on sand. But the closing of the American mind is such that its relativism and historicism, as well as its vulnerability to psychologism and reductionism, are too habitual to be moved by anything so plain as self-contradiction.

In recent decades the social sciences especially have spread the gospels of relativism and historicism. The natural sciences and the humanities, however, have also made their contributions, for all of these commit themselves, one way or another, to "progress" beyond the ways of ancient wisdom. The natural sciences not only make the past look old-fashioned; their methods are also decisive for determining such distinctions as remain between knowledge and opinion. Apparently unable to attain for themselves the universality of the natural sciences and mathematics, the humanities contribute further to their own demise by giving up what Bloom calls "the cosmic intention of placing man in the universe" (369).

History as well as philosophy can serve to illustrate Bloom's point. "Both participants and observers," Bloom says of history,

> are unsure whether it is a social science or one of the humanities. Its matter is resistant to the techniques of the behavioral sciences, since it is particular, and therefore not easily generalizable, deals with the past, and is therefore beyond controlled experiments; but it does not want to be merely literature. (366-367, footnote 17)

History, in short, was taken to be close to "the truth of things" (367, footnote 17). But once everything is historicized, including history itself, history's identity becomes unclear.

The reaction of historians to Bloom's diagnosis will be worth hearing. Meanwhile consider why he thinks philosophy's fate is similar. "Philosophy," claims Bloom,

> once proudly proclaimed that it was the best way of life, and it dared to survey the whole, to seek the first causes of all things, and not only dictated its rules to the special sciences but constituted and ordered them. (377)

Intimidated by the natural sciences, historicism, and relativism, philosophy has also been "dethroned by political and theoretical democracy." Thus, Bloom finds it "bereft of the passion or the capacity to rule" (377). In an age decisively controlled by the natural sciences and the technologies they spawn, this anti-philosophical outcome is one that Bloom deeply regrets, for unless we know what is good—which science cannot tell us, but which we might learn from history and philosophy rightly understood—American life will drift and, indeed, decline.

Insofar as the American mind is gripped by relativism, historicism, and a subservience to scientific "progress" that leads to the forsaking of reason's self-confidence, our culture seems ready to answer Bloom's question about Socrates by responding that Socrates was wrong. As Bloom grasps it, Socrates' self-understanding entailed and intended human reason's rising above time and circumstance to know "the truth—the good, the bad and the ugly." That ancient thinker reasoned his way to the insight that the human mind, when it functions well, can know reality. In the knowing, moreover, Socrates found the highest human fulfillment. Our essential nature, Bloom adds, is such that

man is the particular being that can know the universal, the temporal being that is aware of eternity, the part that can survey the whole, the effect that seeks the cause. (292)

This venerable Socratic vision, Bloom argues, supported philosophy and human life for centuries. We live off its capital. In fact, we are consuming the principal, because we are non-philosophical, close-minded inheritors of Europe's Enlightenment. Its leading lights—Bacon, Descartes, Hobbes, and Locke, to mention only a few of those "moderns"—had their quarrels with Plato, Aristotle, and the other "ancients" who took their inspiration from Socrates. But whatever the differences concerning the content of knowledge, the Enlightenment held fast with the ancient tradition in the confidence that reason, rightly employed, could still provide genuine knowledge.

That tradition gave Americans their treasured views about human rights, freedom, and equality. Bloom's fear is that these beliefs are now like cut flowers. They will wilt because they no longer grow in soil where confidence in reason's power to know can put down deep roots. How we planted and harvested this poisonous crop is complicated, but Bloom stresses two dimensions especially. First, our American experience with democracy left us self-satisfied. We came, for example, to hold as self-evident the truth that we have certain inalienable rights. Content as we were to grant all persons the prerogative to think for themselves and to form opinions as seemed individually appropriate, we failed to promote sufficient thought about how and what we know and about the difference between knowledge and opinion.

Second, particularly from the latter half of the nineteenth century onward, American intellectuals began to encourage what Bloom dubs "the German connection" (141-156). Ideas imported from Germany did not affect everyone at first, but their spread from influential intellectual circles was wide, and before long Nietzsche's death of God, Weber's fact-value distinction, and Freud's psychoanalytic practices were common currency. In general, this German tradition—its beginnings in Kant, Hegel, and Marx have recently culminated in Husserl, Heidegger, and Habermas—attacked, sometimes unintentionally and sometimes intentionally, the confidence in reason that characterized philosophy from Socrates to the American Founding. Democratic self-satisfaction plus a German-inspired criticism that led reason to undermine itself—that combination set us up for the conspiracy of relativism, historicism, and epistemological skepticism that closed the American mind.

Much depends on whether this closing can be reversed, a challenge, Bloom believes, that enjoins us to find Socrates right, not wrong. The crucial matter next becomes how and to what extent that aim can be achieved. Although Bloom provides useful counsel, his signals are mixed, as further reflection on Socrates will show.

Can We Know Things As They Are?

"The philosopher," states Bloom, "wants to know things as they are" (279). Socrates embodied that spirit; it prodded him to ask question after question. Specifically, to know things as they are he had to explore how people thought they were. Even the most dearly held assumptions, including what was most "obvious," became the subject matter for his investigations.

Bloom wants to revive that questioning spirit. Its inspiration would open the American mind. In American life today, moreover, the Socratic spirit would direct its interrogation at relativism and historicism, unfortunately our least questioned intellectual assumptions. Furthermore, if those assumptions are found wanting, as Bloom believes philosophy can demonstrate, then there is a way beyond them. Presumably true philosophy can restore souls that have been impoverished by the skeptical and ultimately nihilistic tendencies which render natural rights mythological, pronounce God dead, destroy confidence that there is a metaphysical difference between good and evil, and, in a word, so disenchant the world that men and women are uprooted from nature and led into a void where nothing but "worldviews" and "values," whatever they may be, are left to guide us (208).

Much of this program makes good sense. The philosophically questioning attitude of a Socrates is essential for knowing, and it always should encompass the things that we most comfortably assume. Thus, it is important to remember that those who most profoundly found reason leading toward relativism and historicism did not easily embrace those "isms." Bloom properly acknowledges, for instance, the fear and trembling that accompanied Friedrich Nietzsche and Max Weber as they did their work. The points that brought them *Angst* we Americans appropriated cheerfully and uncritically. Thus, we created what Bloom calls "nihilism, American style," a way of being too easily and too much at home with relativism and historicism for our own good. Unless we identify and, as far as possible, validate the reasons for our beliefs, a process which involves responding sensibly to the most powerful objections that can be brought against them, we are still very much in the cave of ignorance that Plato described in his *Republic*. Whatever its attractions, that cave is not the best place to be.

Philosophy and history both can and should engage in a Socratic questioning targeted especially at what is currently taken to be most obvious, correct, and beyond question. Bloom sees correctly, moreover, that there are "great questions that must be faced if one is to live a serious life: reason-revelation, freedom-necessity, democracy-aristocracy, good-evil, body-soul, self-other, city-man, eternity-time, being-nothing" (227). Practiced well, philosophy and history show what these alternatives mean and what costs must be borne by the unavoidable, often tragic choices they involve.

The next step in Bloom's program, however, is more problematic. For amidst the considerable finger-wagging polemics that fill much of his book there is a key and arguable assumption. It is that the criticism of relativism and historicism will indeed take us back to a version of the self-confidence about reason that characterized the ancients and the moderns alike—at least until the German juggernaut got rolling. If carried out, this restoration would be replete with authoritative, trans-historical, and lasting knowledge about "the truth—the good, the bad and the ugly." Bloom may be correct about this. The evidence, however, will accrue only in the inquiry itself. As far as that inquiry goes, *The Closing of the American Mind* is more a promissory note than a convincing demonstration.

For one thing, Bloom pays insufficient attention to the rationality that dwells in relativism and historicism. Granted, a corrective is needed to prevent this pair from becoming unwarranted first principles that bully everything in their way. Still, it does not follow that we would be wise to reject many of the most profound effects that relativism and historicism have had on reason's view of itself. It was no accident, as the history of philosophy indicates, that reason eventually criticized itself in ways that left it rightly dubious about achieving the aims to which Bloom would have us return.

If for centuries philosophers held in common a view of reason's potential, they were not noted primarily for agreement among themselves. On the contrary, Bloom's philosophical giants thought their predecessors and peers were often in error about the most fundamental matters. These matters included the intense disputes that always take philosophy back to the beginning: those involving the meaning of philosophy's basic terms—for example, "the truth—the good, the bad and the ugly," and eventually "philosophy" itself. Had it been otherwise, not many philosophers would have bothered to write. Thus, lamentable though the outcome might be, it is anything but unreasonable, let alone unnatural, that the accumulated disagreements led some philosophers—not all of them German by any means—to think that the human mind was less capable of transcending time and circumstance than many thinkers had believed.

This skepticism, however, went too far. Now we see that skepticism itself must be subject to suspicion, questioning, and restraint. Yet it is unwise and hence undesirable to imply that one can simply leap over the chasm of doubt. That Allan Bloom attempts such a leap does more credit to his courage than to his philosophical insight. When Bloom asserts that we can actually discover "the truth according to nature" (254), he is at once more and less than Socratic, because apparently Socrates himself neither overcame nor even wanted to overcome completely the awareness that he was ignorant. His, of course, was a deeply thoughtful ignorance. He sought reasons for beliefs and tested both reasons and beliefs as far as possible. Nevertheless, whatever knowledge Socrates claimed to have, he took it to be tentative, finite, fallible, and subject to correction.

The twin insights that human judgment can be mistaken and that reason can be self-corrective lead to the vision that truth is more than opinion. But whether human minds, individually or collectively, ever grasp truth more than partially remains uncertain. Hence truth may be not so much what reason discovers as what it strives for and grows toward but never wholly attains. This fully Socratic stance, more thoroughly questioning than Bloom's attempt to revive confidence that we are able to discover "the truth according to nature," would produce an American mind open to insights beyond those Bloom has in mind. That is not entirely surprising, however, because Bloom's interest as a philosopher—indeed, as the political philosopher that he shows himself to be— is precisely the achievement of "certitude" (41). It is arguable whether that state of mind should or even can exist. But if it were realized, we would be free from doubt. Things would be beyond question. Thus, we need to ask, is Bloom seeking to open the American mind only to close it all over again, once he and like-minded rationalists have found the certitude for which they yearn?[1]

For too long, thinks Allan Bloom, we have been insufficiently convinced that "there are some things one must know about if one is to be educated" (320). Nihilism, American style, inhibits that disposition. "A parable for our times," continues Bloom, is that the United States has

great universities—which can split the atom, find cures for the most terrible diseases, conduct surveys of whole populations and produce massive dictionaries of lost languages—[but] cannot generate a modest program of general education for undergraduate students. (340)

This legacy of the sixties makes it exceedingly difficult "to recover the knowledge of philosophy, history and literature that was trashed" (321). Links broken from tradition are not easily repaired. Attempts to mend this chain are an essential and worthwhile part of Bloom's efforts to reverse the closing of the American mind.

Both history and philosophy contend with "the truth—the good, the bad and the ugly." Why does the United States have the particular traditions, rites, beliefs, and values that center our national culture? Only as the reasons are probed will the American mind be open to encompass our full inheritance. Historical and philosophical approaches will converge as that analysis goes forward: neither can move toward completeness without the other. But the enterprise is risky, because it can cause the thoroughly Socratic effect of leaving us all less satisfied with who we are.

Note

[1] The possibility of an affirmative answer to this question is enhanced by the fact that Bloom is of the Straussian persuasion in political philosophy. On this view, political circumstance often requires that the philosopher, much as he or she loves the truth, is not always able to speak it plainly with impunity. But there will be a few who can understand what is really going on within and between the lines. Bloom's Straussian book may be intended to mean both more and less than its pages suggest at first. Bloom's aristocratic rationalism suggests that there are those who know best and presumably others should obey their direction. That suggestion may be well and good. It bears careful watching, nonetheless.

Works Cited

Bloom, Allan. *The Closing of the American Mind: How Higher Education Has Failed Democracy and Impoverished the Souls of Today's Students.* New York: Simon and Schuster, 1987.

Turner, Frederick Jackson. "The Significance of the Frontier in American History." 1893. *The Frontier in American History.* New York: Holt, 1920.

Two Wise Men Bearing Strange Gifts:
On the Educational Crisis in America

Frank Caucci

Both Allan Bloom and David Solway[1] attempt to explicate what they perceive in the social mirror of the modern zeitgeist. Indeed, a major thesis common to *The Closing of the American Mind* and *Education Lost* is that the prevailing mythology is largely to blame for the crisis in education today. In attempting to denounce the ubiquitous, ostrich-like philosophy of our day, their endeavor is largely Voltairian. Whether their social philosophies, assuming that they are at all enlightened, remain Voltairian in scope is what this essay seeks to address.

Even prior to an actual reading of the two books, one immediately notes the gloomy tone of their respective titles, which further carry a message of loss. While Solway's title brings to mind Milton's *Paradise Lost*, Bloom's title suggests a shift in the American psyche from a position within an edenic setting to an extramural one. Another appropriate reference might well be Bosch's *Garden of Delights* triptych in which the extreme panels depict an anterior/posterior, or garden of Eden/garden of Satan dichotomy. To this tone sustained throughout the works, there corresponds an underpinning of nostalgia for a much better state in the past. For in the subjective accounts of Bloom and Solway, today's students have closed their minds and souls, and lost the spiritual sense of what an education should be. Just as Bloom drones a chastisement of the lifestyles and attitudes of university students, pointing out that "they are in a no-man's-land" (*The Closing of the American Mind*, 37) and predicating a decline of the American ethos, Solway feels compelled to view himself more like a dentist than a teacher to the students he has taught over the last generation. His retrospective diagnostic of the past fifteen years is that students had been "subject to rampant narcolepsy" (*Education Lost*, 1), and that "there was little one could do to penetrate a cellular slumber so profound and unconscious of itself as to provoke [...] a sense of inexpressible wonder" (2). In fact, Solway's general statements about students make the reader wonder how he could possibly doubt his own cynicism (126), especially when one stumbles on characteristic passages such as the description of the good teacher who in his view:

rejects the statistical heresy of our poll-dominated age and seeks out the reclaimable or mentally endowed student who justifies his expenditure of time, energy, and faith. As for the uncountable and unaccountable rest, he may think of them as [...] poor unfortunates not responsible for the inner devastation of which they are incorrigibly unaware, as eggs slotted in the refrigerator shelf to be cracked later to make the social omelette, as drones and grazers, as History's forgettables, or as the parents of a future generation of computer technicians (2).

This combined criticism reiterates the familiar message that students today know less than used to be the case. Yet neither author appreciates the fact that education has never been as broadly-based as at the present time, with a 400 percent increase in the number of American students from the 1950s to the 1980s. Wayne C. Booth reports that just fifty years ago, one-third of Americans entered high school let alone graduated ("Cultural Literacy and Liberal Learning," *Change*, July/August 1988: 13). In Canada and Europe, the figures were even lower. Solway prefers to explore an apparent corollary to this reality, namely that with some notable exceptions, he has taught a high proportion of mentally defective students who required much remedial learning. His feeling regarding the quality of student papers is that, rather than simply address the problem of literacy, they invoke the very notion of barbarism to which he devotes an entire chapter. He defines barbarism as constituting an absence of memory and a radical silence, just as speech is a condition for civilization, and concludes that speech and memory must be confronted in order to ward off barbarism in today's students (60-2).

Bloom attributes to the American freshman the qualities of having a clean slate and leading spiritually empty lives. On the other hand he views European students as spiritually equipped, reaching the university ready to specialize (47-8). This type of subjective appreciation sets the tone of the entire book. His vulgarizations are especially frustrating when one looks at their comparative import: Bloom makes no qualitative distinction between the elements of the comparison themselves. For instance, while it may be argued that Americans have been educated and socialized through a national mythology of democracy, European society has been more aware of a class system which is the product of three millennia. Nor does he talk about quantitative differences in the two groups, that is the high percentage of American high school students admitted to higher education, as opposed to the correspondingly low percentage of European youths entering the university. This reflects the traditionally more egalitarian American model as opposed to the relatively more elitist European model.

In a sense, then, Bloom is comparing the general lack of preparation of American students reaching the university in large numbers with the better educated Europeans entering their institutions in comparatively low numbers. The comparison is further inappropriate when one considers that some of the parameters on either side are based on knowledge of European civilization and culture. In effect, Bloom is arguing that more Americans attend university than Europeans; that Americans are at the same time less knowledgeable about European culture and civilization than Europeans, and that Americans are therefore less spiritually and culturally ready than their European counterparts.

This type of syllogism is the very foundation of Bloom's premise. But the quantitative differences between the two continents are decreasing. European universities are experiencing the same phenomenon of unprepared freshmen as in North America—a fact further pointing to the flaw in Bloom's comparison. The American model necessarily breeds a tradition different from the European and, in my opinion, does not lend itself to the type of comparison made by Bloom. In view of this, it might be interesting to reexamine the European model in the next decade—particularly if the present rate of Americanization is sustained.

Bloom's generalizations about European countries are based on personal conviction rather than fact. His comments tend to represent as sympathetic a view of French, Italian, and British national cultures as an antipathetic one of twentieth-century Germany. One of his central theses is that American intellectuals have been negatively influenced by German thought, whose foundations were shaken by Heidegger's revolt against Aristotle and Plato and by the decision of German universities to serve the culture of the people. According to this view, which William Buckley calls "provocative but reductive" (*Profession 88*, 47), the death of reason seemed assured. For Bloom, this series of events helped facilitate the closing of contemporary American students to European civilization and culture, and to promote a parochial form of nihilism in American higher education.

I wonder whether Bloom's belief isn't distorted because of his own Germanophobia. He seems dismissive of the many revolutionary movements brought about by the literary and artistic intelligentsia of twentieth century Europe, which either expressed their disdain for the official culture, or represented a cause-and-effect reaction to it. In France alone, Dadaism and Surrealism evolved as appropriate artistic forms out of the horrors of World War I. Existentialism grew out of the turbulent thirties to become the major literary movement of the forties, pitting the self against an absurd universe. The Nouveau Roman of the fifties redefined the vision of the world, stressing the realities of representation and dismissing the anthropocentrism of the previous decade. Much of the best fiction of the sixties and seventies represented society as an anathema, the hallmark of which was alienation. These movements point to an ongoing European crisis which springs from the barbarous side of European civilization.

What emerges then is that such rejection or constantly updated perspective of European society was and continues to be legitimately effected by European minds. It is undeniable that influence and reception act as kinetic forces among the different branches of a civilization. Because this is true, twentieth century German thought alone cannot be responsible for closing the minds of American students to European thought. Among the myriad causes at a time of a new, uneasy but self-scrutinizing nationalism, might it not also legitimately be inferred that the American experience of modernity in the 1960s made it timely to Americanize the study of liberal arts in higher education?

If the Americanization of the curriculum points to a greater degree of national self-indulgence it does so at the expense of national self-effacement, which is the polar opposite. These two polarities have often constituted the dynamics of truly national debates in the past. For instance, and for the sake of argument, one might establish that Bloom's support of the Great Books theory is just as antipathetic to some critics who would decry its pitfalls in contemporary American education, as the classical style of architecture was to Louis Sullivan and the first generation of the Chicago School. Sullivan's vision of America was based on this nation's specificity rather than on a rejection of Europe. Indeed, with the exception of his transcending experience of Michelangelo's genius, Sullivan's sojourn to study at the École des beaux-arts made his decision to leave Europe more important than the one to go to the source. His allegiance was to the future and his philosophy, inspired by Walt Whitman, endeavored to reflect in the plasticity of stone his faith in the character of the young nation and in the perfectability of its democratic principles. His work imparted on his disciple Frank Lloyd Wright a concern about how one might not only toil and play, but live in American society. Little wonder, then, that he viewed the 1892 Columbia Exhibition as reactionary and unAmerican.

The allusions of Bloom and Solway to the lack of preparation of North American students entering higher education do however beg the question of what preparation they should possess by the completion of high school. This immediately brings to mind the controversy E. D. Hirsch has unleased upon the educational establishment. Notwithstanding the critics' caricature of his project as mindless and uncritical, Hirsch's concept of cultural literacy needs to be reckoned with. To date, the discussion has not generated an urgently needed compromise on a cogent method of incorporating cultural literacy into school curricula.[2]

This is not to suggest that the solution put forth by Hirsch is perfect; rather, it offers the potential for expanding or tapering the subject matter in such a way as to ensure that special needs are met. Moreover, the contents do not have to be implemented according to the Gradgrindian pedagogical model decried by skeptics and alarmists alike and satirized by Dickens as a passive enterprise in *Hard Times*, through his image of the contents of a large pitcher being poured into little pitchers. It may be implemented descriptively in a way that would involve students and exclude mechanistic, scholastic, or nonhumanistic methods.[3] Indeed, those who choose to invest Hirsch's approach to cultural literacy with such unenlightened intent are presenting a dramatization of the worst possible scenario in the application of the method.

It should also be kept in mind that this project is not meant as a final educational goal; rather, it is designed to provide a background of literate information which does not have to be in opposition with critical concepts. Hirsch's *Dictionary of Cultural Literacy*, as extensive as it may be, is meant to be a supplementary feature to an intensive curriculum, which is why I disagree with Booth's objection that the author's goal "despite its deep-felt democratic claims, too often sounds not like the education of free men and women, but rather the training of functionaries" (15).[4] Hirsch is far more humanistic:

it isn't facts that deaden the minds of young children, who are storing facts in their minds every day with astonishing voracity. It is incoherence—our failure to ensure that a pattern of shared, vividly taught, and socially enabling knowledge will emerge from our institution. The polarization of educationists into facts-people versus skills-people has no basis in reason. Facts and skills are inseparable. There is no insurmountable reason why those who advocate the teaching of higher order skills and those who advocate the teaching of common traditional content should not join forces. (*Cultural Literacy: What Every American Needs to Know*, 133).

The shared content of cultural literacy is necessary in order for citizens to create the bonds of cohesion which will allow them to identify with the national character—*unum e pluribus* or *a mare usque ad mari*, as the case may be. As such Hirsch's project remains a plausible incentive—particularly in the absence of a national core curriculum, a tradition likely to stay in both the United States and Canada. Surely the contents of his *Dictionary*, with its inevitable addenda and deletions over time, would not represent an insurmountable pool of knowledge for insertion in an academic program that stretches beyond 10,000 hours. One thing appears certain: if a Hirschian type of program is dealt with as an effective tool throughout the formative years of education chances are great that academia will be upgraded, and that much of the present remedial effort disparaged by Bloom and Solway would not be necessary because the school system would have successfully realized a fundamental acculturative responsibility.

On the other hand, if we continue to allow children to develop naturally in the narrower sense of Rousseau and Dewey, and at the present critical juncture of technology when the array of choices is increasingly intimidating, we run the risk of losing them. One would thus have to agree with Bloom and Solway, and indeed with Hirsch, about the need for keeping the past alive. How can we lead a child in our present world without teaching him about his roots and building a solid future on the foundations of the past? The more computers and technology we have, the more it becomes necessary to also acculturate our children and empower them through their cultural patrimony.

Bloom expands his negative characterization of American students by attributing to them a preoccupation of narrow self-centeredness (83), forgetting for a moment that this is due to the times and to a system in which students are the victims. When he argues that students today lack passion I am left wondering whether he would go as far as to condone the passions of a previous generation, which blindly upheld the beliefs of Hitler, Mussolini and Franco. He also believes that they lack prejudice as a result of their failure "to see differences and the gradual eradication of differences" (91). When our campuses are presently struggling with such nation-wide issues as racism and sexism, as well as the crimes which are sometimes motivated by these, it becomes difficult to imagine that students are blind to differences. In the face of such problems, some universities require their campus police to receive instruction on race and ethnicity, as well as on religious and sexual orientations.

Bloom completes his portrait by alluding to the student sense of egalitarianism, according to which "all men—and women—are created equal and have equal rights" (88). He does view this as a form of indoctrination which has bred a misguided sense of openness or cultural relativism. Indeed, the ethos of openness is equated by Bloom to a closing of the mind promoted by an attitude of laissez-faire, an attitude which then encouraged students to abandon the idea on which the university was founded: the rational search for the best life. However, his discussion of student relativism does not take into consideration the historical impact of pragmatism and unitarianism on this country.

Solway's treatment of the egalitarian principle accords well with Bloom's view, despite the fact that it is designed as an attack on pedagogical practice. Invoking Mortimer Adler's *The Paideia Proposal*, he suggests that, because of a democratic bias, its author equates the notions of universal education and quality education (120). His disagreement with Adler is strong, as is his insistence that educational egalitarianism is not equivalent to quality:

our principle of original selection should be democratic in that *everyone* is given a fair chance to benefit from the educational system. But the winnowing process is imperative and when the best students have been determined, the educational apparatus must concentrate its attention, its advantages and its demands upon *them*. No doubt this smacks of oligarchic ruthlessness. Yet it is the *sine qua non* for the existence of a robust democracy (121, author's emphasis).

Certain disturbing questions spring to mind before such a summary conviction. What is a fair chance for everyone? How does it address racial, social, and economic inequalities in a de facto way? Are the inner city children such as those whom Joe Clark has had to contend with given as fair a chance as the privileged children placed in the best private schools of any state? How are children whose complete environment breeds failure given the same fair chance as those whose bright future is practically assured from the start?

Solway admonishes that we should "educate all the educable—but let us not waste our efforts in trying to educate those who turn out to be education-proof" (121). But he fails to determine who should decide that a child is education-proof, and to discuss the legitimacy of such a decision. I believe it was Benjamin Franklin who stated that the doors of wisdom are never shut. Diogenes believed that the foundation of any state is the education of its youth. Abandoning young people who face overwhelming obstacles may be an open invitation to a criminal future. I shudder at the thought that in North America, in two of the most affluent societies in the world we would choose to discard children whose overwhelming circumstances have rendered them disfunctional. It becomes ironic then, that in some programs, these failures should receive an education in prison by way of rehabilitation after having been deemed education-proof in their childhood. The high rate of recidivism corroborates the fact that it often becomes impossible to correct the original wrong at this late stage.

The Adlerian belief that ours should be an educationally classless society is viewed by Solway as the "democratic shibboleth" which has instilled a sense of guilt in teachers who neglect the less gifted (121-2). He believes that this is a misguided position, and that the neglect of the gifted student should be considered an act of criminal negligence (122). Yet it is feasible to argue that if gifted, a student will not become less gifted because his teacher (in all probability less gifted than himself) is neglecting him in the name of egalitarianism. In this light, Solway's criticism of the democratic postulate is a misplaced invective.

It is not surprising that Solway traces back to the sixties the dramatic transformation which occurred in the classroom. He attributes the effect to the likes of Dr. Spock whose philosophy ultimately made the school an arena for greater freedom and openness. The changes were revolutionary indeed, when, the more regimented and hierarchical forties and fifties, in which the concept of academic freedom did not exist, yielded to the democratization of the disciplines. For Solway, those students graduating as teachers then "proceeded to instruct a new generation of illiterates whose precociousness tended to stop at the boundaries of sexuality and folkmusic" (42). And for Bloom, our present educational problems is the result of the experience in American universities in the sixties of the "same dismantling of structure of rational inquiry as the

German universities in the thirties" (313). For both critics, the reforms lacked substance and even "replace[d] something with nothing" (Bloom, 320). Thus, in their minds the winds of change of the 1960s are responsible for the collapse of education.

Bloom attributes many of our present ills to the spread of feminism. He argues in favor of nature and patriarchal culture, contending that "biology is surely nature" (100). He tends to be reductive in ascribing a monolithic value to the women's movement, and views its concerns as confused, wrong, and unnatural, forgetting his all-to-evident bias for culture. "Nature weighs more heavily on women," he concludes. "In the old order they were subordinated and dependent on men; in the new order they are isolated, needing men, but not able to count on them, and hampered in the free development of their individuality" (114). Inherent in his discrediting of feminism is an apparent contradiction. On the one hand, he ascribes a high value to socratic and stoic philosophy in its search for the good life through reason. Yet feminism strives to uphold the principle of egalitarianism between the sexes in order to better the lot of womankind and of society in general, exactly what Bloom would seem to be advocating.

This subtle form of patriarchy rests on the idea of difference, which many feminists consider to be a fundamental and destructive concept. As Colette Guillaumin argues, one must understand the notion of difference in its historical, political, and material context. "Once analysed in these terms, difference is exposed as synonymous with women's oppression."[5] Contrary to Bloom's benign outlook on nature, much of civilization was fashioned as a result of mankind's struggle against nature, both physical and human. Indeed, we have come a long way since the cave man. It is difficult to imagine a lecturer delivering such messages before self-respecting female students, without an outcry.

Another major destructive force reportedly working against education is technology. Both critics feel strongly that our technological era has eroded our cultural patrimony, but Solway goes further, adamantly condemning the pervasive and universal application of technology. He criticizes our mythical conception of technology which must be "de-metaphorized, if education is not to go under, taking our conception of the self along with it in its irresistible vortical drag" (109).

Solway continually contrasts our technological present with the need for the past, as does Bloom with the archaeology of tradition and the soul via history and the classics. To illustrate his idea that technology in fact proscribes the need for time and memory, Solway quotes John R. Clark's study of *A Tale of a Tub*, which attributes to Swift the idea that the "capacity for retentiveness is...the very source of man's humanity; without memory, man loses altogether that sense of locus, of continuity, and of identity that constitutes the self" (140). He designates the nameless protagonist as "the forerunner of technological man [who] lives in a world without a past, without duration, and without memory" (140). Bloom, too, recognizes history as memory, "not to tell us what happened, or to explain the past, but to make the past alive so that it can explain us and make a future possible" (239-40).

These points have been put eloquently, and their veracity can hardly be disavowed. Nevertheless, they have been argued with a great deal of dramatic hyperbole. In the first place, to deny our generation the instruments and inventions of our technological era would be anachronistic and reactionary. Did Pithecanthropus and Homo sapiens reject the use of fire? Did civilized man neglect such technological innovations of the Renaissance as the Gutenberg press, or advances in the use of gunpowder, navigation, and shipbuilding? Do our contemporaries shun the spectacular feats of aeronautics and space technology which might one day help unravel the mysteries of the origin of the universe and improve our understanding of cosmogony? Clearly we cannot undo the fruits of our technological era. Students should be given every educational opportunity to study the past in order to develop a sense of mankind's origins and evolution. But a tempered and discriminate use of technology should never be a hindrance to this pursuit.

How then do our critics conceive of education in general, or of the university in particular? Solway's rejection of the technological model to which he attributes the ills of our present educational system leads him to offer a pre-technological solution. His "new" pedagogy would thus be fashioned after the master of antiquity who was in possession of the promethian flame: it is "the ancient paradigm of rite and drama, the psychological structure of the initiation ritual as applied to the dynamics of teaching" (5). The teacher thus needs to reenact the dramatic rite and be capable of reaching the student through an exceptional personality.[6] In this ideal context, in which standards and instruction are the very highest, the student would naturally be predisposed to learning.

As for the innumerable students who would have to be given up in order to uphold this elitist model, there is no attempt to find a solution. Indeed, Solway emphatically decries our Robin Hoodish attitude in education. For this reason, he insists "that our educational programs cannot be unilateral, that after democratic opportunity has been offered to all, a kind of patrician selectivity must supervene, and that the higher conscience must replace our sense of egalitarian accountability" (128). Solway ignores, however, that like the models whose imperfections he criticizes, so too his own model, which sorely lacks a description of the means to ensure the end he is preconizing, is imperfect and virtually unrealizable in the name of true fairness.

Solway's choice of words in describing the majority of students conjures up the image of a diseased mind. By this view, only the *crème de la crème* should be given a privileged education—without apparent allowances for extraordinary circumstances and exceptional cases. At a recent conference on the Liberal Arts, one professor from an all-Black college proudly insisted that even she had gotten an education and had made it, despite the fact that the odds against her had been overwhelming from the start. If one adhered to Solway's principle, not only would this person not have been redeemed, society would have lost a much needed role model and mentor.

Bloom's premise complements Solway's general idea on education in that he is convinced that the university's vocation is to be undemocratic. He frequently evokes the model of Socrates who distanced himself from the Athenians and whose own thinking remained unadulterated by common opinion and culture to the very end. This explains Bloom's contention that Heidegger and others who put philosophy at the service of contemporary society are responsible for the death of the university. However, if Bloom's vision of the university based on the example of Socrates were to be taken seriously, we would be creating an army of potential dissidents against the very society which supports the university. Moreover, why would society continue to support the university if it became the symbol of an ivory tower at the antipodes from popular culture, undemocratic values, and absolute, anti-social truth? Would this implausible scenario not actually precipitate the demise of the university?

Pedagogically, Bloom is critical of the requirements which universities in the 1980s have imposed in order to repair the damages made by the curricular changes of the 1960s. He does not believe that a core curriculum with its broad inclusions from the various divisions affords students an adequate understanding of universal questions. Nor does he feel that composite courses, interdisciplinary in nature and designed with general education in mind, provide the "independent means to pursue permanent questions independently" (343).

The only viable solution for Bloom remains the Great Books approach which acquaints students with "what big questions were when there were still big questions; models, at the very least, of how to go about answering them" (344). Of course, since Bloom dismisses and defines as misguided the concerns of the feminist movement, he does not seriously concern himself with one of the leading bodies of criticism of our day. Indeed, one of the disadvantages to this approach is legitimately raised by feminism and by reader-response theory: how should a female readership respond to classical models of literature in which women do not figure as protagonists?[7] In the words of Annie Leclerc, women must invent their own language in order to invent woman. Referring to the great classics of the Western tradition, the French feminist states:

I haven't forgotten the names of the great talkers. Plato, Aristotle and Montaigne, Marx and Freud and Nietzsche. I know them because I've lived among them and among them alone. These strong voices are also those who have reduced me the most effectively to silence. It is these superb speakers who, more than any others, have forced me into silence (*French Connections*, 58).

At an age when more than half the student population is female compared with time immemorial when women did not attend university, when the proportion of minority and nontraditional students is increasing dramatically, and when demography is a driving concern in college planning, the Great Books approach seems inadequate and anachronistic. This is quite apart from ethical or scientific issues of our day, or from the issue of the environment which must be addressed if we are to save the Earth in the twenty-first century. In the era of the global village, Bloom's position that student relativism can be checked with a Great Books approach confined to Western tradition is simply misguided. His insistence that these books should be read as they were intended to be read is yet another sweeping statement which ignores the fact that many scholars do not agree on a universal interpretation of the Great Books. For one thing, it is sometimes difficult to objectively apprehend the authors' motivation. Moreover, neither sensibilities nor values nor mythologies remain stable throughout the ages, and dyachronic interpretation merely reflects such change.

In the words of Joseph Campbell, "Myths offer life models. But the models have to be appropriate to the time in which you are living, and our time has changed so fast that what was proper fifty years ago is not proper today" (*The Power of Myth*, 13).

A liberal arts education which exclusively maintains a Great Books tradition is denying modernity for the idol of an established canon. That curriculum also has to keep pace with the new language and concepts of our time which, incidentally, the Hirschian approach does not disregard. Thus, our current state of technological development makes it imperative to be well-versed in concepts which convey the way we relate to our modern world.

In the light of this, the synthesis might be to integrate the three approaches discussed above. An integrated curriculum would thus contain a Great Books component, without excluding such topical concerns as feminism, the environment, space, AIDS-related issues, Western and non-Western epistemologies, and international relations based on the present state of the world. Computer literacy, communication theory, and the media thus become as essential for an understanding of the world we live in as a knowledge of Aristotle's poetics and Castelvetro's interpretation of the unities for the study of seventeenth century French theater, or as significant as Petrarch for the study of Ronsard or the Shakespearean sonnet. The question of modernity is, after all, an old issue at the center of the quarrel between the Ancients and the Moderns. The difficulty resides in establishing a fine balance between exposure to the vast patrimony which we have inherited and to our changing modern world.

Bloom and Solway embody an elitist, undemocratic and oligarchic vision whose philosophic presuppositions iterate fixed truths which are not concerned with social justice and ethical questions. They are at the opposite spectrum from a society of self-educators whose idea of learning is not meant to be for the few whom nature has circumstantially privileged. Their idea of the best human life is not Voltairian. In order to create a happier, more enlightened society in the Voltairian sense, it is necessary to be less abrasive than Solway and Bloom whose will is to exclude large groups of students who are difficult to educate, and more tolerant than they vis-à-vis a society in the throes of fundamental changes. A more holistic approach in the spirit of Dewey, who believed in the whole child, is in order. A more supportive attitude fashioned after Joseph Katz, by which teachers have a greater understanding of the obstacles, conditions, and needs of student living and learning, is more crucial than ever before. *The Closing of the American Mind* and *Education Lost* clearly fall short of approximating these criteria.

Notes

[1]Solway is a Canadian poet and professor of English at John Abbott College, in Montreal.

[2]Universities which offer a core curriculum might wish to follow George Mason's present initiative in studying ways to assimilate Hirsch's program of cultural literacy. If and when its efforts are followed by implementation, the results might provide a degree of tangible evidence for other universities contemplating a similar experience. Whether

or not a Hirschian model would correct what many academics recognize along with Bloom and Solway to be an unacceptable level of general knowledge among North American university students, might thus become clear.

[3]See Alexander W. Astin's article on involvement which he likens to the Freudian concept of cathexis: "Freud believed that people invest psychological energy in objects outside of themselves. In other words, people can cathect on their friends, families, schoolwork, jobs, and so on" ("Involvement: The Cornerstone of Excellence," *Change*, July/August 1985: 36).

[4]One single book of facts spread throughout primary and secondary education is very little indeed, and can hardly be said to pose an obstacle to the development of the spirit. Such basic courses as Chemistry and Biology may likewise be taxed as data-based, even if they do have a practical application.

[5]See *French Connections: Voices from the Women's Movement in France*, translated and edited by Claire Duchen, 14.

[6]It is worth comparing Solway's very personal style of teaching with Paul de Man's contention that "the only teaching worthy of the name is scholarly, not personal" (*The Pedagogical Imperative*, 3).

[7]See such works as *L'Euguélionne* and *Le Pique-nique sur l'Acropole* in which Quebec author Louky Bersianik deals a stinging attack on patriarchal mythology and culture. The *Pique-nique sur l'Acropole*, for example, is a parody of Plato's *Symposium*, in which the discussion centers around a picnic and the points of view center around women. In portraying Xantippe as a strong woman who is doubtful of her husband's philosophy, Bersianik is vicariously giving birth to a new, non-male system of values. Through her canon-bashing, she deconstructs the patriarchal model still present in today's ontology as a result of the theories of Lacan, whom she considers to be the philosopher of the phallus, and of other psychoanalysts for whom woman is an incomplete being.

Works Cited

Astin, Alexander W. "Involvement: The Cornerstone of Excellence." *Change* July/ August 1985: 35-39.

Bloom, Allan. *The Closing of the American Mind: How Higher Education Has Failed Democracy and Impoverished the Souls of Today's Students.* N.Y.: Simon, 1987.

Booth, Wayne C. "Cultural Literacy and Liberal Learning: An Open Letter to E.D. Hirsch, Jr." *Change* July/August 1988: 12-21.

Buckley, William K. "The Good, the Bad, and the Ugly in Amerika's Akademia." *Profession 88*: 46-52.

Campbell, Joseph. *The Power of Myth.* Edited by Betty Sue Flowers. New York: Doubleday, 1988.

Duchen, Claire, ed. and trans. *French Connections: Voices from the Women's Movement in France.* Amhurst: The U of Massachusetts P, 1987.

Hirsch, E.D. Jr. *Cultural Literacy: What Every American Needs to Know.* Boston: Houghton, 1987.

Johnson, Barbara, ed. *The Pedagogical Imperative.* New Haven: Yale UP, 1987.

Solway, David. *Education Lost: Reflections on Contemporary Pedagogical Practice.* Toronto: The Ontario Institute for Studies in Education, 1989.

The Good, the Bad, and the Ugly
in Amerika's *Akadēmia*

William K. Buckley

I am not moralizing.

Allan Bloom, *The Closing of the American Mind* 22

To pass from the overheated Utopia of Education to the realm of teaching is to leave behind false heroics and take a seat in the front row of the human comedy.

Jacques Barzun, *Teacher in America* 17

Their world was also my world, their difficulties my difficulties, and if they were going to connect the world of the novels with their world. I had to acknowledge the same or similar connections.

Wayne Burns, *Journey through the Dark Woods* 115

"I am just an American Jewish kid," Allan Bloom has said, "to whom the ideas of great thinkers were made available, but I fear that the opportunities I had will no longer exist" (Interview). There can be no doubt that Bloom means what he says here, and, in fact, there can be no doubt that we know him to be a scholar who passionately loves the great books. But surely he is being modest when he says that he was *just* a kid "to whom the ideas of great thinkers were made available." *The Closing of the American Mind* has won the Jean-Jacques Rousseau Prize in Geneva, and Bloom's analysis of our "spiritual malaise" has been read in this country by probably half a million people. He has attracted congratulatory raves from the Right and bitter denunciations from the Left. The *National Review* has devoted its annual campus issue to him (where Hugh Kenner hopes for big sales of the book), while *Harper's* has Benjamin Barber proclaiming that Bloom has written "one of the most profoundly anti-democratic books ever" (62). Bloom is too complex, however, for either the Right or the Left to adopt him as their Jeremiah. He is not the academy's ayatollah. Tongues are not cut out from students' mouths at the University of Chicago for uttering Western "liberalisms." Nor is he the Frankfurt School sociologist, although many of his comments on American culture can be traced to the influence of this school. He dismisses thinkers like Marcuse and Adorno quickly and without any discussion. That he is no "liberal" may, at first glance, seem obvious, with his offhanded pan of Freud, Marx, and the social sciences. That he is a

Reprinted with permission of *Profession '88* and the Modern Language Association. Expanded essay.

"conservative" may be strongly argued, since he is codirector of the John M. Olin Center and says things like "students...no longer have any image of a perfect soul" (67) and modern American political thought has betrayed the original intentions of the "Founders" (31; see also Bork). What makes *The Closing of the American Mind* more controversial than E.D. Hirsch's *Cultural Literacy*, and less likely to be adopted wholeheartedly by either Left or Right, is its sharper criticisms of American democracy. And to many of those criticisms we can say yes:

1. Students "live comfortably within the administrative state that has replaced politics" (85)—yes.

2. "[P]assionlessness is the most striking effect...of the sexual revolution" (99)—yes.

3. Students are "full of desperate platitudes about self-determination....[T]his is a thin veneer over boundless seas of rage, doubt, and fear" (120)—yes.

4. "There is a whole arsenal of terms for talking about nothing—caring, self-fulfillment, expanding consciousness" (155)—yes.

5. "The humanities are like the great old Paris Flea Market where, amidst masses of junk, people with a good eye found castaway treasures that made them rich" (371)—yes.

6. The humanities "suffer most from democratic society's lack of respect for tradition and its emphasis on utility" (373)—yes.

7. "American life-style has become a Disneyland version of the Weimar Republic for the whole family" (147)—perhaps.

8. "Historicism and cultural relativism actually are a means to avoid testing our own prejudices" (40)—yes.

Yet there is much in the book to which I can respond no:

1. America has no "deep necessity" to read its own authors (54)—no. What of Cooper, Twain, Crane, Whitman, Melville, and Hawthorne? If not found in high school courses—and most are—then they are found in required college courses.

2. Rock music ruins the imagination of students and makes it difficult for them "to have a passionate relationship to the art and thought...of liberal education" (79)—no. My students have always reacted passionately to the books I teach—from Rousseau to D. H. Lawrence. They use rock music to escape from their passions.

3. Kids don't have "prejudices against anyone" (89)—not where I teach. Judgments about race, sex, and religion are strong and deep here, and they don't spring from what Bloom calls "aristocratic" sentiments "within the democracy" (89).

4. "Freud and D. H. Lawrence are very old hat" (107)—not for my students, no matter where I have taught. Both still outrage.

5. Heidegger's revolt against Aristotle and Plato and the decision by German universities to serve "German culture" spelled death for reason and introduced nihilism into American higher education—provocative but reductive. The "Nietzscheanization of the Left" has been shown by Wilhelm Reich to be only one manifestation of a much broader phenomenon: all mass psychologies, whether Left, Right, or center, are based on organized mysticism, repressive idealisms, and politically staged events. The nihilism I feel in my students as they struggle to respond to Céline or Lawrence is really the hard and angry reaction to the most repressive aspects of idealism in their lives.[1] Nihilism is pleasure anxiety, the energizing core of patriarchal religions, and it was precisely this kind of anxiety that Hitler and Lenin counted on in setting up their governments (Reich shows us in *The*

Mass Psychology of Fascism certain pamphlets distributed to German students in the 1930s that are full of religious mysticisms, silly patriotic ideals, references to Nietzsche, and careful recognitions of sexual repressions and how students might satisfy them in order to be more effective and obedient servants to the fuhrer figure). Nihilism in America is not the revolt against Aristotle and Plato but the manifestation of inner struggles against what can be a ruthless economy. Far from projecting what Bloom calls an "ambiguous image" (297), the natural sciences in our American universities actually tap into the full emotional content of political mysticisms and exploitive economics in order to forge whatever economic and military policy is deemed expedient.[2]

6. Our students are free to read "in any way they please" (374)—not in my classes; nor was I ever allowed to read this way in the classes I attended at college in the 1960s and 1970s. And my colleagues today do not let this happen in their classes.

7. The "fate of freedom in the world has devolved upon our regime...[T]he fate of philosophy in the world has devolved upon our universities" (382)—let's just say that these statements are a little self-conscious.

More tempestuous than Hirsch's *Cultural Literacy* and more ambitious than Barzun's *Teacher in America*, *The Closing of the American Mind* remains, curiously enough, too much the general swipe—despite the lengthy descriptions of American life in part 1. Sometimes the book is the leisured and cranky lament, characteristic of the small-town editorial page; in other places it is the thick treatise. What makes *Closing* so popular, however, is that it just might be the last and most eloquent twentieth-century protest against the scientific discoveries of the nineteenth century. And in its genuine pain at seeing the mute and brutal reality of things surround culture, "as the puppet-show of fancy was surrounded by the inn," as Ortega y Gasset called it (144-45), the book becomes more howl than argument, more condemnation of history than level-eyed tangle with fact. Bloom's complaints are not new: we read much the same in Veblen, Marx, Freud, Marcuse, and Adorno and in the essays by our colleagues in the last issues of *Profession* (in *Profession 87* Wayne Booth's "Reversing the Downward Spiral: Or, What Is the Graduate Program *For?*" divides us with more compassion into the "Ancients" and the "Mods"). What *is* new, however, is how we come to know Bloom's views. Through his commonplace dichotomies we come to see his vision of our *akadēmia*; by his clear view of the "good" and his descriptions of the bad and ugly, we come to see our post-Socratic Amerika.

The Good (The True Socratic Teacher Who Fights with Right Reason the Culture of Relativism)

It is difficult to discover just what Bloom means by "the good," a phrase that appears with regularity in his book as the offered cure-all for our pursuit of nihilism. That's because in true Socratic fashion Bloom refuses to be specific about "things of Being." Perhaps the good is the "fulfillment of the whole natural human potential" (37). But what is that? Perhaps it is the United States, which, he says, is one of the "highest and most extreme achievements of the rational quest for the good life according to nature" (39). Sweden, France, and England would disagree. We can guess with relative accuracy that the University is a good if it provides a place where Reason can be contemptuous of public opinion. More likely, however, the good are only those men who do *not* live "off the gradually dying energy provided by the original philosophic dynamos"

(311), men who still believe with Plato that eros leads to philosophy, which in turn leads to "the rational quest for the best regime, the *one* good political order vs. the plurality of cultures" (305). Now this quest for the "*one*" good political order goes far beyond any of the blueprints for literacy drawn up by Hirsch or Paulo Freire. To discover what kind of men pursue the best regime, and what political order they want, we must finally turn to Plato's *Republic*— especially since Bloom admits that the *Republic* is "*the* book on education" for him (381).

Socrates. [E]ducation is not truly what some of its professors say it is. They say they are able to put knowledge into a soul which hasn't got it—as if they were putting sight into blind eyes.
Glaucon. They do say so.
Socrates. But our argument points to this: the natural power to learn lives in the soul and is like an eye which might not be turned from the dark to the light without a turning round of the whole body. The instrument of knowledge has to be turned around, and with it the whole soul, from the things of becoming to the things of being, till the soul is able, by degrees, to support the light of true being and can look at the brightest. And this, we say, is the good?
Glaucon. We do.   (126)

Now, at last, we are close to understanding. To be able to turn people around in just *this* way, an efficient and powerful political structure is necessary.

Socrates. So we who are designing this state will have to force these naturally best minds to get what we have said is the greatest knowledge of all, to go on up till they see the good, and, when they have seen enough, we will not let them do as they do now.
Glaucon. What is that?
Socrates. They may not keep to themselves up there, but have to go down again among those prisoners and take part in their work and rewards, whatever these may be.
Glaucon. Then are we to wrong them by forcing them into a worse way of living when a better one is within their power?
Socrates. Are you keeping in mind, my friend, that this law of ours is not to make any one group in the state specially happy, but the state itself? Everyone is to give to all the others whatever he is able to produce for the society. For it made these men so, not to please themselves, but to unite the commonwealth.
Glaucon. I see. I was overlooking that.
Socrates. But note, Glaucon, there will be no wrong done to the philosophers in this. We have just arguments to give them when we force them to become guardians.   (127-28)

Now we see, clearly, the good: the state itself. And it was Plato's devotion to this goal that drove him to say "we will keep a sharp eye on these makers of stories" (49). What would a Platonic state do with William Blake, Céline, or Allen Ginsberg? It would not let them "do as they do now." The pursuit of the good, therefore, is that focusing of the ancient "sharp eye" on the dangers that the imagination poses to the ideal state or the ideal university. Zamiatin's *We* pointedly describes the phenomenon:

REJOICE!

For from now on we are *perfect*!
Until today your own creation, engines, were more perfect than you.

WHY?

For every spark from a dynamo is a spark of pure reason; each motion of a piston, a pure syllogism. It is not true that the same faultless reason is within you?

The philosophy of the cranes, presses, and pumps is complete and clear like a circle. But is your philosophy less circular? The beauty of a mechanism lies in its immutable, precise rhythm, like that of a pendulum. But have you not become as precise as a pendulum?...

Yes, but there is one difference:

MECHANISMS HAVE NO FANCY.

Did you ever notice a pump cylinder with a wide, distant, sensuously dreaming smile upon its face while it was working? Did you ever hear cranes that were restless, tossing about and sighing at night during the hours designed for rest?

NO!

Yet on your faces (you may well blush with shame!) the Guardians have more and more frequently seen those smiles, and they have heard your sighs. And (you should hide your eyes for shame!) the historians of the United States have all tendered their resignations so as to be relieved from having to record such shameful occurrences.

It is not your fault; you are ill. And the name of your illness is:

(166)

FANCY

The Bad (Sometimes the Masses Awash with Opinions and Sometimes Intellectuals Who Deny Man "Eternity")

The mass-minded American student is an easy individual to condemn. As an obvious target, his mind is so weak that it neither recognizes the attack on it nor allows space for such a critique to thrive. Even those of us who think we are free from the diversity of propaganda discover that our ideas have not escaped the power of its reductive force. That's why teaching is such hard work. The crowd out in front of us must fight the swallowed-whole notions of its culture if it is ever to break free and really read a great book—and so must the teacher fight. It's easy, then, to use Tocqueville's *Democracy in America* to attack what we already know: that the American mind is conformist. It is much harder to analyze the effects of our conformity, which seem to interpenetrate our very analysis of it. Even Bloom has been bamboozled by the media's hype of the sixties as the so-called decade of revolution. Our language has been so thinned out by a consumer economy, so absorbed by the black hole of propaganda, that words like *revolution* can now be used to sell dishwashing liquid. That's why Bloom's "report from the front" (22) will be used and popularized according to the needs of a well-oiled state. Surely Bloom realizes that, true to Tocqueville's descriptions, *Closing* will be shelved as just one more opinion and that the economic, business, and military interests of an industrialized nation will quietly and efficiently use his ideas in any way that it wants and then jettison them from the arranged public climate when they are no longer expedient. Marcuse's

"Beyond Tolerance" gives us detailed and effectively reasoned descriptions of this aspect of democracy.

E. D. Hirsch's solution to our illiterate conformity is to require that all our students know "what literate Americans know" (146), and what literate Americans know he provides in a lengthy, alphabetically arranged list of facts, ideas, names, and books (e.g. "Adonis," "adrenal gland," "adrenaline," etc. I note with surprise that Blake is on the list but not Ginsberg, "adultery" but not "alcoholism," Dickens but not Hardy, "circumcision" but not "circulation"; see also Scholes's responses to the list). Hirsch's plan is to teach the list not "as a series of terms, or a list of words," but as a "vivid system of shared associations" (127): all to bring us close to the "Ciceronian ideal of universal public discourse—in short, achieving fundamental goals of the Founders at the birth of the republic" (145). This sort of sloganeering reminds us of Bloom; Bloom's solution, however, is more radical: we must tell the student "what he *should* study" (338). And that "*should*," of course, means studying not the "multiversity smorgasbord," the traitorous social sciences, or the big bad MBA programs but a completely interrelated system of disciplines that will satisfy our need for what Bloom calls "high-level generalism" (343). I think he means that liberal education must go back to discussing "a unified view of nature and man's place in it" (347). I can't believe that our place in nature is *not* being discussed at schools across the land—given the American love for sweeping pronouncements. But Bloom is convinced that the bad is "cultural relativism," which "succeeds in destroying the West's universal or intellectually imperialistic claims" (39); that Marxism, Freudianism, and behaviorism (presumably the work of B. F. Skinner) are abstractions not grounded in experience; and that the growth of these relativisms is destroying the university by destroying high-level generalisms. I find it baffling that Bloom condemns Marx and Freud, those high-level generalists whose first analyses of "the mob" have helped Bloom come to the conclusions he has reached. Moreover, what could be more grounded in experience than the descriptions found in Freud's "Infantile Sexuality" or Marx's "Estranged Labour" or Skinner's "What Is Man?" Only Charles Darwin was more worried about our place in nature.

The bad is not the mob waiting to tear down the walls of the university but the efficient removal of our individuality by institutions that find it necessary to anchor their policies in political idealisms—this is the real cause for our modern feelings of alienation. The "antidote" is not "the heroic—Homer, Plutarch" (256), as Bloom says it is, or a more clever way of feeding state lies to children. Prince Hal's pursuit of the heroic led him back to the Inn, where Falstaff waited with a mug of ale and a speech on missing limbs. Surrounding the Ideal, always, is the Inn, *Don Quixote* keeps telling us, and the Inn offers itself as a refuge for those battered by the high expectations of civilization. Perhaps our universities should offer a haven, too, to those who feel battered.

Wayne Burns's *Journey through the Dark Woods* is probably the most remarkable autobiography ever penned by a college teacher, and I offer a quote from it now as a response to Bloom's Platonic solutions to our academic problems. Both Burns and Bloom have looked at the same problems, and they even say similar things about American life, but where Bloom says, with Plato, "Till philosophers become kings...only then will this our republic see the light of day" (*Republic* 97), Burns, after giving us remarkable political and social observations of the university from 1940 to 1980, says something quite the opposite:

> I don't think you can speak of the survival of education or society apart from the survival of individuals. For my part I feel no concern for the survival of even. . . the university, except in so far as it sustains and nourishes individual students and teachers. . . .
>
> To ask, or to demand, or to expect that a University of some 30,000 students can be humanized is to me sheer naiveté. And to persist in this demand or expectation is sheer folly, and can only lead to still further institutionalization of students and teachers alike.   (195-96)

I believe I did, in my undergraduate classes, manage to combine theory with practice in such a way as to deepen, without restricting, their responses to the novels. But in the process I ran into unforeseen consequences, since I found it impossible to effect the combination without having my theory of fiction turn into a theory of life. I didn't want that to happen, or at least I didn't want it to happen in the way it often did happen. For I had no lust for power, no desire to become some kind of guru. The most I wanted to do was provide the students with a way of understanding fiction that was also, as I believed it had to be, a way of understanding life in all its dismaying complexity.

Yet if I wasn't forcing I was inevitably persuading. I couldn't do anything else. In consciously setting myself up as the teacher as revolutionary, committed to helping the students who wished to follow the novelist as revolutionary wherever he might lead, I had, in effect, committed myself to going places with students that teachers do not ordinarily go. In asking them to be naked I had to be naked too; or more accurately, I had to be naked first, since I, as the teacher, couldn't ask them to do what I had not yet done. I couldn't, in other words, ask them to make connections I hadn't made.   (114-15)

The Ugly (The Nihilists—Dangerous Souls to the Body Politic)
Bloom: Isn't it true that under your powerful influence the German university abandoned reason when it began to attack Socrates himself?
Nietzsche: That may be so, but a philosopher—as you have said—should not have any allegiance to institutions. I place myself outside *akadēmia*, as did Socrates.
Bloom: But you have destroyed the tragic sense of life, the noble instincts. You have cut the common thread linking us to the real Greece.
Nietzsche: Indeed. But what is the real Greece?
Bloom: It is reason itself, and reason is now rejected by philosophy itself. Your opinions are separated from knowledge, and, as Plato said, they are therefore "ugly things" [*Republic* 115].
Nietzsche: Wasn't it reasoning that led me to my reasonings? My ugly things?
Bloom: Yes, but your disciple Heidegger has betrayed the spirit of philosophy and put the university at the service of German culture. And now the very idea of the university in America is close to being destroyed as a result.
Nietzsche: Then he must assume responsibility for his own reasoning.
Bloom: And you must assume yours!
Nietzsche: Indeed, I do. Which is?
Bloom: You have attacked the ideal state.
Woody Allen: Could I break in here? Where is the ideal state?
Bloom: In our noble instincts.

Allen: My mother once told me that my Aunt Gladys had noble instincts and that's why she never got married. She spent her whole life ogling ideal women in the Sears *Catalog* and eating chocolates.

Bloom: You are trivializing, as usual! And you are not very amusing either. Both you and Nietzsche have lost true inner-directedness.

Allen: I'm sentimental, for Christ's sake! about my old neighborhood! and 1940s big band music, delicatessens, food, smells, really attractive women! That's nihilism?

Bloom: Yes. You give us nihilism as something we want to feel cozy about.

Allen: That's what I'm showing in my movies! Everyone wants me to be serious. Nobody wants me to be funny anymore!

Karl Marx: None of you have got it yet. If our ideas are ugly, gentlemen, then they reflect the ugliness of those in power. Professor Bloom, you remember the discussion between Socrates and Thrasymachus over the keepers of the sheep?

Bloom: I do.

Marx: And do you remember that Thrasymachus's point was that "justice is simply what is to the stronger man's profit?" [*Republic* 26]

Allen: Sounds like my agent.

Bloom: I do.

Marx: And that the unjust man will always outdo the just man, especially where money is concerned?

Bloom: Yes.

Marx: And that injustice will often get more for one man than justice will get for another?

Bloom: Yes.

Marx: Well?

Bloom: Well, what?

Marx: Don't you see the irony?

Bloom: We must still define justice according to all things good and unchanging.

Marx: Who must?

Bloom: The philosophers, the true guardians of the state.

Marx: And I'm not a philosopher?

Bloom: No. You are an economist.

Marx: And you?

Bloom: I am a philosopher, and I am in "love with knowledge of the unchanging" [*Republic* 102]. And even though all of you may be philosophers in one degree or another, your natural science and your historicism are destroying the academy. There is no common concern and search for the good today. We must, like all those men in the Platonic dialogues, think together for the establishment of the true republic.

Marx: Come now, the watchword is *Kritik*. Utopias of whatever kind are abstractions! That's why we must clarify our consciousness by waking it up from its dream world! Everywhere the state presumes that Reason has been realized! When what is really going on is the conflict between the workings of the State and our real conditions (9-10).

Bloom: Don't you think philosophy should get beyond your reduction of everything to dialectics?

Marx: How? We can't tell the world, "Here is the truth, bow down before it!"...We only show the world what it is fighting for..."religion is the catalogue of the theoretical struggles of mankind...the political state is the catalogue of its practical struggles." (9-10).

Bloom: Then what do you believe in?

Marx: Consciousness!

Bloom: And resolution? The sublime?

Allen: I've got a sublime resolution. "The lion and the calf shall lie down together but the calf won't get much sleep." (WF, 25)

Bloom: Even Marx takes religion seriously.

Allen: Wait a minute! "I have been known to have some reasonably profound insights myself, although mine invariably revolve around a Swedish airline stewardess and some handcuffs" (SE, 33)

(Groans)

O.K., O.K., seriously people, "the great appeal for me of this wisest of all Greeks was his courage in the face of death...Socrates' brave death gave his life authentic meaning; something my existence lacks totally, although it does possess a minimal relevance to the Internal Revenue Department!" (SE, 33)

Bloom: Look, this really isn't funny anymore. You destroy philosophy in "Hannah and Her Sisters" when you say that "Socrates screwed little Greek boys." And was that white bread and mayonnaise really necessary?

Allen: Oh, for Christ's sake! I'm putting words in the mouth of a self in a movie the way Plato put words into Socrates' mouth!

Noam Chomsky: Precisely! Management! The powerful "are able to fix the premises of discourse, to decide what the general populace is allowed to see, hear, and think about, and to 'manage' public opinion by regular propaganda campaigns!" (xi).

Bloom: Whatever we acquire *over* the natural in man's humanity is fruit for the real culture (190). History is not a catalogue of deeds or products, or manufactured news items, but a dimension of man's being. History is a union of nature and political order, and that union is forced together by the legislator (190).

Jean Baudrillard: I've listened long enough to all this! Can't any of you see that the structure of our world is beginning to go far beyond the old way of organization? The U.S. is Utopia achieved! But of a special kind, where "everything is appropriated and simplified into the translucence of abstract 'happiness,' simply defined by the resolution of tensions..." (SW, 34). America is the ecstatic critique of culture, where, like deserts, vanishing points live at the end of freeways and consumption! Astral America exists! "The lyrical nature of pure circulation...The direct star-blast from vectors and signals, from the vertical and the spatial. As against the fevered distance of the cultural gaze" (A, 27). The exhilaration of obscene obviousness! It is no longer a question of nihilism or meaning! But one of repetition and the hyperreal! This is the era of simulation! All forces have joined the power of the sign. "All the great humanist criteria of value, all the values of a civilization of moral, aesthetic, and practical judgement, vanish in our system of images and signs. Everything becomes undecidable, interchangeable." Our history is the "generalized brothel of substitution and interchangeability!" (SW, 128).

Sigmund Freud: Gentlemen, gentlemen, please! We must get beyond our pleasure principles here. Do you all really believe in the human instinct for perfection? Such a "benevolent illusion!" (615). Repressed instincts will never tire at finding "complete satisfaction, which would consist in the repetition of a primary experience of satisfaction" (616). Even in horror Utopias!

Bloom: Now I know why you are so popular in America, doctor. Your account of sublimation makes us *regret* civilization. It suggests the decline of the West, personal failure, and guilt (231). Yes?

Freud:

Bloom: Well?

Freud: Do you understand the irony? The tension between consciousness and regret? Knowledge and loss? The Totemic Meal?

Baudrillard: The drugstore!

Marx: Productive Forces!

Chomsky: Flak!

Allen: The delicatessen!

Nietzsche: Socratic lobotomies!!

Bloom: We still must define the State according to all things good and unchanging.

The rest: Who must?

Bloom: The philosophers.

The rest: And we are not philosophers?

Bloom: No, I've said. You are not. I am. Because I remain in love "with knowledge of the unchanging" (Republic, 102).

Bloom is a passionate thinker, reader, teacher, and idealist, who, like Plato, feels he is writing at a time when his country is doomed. These are reactionary times in Amerika, years in a decade marked by an age-old complaint hollered out by the editors of the inaugural issue of the *National Review*: We shall stand athwart history and yell "Stop!" Unlike E. D. Hirsch, Bloom reasons around history and back to the sweet dreams of an old Greek. *The Closing of the American Mind* is plagued by a generalized vision that sees only two kinds of American students and teachers: those who are subject to mob opinion and those who read and apply the classics. Bloom's proof for this division is to describe his students' behavior on one day in the 1960s, when they *"looked down* from the classroom on the frantic activity outside, thinking they were privileged"* (332). In 1973, I had the opportunity to *look down* too, from an outside stairwell attached to a university library building, and I witnessed with detachment how a mob coiled itself up and then lunged into the closed front doors of an administration building. It was "Stop-the-War Day." I did not join the mob, nor did I feel superior. I went home and found myself reading Lucan's *Civil Wars* and Freud's "Group Psychology and Analysis of the Ego." There were many reactions that day, however, other than the mob's choice or my bookish one. A lot of teachers and students were in the library; a lot of students walked by the riot, on their way to work. Quite a few people stood around and cheered; some were even taking a nap in the sun on a grassy hillside overlooking the scene. The whole event was rich in irony—and had you witnessed that event from a great distance away, I have no doubt that you would have found it as ironic as Icarus's unnoticed fall in Breughel's painting. There were so many individualized actions that day, and individualized actions, anchored as they are in reality, are always in conflict with ideal prescriptions.

When Socrates tells Glaucon that justice is to be loved for itself, Glaucon responds, "But the masses, Socrates, don't think so. They put being just with hard work, as one of the things to be done only for what is to be got out of it, rewards and a good name" (33). Such realism is too much for Socrates. He responds that he is not "very good at learning such things" (33). Realism is, perhaps, too much for Bloom, as it is for most of us—as it was for Don Quixote. Like Husserl, who planned in *The Crisis of the European Sciences* to secure for eternity reason and truth against all doubt, so has Bloom planned, in *Closing*, to encase the imagination within prescribed consensus and to secure the university against change. But if it is true (and I think it is) that, as Wayne Burns says, our students' world is also our world and "their difficulties" are our difficulties, and if as teachers we acknowledge this, then and only then can we leave the "overheated Utopia of Education" and "take a seat in the front row of the human comedy" (Barzun 17).

Notes

[1]"Away from the animal; away from the sexuality!" are the guiding principles of the formation of all human ideology. This is the case whether it is disguised in the fascist form of racially pure "supermen," the communist form of proletarian class honor, the Christian form of man's "spiritual and ethical nature," or the liberal form of "higher human values." All these ideas harp on the same monotonous tune: "We are not animals; it was we who discovered the machine—not the animal. *And we don't have genitals like the animals!*" All of this adds up to an overemphasis of the intellect, of the "purely" mechanistic; logic and reason as opposed to instinct; culture as opposed to nature; the mind as opposed to the body; work as opposed to sexuality; the state as opposed to the individual; the superior man as opposed to the inferior man.

How is it to be explained that of the millions of car drivers, radio listeners, etc., only very few know the name of the inventor of the car and the radio, whereas every child knows the name of the generals of the political plague?

Natural science is constantly drilling into man's consciousness that fundamentally he is a worm in the universe. The political plague-monger is constantly harping upon the fact that man is not an animal, but a "zoon politikon," i.e., a non-animal, an upholder of values, a "moral being." How much mischief has been perpetuated by the Platonic philosophy of the state! It is quite clear why man knows the politicos better than the natural scientists: He does not want to be reminded of the fact that he is fundamentally a sexual animal. *He does not want to be an animal.* (Reich 339)

[2]See Reich, chapters 7 and 8.

Works Cited

Allen, Woody. *Without Feathers.* New York: Random House, 1972.
———. "My Apology," *Side Effects.* New York: Random House, 1975.
Barber, Benjamin. "The Philosopher Despot." *Harper's* January 1988: 61-65.
Barzun, Jacques. *Teacher in America.* Indianapolis: Liberty, 1981.
Baudrillard, Jean. *America.* London: Verso, 1988.

_____ *Selected Writings*. Stanford UP, 1988.

Bloom, Allan. Interview. *U.S. News and World Report* 11 May 1987: 78.

_____ *The Closing of the American Mind*. New York: Simon, 1987.

Bork, Robert H. "Neutral Principles and Some First Amendment Problems." *Indiana Law Journal* 47 (1971): 1-35.

Burns, Wayne. *Journey Through The Dark Woods*. Seattle: Howe Street, 1982.

Freud, Sigmund. "Beyond the Pleasure Principle." *The Freud Reader*. New York: W.W. Norton, 1989.

Herman, E. S. and N. Chomsky. *Manufacturing Consent*. New York: Pantheon, 1988.

Hirsch, E. D. Jr. *Cultural Literacy: What Every American Needs to Know*. Boston: Houghton, 1987.

Marx, Karl. "For a Ruthless Criticism of Everything that Exists." *The Marx-Engels Reader*. W. W. Norton, 1972.

Ortega y Gasset, José. *Meditations on Quixote*. New York: Norton, 1961.

Plato. *Plato's Republic*. I. A. Richards, ed. and trans. Cambridge: Cambridge UP, 1966.

Reich, Wilhelm. *The Mass Psychology of Fascism*. New York: Farrar, 1970.

Scholes, Robert. "Three Views of Education: Nostalgia, History, and Voodo." *College English* 50 (1988): 323-32.

Zamiatin, Eugene. *We*. Trans. G. Zilboorg. New York: Dutton, 1924.

Culture and Democracy:
Strange Bedfellows and Their Offspring

Milton R. Stern

Cultural Literacy by Professor E.D. Hirsch of the University of Virginia and *The Closing of the American Mind* by Professor Allan Bloom of the University of Chicago are in the great tradition of self-flagellation (without pain) common to academics. They echo the complaint of the ages: "The cultural power of our higher educational institutions has perhaps never been lower or feebler than at present." That was Nietzsche in *The Birth of Tragedy* 1872.

What Every American Needs to Know

Professor Hirsch has given his book the dashing subtitle, "What Every American Needs to Know." After a few useful chapters addressing the importance of something more than simple literacy, the book tells us what we need to know to make all of us culturally literate. As you probably know by now, it contains a list, a list of people, places, names, quotations, ideas, which covers a waterfront—Professor Hirsch's waterfront, to be sure, which may be on Chesapeake Bay, or even closer on Pamunkey River. This list has been found offensive by some people, and they take potshots at the book. At the same time, it is a very tempting book. It's "Trivial Pursuit," at another level, presumably "Profound Pursuit."

The *Wall Street Journal* took its licks at *Cultural Literacy* and *The List*, pointing out that it included the line, "Regret that I have but one life to lose for my country, I only," but didn't identify Nathan Hale as the author. I discovered myself that it did list Hale alphabetically between "Haiti" and "Half a loaf is better than none" (I don't know why that doesn't read, "Loaf, half a, is better than none," but there we are, or there Professor Hirsch is). The *Wall Street Journal* story was patronizing, but I am sure that everyone who looks at the list will have that same mischievous curiosity—what did he leave out that I know and what did he put in that he shouldn't have? Thus, you may ask, why didn't he put in the Grateful Dead, if he put in Elvis Presley? I might add that he does not have the negative attitudes toward contemporary art and music, rock, jazz, synthesizer, you name it, in which Professor Bloom seems to revel.

Adapted from the keynote address of the National University Continuing Education Association (NUCEA) regional conference an *A Multicultural Society*, October 13, 1987, Salt Lake City, Utah. It was delivered soon after the publication of both books discussed.

The *Wall Street Journal* was condescending, and one thing I rather liked about Mr. Hirsch's book is that it does not condescend. It takes a forthright position, saying, here's a whole list of things, ideas, names, places, scientific discoveries, medical terms, that culturally literate American adults should have in their awareness. Professor Hirsch's list was compiled with the help of two other members of the Virginia faculty. One wants to check it constantly, quarrel with it and have fun with it. But it does help to achieve his purpose to some degree by creating discussion about what makes for cultural literacy.

I thought that the Note on the Scientific Terms by Dr. James Trefil was particularly helpful in this regard. Trefil made the point that people—the ordinary run of non-scientific mortals—need help. Even when he writes, as he says, for the "well educated, highly literate readership of *Smithsonian* magazine,"—he finds himself reluctant to use the word *proton* without glossing it ("One of the elementary particles that forms a nucleus of an atom"). Without that extra phrase, he says, it just won't be understood. And he goes on to say that if a political scientist were to proceed on comparable assumptions, "He or she would have to pause to explain every time a term like United States Senate appeared in the text."

His point is well-founded—that cultural ignorance about scientific terms among the otherwise culturally literate is general. With that in mind, I went over the list, obeying the natural temptation to ask what is left out that is scientific. My basic criticism of the book, its basic weakness, is that it is—it must be— particular to the people who compile it in their time and place, in terms of their own culture. On that score, while the word "reactor" is in—and I am sure that Professor Trefil felt that that doesn't need too much of an explanation when he writes for the *Smithsonian*—the word "reaper," McCormick's reaper, that is, is not in. Were this book written in 1887, instead of 1987, I am sure that the word "reaper" would have been there, and many other farm terms would be part of the cultural literacy of the "culturally literate audience." Not today.

My search also gives me an opportunity to point out that, while Franklin Pierce isn't listed, the only Pierce that is shown is a misspelling of Charles Sanders Peirce—ah, there, Professor Hirsch or Trefil. But let me not trifle with Trefil.

It's the kind of thing that everybody can enjoy. Classical music? Franz Schubert, but not Arnold Schoenberg. It includes *crème de la crème*, but not *crème Anglaise*. You can pick and choose: What's your cultural index, what's your cultural background? Where, quite literally, are you coming from? Professor Hirsch has a bias in certain directions, but that's rather engaging. He admits to his biases, and he doesn't argue that his list is at all perfect, or even perfectible. But he says, "Here's something that would be useful to know, and if you quarrel with my list, well that is the sign of active stimulation, and it helps the cause of cultural literacy."

Yet, the whole exercise conduces to pathos. I was in a bookstore in Marin County a few weeks ago, and a woman came in looking as she said, for a book which lists all those things that every cultivated person—"cultured person," is the phrase she used—has to know. And so, the clerk referred her to Mr. Hirsch's book, and there was the list. She said, "But I want them explained. I want definitions." "Ah," he said, "We don't have that book."

Well, you know, there are such things as encyclopedias, and dictionaries, but I don't really think that the encyclopedia is what she had in mind. She meant, "If I have to know these things, can I learn them in a hurry and be ready by Sunday for the brunch bunch?"

There are many books like *Cultural Literacy*, of course; Mr. Hirsch has the merit of being somewhat modest in his approach. He recently went into business for himself down in Virginia, as I understand from the *Chronicle of Higher Education*; he is going to help the poor lady in the bookstore. I wish him luck. I hope that he doesn't discover what some people find—that there are worse things than selling out, and one of them is finding no buyers.

A question one must address is, can one *teach* or *learn* cultural literacy? Cautiously, I think so, but I think that the question calls for a long longitudinal research.

More to the point is method. It is education by inquiry that we need: Courses in critical reasoning, like the one I taught for twelve years at N.Y.U. called "How to Read and Think." I used *The Declaration of Independence*, Mill *On Liberty*, Thoreau's *Walden*, Shaw's *St. Joan*, Sophocles' *Oedipus*: There are more ways than cramming to become culturally literate.

Bloom's Closed American Mind

Allan Bloom is a polemicist, a master of invective and of hyperbole to the point of one's not being sure that he is speaking accurately, or wants to be taken seriously. He sounds like an impetuous college teacher in the classroom in full cry after an idea which he regards as important. In that circumstance you can move readily, as Judge Bork recently told us, into hyperbolic comments, deliberately provocative and speculative and not to be taken at all that seriously. Yet, there they are on paper, and they sound serious, and that bothers me from time to time in Allan Bloom's book.

His paragraphs are—well—impetuous. He has a habit of piling up dubious propositions on top of each other to arrive in the last sentence at what may only be called irrelevant, intemperate and illogical conclusions. He reminds me of that definition of an expert as one who avoids small errors, as he swoops down on the grand fallacy. Let me give you an example: He alleges that American intellectuals—and I really didn't think he'd find too many of them, but he does—really are dazzled by a nostalgia for the Weimar Republic. And he argues further that, after the war, meaning World War II, "While America was sending out its blue jeans to unite the young of all nations, a concrete form of democratic universalism that has had liberalizing effects on many enslaved nations, it was importing a clothing of German fabrication for its souls which clashed with all that, and cast doubt on the Americanization of the world on which we had embarked, thinking it was good and in conformity with the rights of man. Our intellectual skyline has been altered by German thinkers even more radically than has our physical skyline by German architects."

Does that give you the flavor of Allan Bloom? Let me quote a bit more, "The great influence of a nation with a powerful intellectual life over less well-endowed nations, even if the armies of the latter are very powerful, is not rare in human experience. The most obvious cases are the influence of Greece on Rome, and of France on Germany and Russia. But it is precisely the difference between these two cases and the example of Germany and the United States that makes the latter so problematic for us. Greek and French philosophy were universalistic in intention and fact. They appealed to the use of a faculty potentially possessed by all men everywhere and at all times. [He means the mind, I think.-MRS] The proper noun in *Greek* philosophy [He means a proper *adjective*, but let's not quibble.-MRS] is only an inessential tag, as it is in *French* Enlightenment. (The same is true of *Italian* Renaissance, a rebirth that is proof of the accidental character of nations and of the universality of Greek thinkers.) The good life and the just regime they taught knew no limits of race, nation, religion, or climate. This relationship of man as man was the very definition of philosophy. We are aware of this when we speak of science, and no one seriously talks of German, Italian or English physics. And when we Americans speak seriously about politics, we mean that our principles of freedom and equality and the rights based on them are rational and everywhere applicable. World War II was really an educational project undertaken to force those who did not accept these principles to do so."

You can really tune in on the flavor and nervous energy behind those words, but accuracy? My gracious, what does he mean in that last sentence? Is he serious? It's all very well for Professor Bloom as he does, to remark that we've been led astray. But we didn't even get into World War II until we were attacked at Pearl Harbor. The 1939 War had been going on for a couple of years, a few million people had already lost their lives in Western Europe and Russia. We didn't start World War II, but we entered it, and, Bloom says, we fought it as, "an educational project undertaken to *force* those who did not accept these principles to do so." General Marshall was more modest, and so was Sergeant Milton Stern.

I have a feeling that Mr. Bloom is fighting in the right war, the war against ignorance, but as a recruit, and he's misunderstood his role. He hasn't yet gone to boot camp, let alone ROTC. He says in his introduction that he wants to be more than a Jeremiah, and regards the book he has written as, "a report from the front." Well—the University of Chicago as frontlines? More likely, first grade and sixth grade teachers in the ungolden ghetto surrounding the University in southside Chicago. I have no doubt that he has, as he says, spoken to many thousands of students. He's seen them, he's talked to them, he's taught them and he's despaired of them—as those of us who relate to them sometimes do.

Professor Bloom feels that cultural relativism is the great enemy. He is a Neoplatonist, almost to the point of cabalistic mysticism. He reminds me a bit, although his prose lacks Barzun's elegance, of Jacques Barzun's *House of Intellect*. A generation ago, I reviewed that book for the NUCEA *Spectator* under the title "Down with Philosopher Kings." Barzun, too, was full of despair, but he didn't relish it as Bloom does. If you're a democrat, small "d," you find this new version of élite literacy, pronounced, "éliteracy," hard to take.

Bloom obviously does not believe, as Karl Popper has observed, that Plato is the chief enemy of the open society, but rather Bloom believes that the open society is the enemy of culture, as he understands culture. With Matthew Arnold, he's gone back to the Greeks; and his view of the Greeks really lacks reality. Here was a society based on slavery. Here was a society in which—something he ignores—body and mind were regarded as a harmony. But it is Mind only on Bloomsday. Here was a society whose goal of the golden mean was expressed as a goal because the Greeks so rarely arrived at it, even temporarily. That they were extreme in their behavior, one has only to read Arnold Toynbee, in any of several books, to discover. One can go back to Herodotus. One sees what Greek life in the Golden Age was really like: It was vital. My God, it was vital, and that which we have from it is vital, too, but Professor Bloom's view is a phantom image. Herbert Muller pointed out in *The Uses of the Past,* that

"Philosophy, the rare love of wisdom, the fine flower of serenity, has commonly flourished in ages of disruption or decay—in the sickness of China, Rome, and Islam as of Greece; and it has commonly aggravated the sickness by inducing thoughtful men to turn their backs on the basic social problems of cause and cure... Given such tendencies to withdrawal, Plato's realm of ideal essences naturally became a refuge from the actual world of change and uncertainty. Here the mind is free to contemplate, follow the gleam of the heart's desires. Or here, in other words, it is relieved of its natural responsibilities."

Let me paraphrase that wonderful quatrain of Clarence Day, who wrote:

When eras die, their legacies
Are left to strange police.
Professors in Chicago guard
The glory that was Greece.

International Sensibility and World Culture

Let us not abandon our natural responsibilities. Let these two books serve as a preamble to that serious question that concerns us—of a multi-cultural society, of what might be the appropriate policy (philosophy is too imposing for me) that we should frame as we consider our continuing education students, in terms of the many roots we know our people stem from—the many individual cultural backgrounds that they have. Bloom's position is fairly conventional— even useful, as far as it goes, but also static. He makes no allowance for that luminous vision advanced by a philosopher of quite a different stripe, Suzanne Langer, when she said:

A new culture is probably in the making, which will catch up with the changed human environment that our runaway, freewheeling civilization has visited on us. But one cannot force the emergence of a real culture. It begins when imagination catches fire, and objects and actions become life symbols, and the new life symbols become motifs of art. Art, which formulates and fixes human ways of feeling, is always the spearhead of a new culture, for culture is the objective record of developed feeling.

We do not know what the driving force and the sustance of the next cultural epoch will be, but I suspect that, as so often in nature, the same development which is breaking the old frame of our thinking will fashion the new one: namely, the development of science. [And then she expands.-MRS]...Science is not native or exotic; it belongs to humanity and is the same wherever it is found. Only it is not likely to beget a culture unless, and until, a truly universal artistic imagination catches fire from its torch and serves without deliberate intent to give shape to a new feeling, such as generally initiates a new epoch of society.

Bloom is protecting what is, or never was—in the fussiest kind of way. He has no sense of the future! But we others alive today are in the process, if you like, of the formation of a new world culture. Economics as well as science are propelling us in this direction.

I remember Germaine Brée, a distinguished professor of French, most recently, I believe, at the University of Wisconsin; but, when I knew her, at New York University, speaking at a memorial service for Camus in 1960; she pointed out his great attraction for young people lay in his awareness of what she called "a developing international sensibility." This we must take into our consciousness. In complex ways we in continuing education will deal with, will research, will develop, and will probably produce the kinds of awkwardly imbalanced list that Professor Hirsch produced, but with good purpose, and more embracing.

In order to develop useful programs in continuing education, we will have to send back emissaries to earlier schooling. We will have to relate emphatically to teachers in lower grades, well before high school. It seems to me that what we (here "we" used broadly as representing all of higher education) have to do, both in continuing education as we deal with immediate crash program approaches and also in teacher training, is to deal with the teachers in our primary grades, because, unless we do, we do not set the stage properly. The complaints that have been made are real and serious about the lack of ability of a fourth grade teacher to teach composition because he or she doesn't know it. But, this is just part of the problem. Cultural literacy is a major theme. But that cultural literacy is now *multiphasic* and it must be dealt with in those terms. Is this a harder job to deal with? I suppose so. But if it is that difficult, it is exciting and worth a lifetime.

Kultur is the most ambiguous word in any language, and it is surely not the same as *la culture*. But let us recognize that as we speak of a multicultural society, we are approaching that dream expressed many times in this 20th century, an embracive world culture, a non-differentiated human culture. We must not abandon our roots, but we must cultivate the whole garden of earth.

A Feminist Reads
The Closing of the American Mind

Susan Bourgeois

The Invisible Woman reads the Eastern-establishment professor who is still angry because the Cornell administration didn't adhere to his advice in the 1960s.

While my subtitle oversimplifies a complex book, I think the *raison d'etre* for writing *The Closing of the American Mind* is Professor Bloom's tremendous pique at the universities of the 1960s for becoming more inclusive in curriculum and expanding their responsiveness to student populations other than that of white men between the ages of 18 and 22. Professor Bloom says the same thing, but from his perspective the thesis reads differently: the universities in the 1960s abandoned their mission to provide young white men at major universities with a classical education that would coherently take them through the thought of the Enlightenment, the basis for the establishment of our American government. The abandonment of the study of classical humanities, in turn, causes these young men, our natural leaders, according to Bloom, to be ill-educated for their lives.

My disagreement with the syntax of Bloom's thesis is its exclusivity. I believe everyone—women, blacks, Hispanics, students in public colleges and universities in the Midwest, even—needs to read Plato, Aristotle, Aristophanes, Shakespeare, Hobbes, Locke, Rousseau, De Tocqueville, etc., the entire canon of the classical period, the Renaissance, and the Enlightenment. I also believe these same students must read Julian of Norwich, (to hear of God, the Mother, for perhaps the first time) Sappho, Wollstonecraft, the African tribal tales that have survived, native American tales in which the philosophical basis for a religion of the earth is reflected, a basis for life that preceded Rousseau's and subsequent Romantics' attachment to nature by centuries.

The addition of women's writing and philosophical points of view and that of other major population groups that are contributors to this country is what Bloom calls pejoratively the smorgasbord approach to education. Once again, the syntax of the description makes all the difference. This essential enrichment of the humanities curriculum reflects the true composition of our heterogeneous society as it currently exists and includes a more sympathetic philosophical basis of life for those of us who don't look like Thomas Jefferson and James Madison.

According to Bloom, rationality is the goal of a classical/Enlightenment view of life, and rationalism accompanies the diploma at the end of a classical education. Rationalism may not be the natural product of a woman's education. We do not necessarily move from acceptance of authority to subjectivism to rationalism. Some of us accept authority briefly and then stay in subjectivism, gathering more and more knowledge based on the accumulation of comparative experiences. Others of us who have gained a great deal of education in a male-dominated system are as rational as the next fellow and can take a place in the disciplines of modern universities, perhaps reserving other knowledge—real, owned knowledge, the subjective and intuitive—for safe, woman-only space.

Sonia Johnson, a brave, contemporary feminist activist and thinker, has come to believe that women cannot change established, male dominated ways of thinking by supporting sympathetic political candidates or simply by endorsing and working for feminist causes. She sees as essential a full-scale revolution by women to change the system. To even say "the system" or "the establishment" evokes the furor of the 1960s—a furor that, in fact, was not always rational but that was based on a perception of the genuine inequities of education and opportunity coming out of the 1950s and previous decades. Johnson and other modern writers echo Mary Wollstonecraft who wrote in the eighteenth century, "till society be differently constituted, much cannot be expected from education [for women]" (21).

As a woman, I have been moved by both Mary Wollstonecraft and Sonia Johnson, but until I read Bloom, a contemporary intellectual expositing his single-sex education and culture, dismissing feminist criticism in two pages, and assuming, as Rousseau did two centuries earlier, that power would *always* be masculine, did I feel for sure that they are right. The inescapable irony and pain for a female reader, a female professor who teaches women students as well as men, is that an expert on the history of philosophy can ignore almost utterly any contributions of women thinkers to civilization, that a contemporary university professor can write, in general, as if co-education has not yet come about. Perhaps the irony is compounded for me because I attended college as an undergraduate during the late 1950s, the last of the period which Bloom considers the golden age for classical and enlightenment education. My mind was opened in a small state-supported college in the Ozarks. I studied World Literature (read: Western Literature) and History of Civilization (read: Western Civilization), and I was hooked on rationalism and the joys of life-time education. I graduated, *cum laude*, with a major in English and a minor in history; and, as far as I knew then, there had been perhaps two women writers worth reading and no women artists nor intellectuals of any kind. I believed that I was included when writers spoke of "mankind," and I always used "he" for every singular pronoun reference. And wasn't I used to identifying always with male protagonists from all my childhood reading? Why not continue thus forever? Bloom has.

The reason, of course, not to continue in this mode is that the women's movement and the feminist scholarship that it encouraged has brought forth the work of notable women in all areas of intellectual and artistic endeavor—women whose work has not been anthologized, referred to in texts, or presented as primary sources, until the last fifteen years. In addition, there has been and is a great psychological loss in the thinking of Americans about the quality of women when little or no attention is paid by writers to non-sexist language. If women are always assumed to be part of "mankind" and the pronoun is always "he" when the referent is "a person," exclusion is reinforced in a not-so-subtle way.

Rousseau:

One of the philosophic sources Bloom refers to with great frequency and whose work encourages the exclusion of women from the mainstream of life and certainly from access to power is Jean-Jacques Rousseau.

Saul Bellow points out in the Foreward to *The Closing of the American Mind* that Bloom tells us the intentions of Machiavelli, Hobbes, Locke, and Rousseau as they apply to modern democracy, and Bloom does this very well indeed. Rousseau emerges as rather the hero of this grouping, a fact which is significant to a female reader. Rousseau's book *Emile* was until the 1950s, at least, used as one of the commendable models of early childhood education in schools of education. Rousseau, the perfect romantic model, advocates taking male children away from strict discipline and rote memorization, returning them to nature—no swaddling clothes, no strict feeding schedule, no schedule for learning except that that nature shows as timely. This was great for little Emile, but what of the book's other character, Sophie? She inhabits a much smaller section of the book because she is going to learn so much less. Rousseau, excellent observer of nature that he is, describes Sophie's precociousness as compared to male children and generalizes on the superiority of intellect of all female children. But here is where Rousseau disregards nature, as he doesn't see fit to encourage nature's greater early intellectual gifts for female children. Rather, he makes sweeping generalizations from his observations of women after they have been socialized, reflecting on their coyness and slyness and concluding that women must be educated only to be pleasing to men and must always be kept under close supervision. Bloom responds briefly to feminist criticism of Rousseau occurring in college courses. He says Rousseau is used "as evidence of the misunderstanding of woman's nature and the history of injustice to it" (66). But Bloom resents this approach to Rousseau's work and to the works of other historical, sexist writers. He caustically adds: "But never, never, must a student be attracted to those old ways and take them as models for him or herself" (66). (This quotation is notable because it is one of two or three times in Bloom's 382-page text that he uses non-sexist pronouns.)

Mary Wollstonecraft:

When Mary Wollstonecraft wrote *A Vindication of the Rights of Women* in 1792, she laid the philosophical principles of feminism and set up criteria for the rational education of women, criteria that took issue with the writing of Rousseau. To read her work in conjunction with Bloom is both instructive and disheartening—disheartening because one can see how timely many of her points remain after 200 years. For example, Bloom notes with approbation that Rousseau is one of the philosophers who sees music as necessary to minister to men's passions because "the passions...had become thin under the rule of reason and that, therefore, man himself and what he sees in the world have become correspondingly thin" (73). Wollstonecraft, however, objects to

Rousseau's voluptuous reveries about women as woman is considered only a bearer of ministering "airs," including music (25). She correctly concludes that this view of women causes them to be regarded only with the warm emotions we feel when we see children or animals playing. This view precludes women being taken seriously enough to place them in "that world where sensation will give place to reason" (Wollstonecraft 25).

Wollstonecraft does agree with Rousseau on the importance of love between men and women but cries out for a rational element: "tumultuous passion...should not be allowed to dethrone superior powers or to usurp the scepter which the understanding should ever coolly wield" (27).

Bloom, by excluding the mention of women as students of reason, seems to acquiesce in Rousseau's exclusion of women from serious, rational study. Rousseau believed that "all was right originally," assuming women's second-class status because of Eve's second place in human creation (Wollstonecraft 15). Wollstonecraft says that when Rousseau wants to stop an "unnatural" progress of reason in men, he is ignoring the fact that women have gotten little to eat of the tree of knowledge. "From the imperfect cultivation which their understandings now receive, they only attain a knowledge of evil" (20) because every woman, no matter how smart or good, is subject to every man, no matter how ignorant or depraved. It is Rousseau's and Bloom's opinion that virtue or true education for men comes only from the natural use of reason. Wollstonecraft says that this is also true for women (21). She trusted that the equal rational education of women would change not only any negative, culturally-imposed characteristics of women but would also change male-dominated society.

Women's Movement:

Today's feminists share this goal of equality, and while education is no longer the only path, there is a primacy to education. Education for positions of power in America must expand from the Eurocentered Eastern universities in which coeducation is still somewhat an anomaly. Having a very different perspective on why universities need to be transformed, Bloom's description of the women's movement is sometimes limited, sometimes distorted, and sometimes simply false. For example, he states that women's liberation was a liberation form nature, rather than from societal conventions, and he calls on Freud for support. "The negative sentiment of imprisonment was there, but what was wanted, as Freud suggested, was unclear" (100). Bringing up the cliché that women don't know what they want is as serious as any other thoughts Bloom devotes to women. I am shocked that freedom from imprisonment and limitations is not considered a sufficient goal for a women's movement. The virtual universality of images of imprisonment and enclosure in literature by women has long been noted by literary critics. From the Middle Ages to the twentieth century, women have written of confinement and restrictions imposed by their male associates, confinement that often could and can only be escaped by insanity or death.

According to Bloom, women, however, are going against nature when they say "biology should not be destiny...It is not self-evident, *although it may be true*, [emphasis mine] that women's roles were always determined by human relations of domination, like those underlying slavery's" (100). Although our laws now provide civil equality in many arenas, there is a history of unequal laws in this country, and there are current laws and regulations "protecting" women from hazardous (and higher-paying) jobs during their child-bearing years, for example. Such laws continue to reinforce the domination of men in higher paying jobs and to reinforce the perception that women are unable to make their own choices.

Bloom regards the women's movement as unnatural, as he does the other movements coming out of the 1960s, because it seems to him to express "the longing for the unlimited, the unconstrained...forgetting nature and using force to refashion human beings to secure that justice" (100). A good bit of the double standard applied to gender is apparent in this comment. Women's speaking out and, yes, shouting for equality and freedom from restraint would hardly be regarded as the use of force in other circumstances. Women learned from the civil rights marches that there is a more effective way to gain rights than gradualism. For women to acquire the rights John Stuart Mill described in "On Freedom," rights circumscribed only by the avoidance of harm to others, is long overdue. These rights never seem "unlimited" and "unconstrained" to Bloom when defining the rights of men.

As Bloom continues to calumniate the women's movement, he associates women's complaints about men's sexual crimes with an unnatural stifling of men's necessary sex drive (101). In a bizarre, sarcastic list, he goes through accusations women make and culminates the list with an accusation against victims and mothers of victims:

Women are made into objects, they are raped by their husbands as well as by strangers, they are sexually harassed by professors and employers at school and at work, and their children, whom they leave in daycare centers in order to pursue their careers, are sexually abused by teachers. (101)

All of these crimes against modern woman have really occurred, according to Bloom, because the feminist movement has suppressed old-fashioned feminine modesty—the trait that used to keep men under control. It is very disconcerting to read an author, especially one as knowledgeable as Bloom, subscribing to the primitive idea of the culpability of the victim. He embroiders on the theme, blaming women's desire for independence and meaningful work as the primary cause for disjunction between the sexes (102).

Bloom also misconstrues the feminist objection to pornography as an objection to the natural order of things, "because it is a reminiscence of the old love relationship, which involved differentiated sexual roles—roles now interpreted as bondage and domination" (103). Much of pornography involves very literal bondage, torture of women, and sometimes even murder—facts never recognized by Bloom as he breezily summarizes the content of pornography: "It [pornography] caters to and encourages the longing men have for women and its unrestrained if impoverished satisfaction" (104).

While it would be all right to protect women from ravishment and brutalization "because modesty and purity should be respected and their weakness protected by responsible males, [it is] quite another to protect them from male desire altogether so that they can live as they please" (104). Bloom is begging the question indeed when "pornography" and male desire are made synonymous. And the objectification intrinsic in the "they" of "so that *they* can live as *they* please" unconsciously posits the objectification of women that pornography almost invariably illustrates. What sort of creatures does Bloom take us to be that we are not to be protected as citizens to legally live as we please?

Bloom also makes too large an assumption about women's expectations in their relationships with men. He says that with the disappearance of women's modesty, men were free to have sex before marriage. Therefore, there is no commitment on a man's part to a continuing relationship, but Bloom thinks that women, nevertheless, expect a large emotional commitment. "Women can say they do not care, that they want men to have the right motives or none at all, but everyone, and they best of all, know that they are being, at most, only half truthful with themselves" (132). Bloom has no qualms, apparently, about doubting women's words and sincerity when they do not fit his picture of the pre-1960s role for women—modest, married, and manageable.

Bloom makes the disclaimer that the old family arrangements were not necessarily good, but avers that nothing better has replaced these arrangements. From a very Hobbesian definition of man, Bloom says that if women and children can no longer be regarded as property for a husband to protect, women should not expect a man to act as a faithful mate and father. "The father will almost inevitably constrict his quest for property, cease being a father and become a mere man again, rather than turning into a providential God, as others ask him to be" (130). A contemporary woman's desire for her husband or lover to treat her as an individual and to share the labor and the financial responsibility of childcare should not be concomitant with asking him to be "a providential God." Rather, this is the simple job description of an adult parent. Once again Bloom blames women for the wrongdoing of men if men fail to contribute to the support of their children. "And a woman who can be independent of men has much less motive to entice a man into taking care of her and her children." (131). The use of "entice" smacks of real misogyny and "her children" coopts the attitude of many men toward their children if the husband and wife separate.

Bloom continues with his blame of women, saying we set up our own situations, creating a self-fulfilling prophecy: "They may hope otherwise, but they fully expect to pursue careers, to have to pursue careers, while caring for children alone. And what they expect and plan for is likely to happen" (131). What we, in fact, plan for is to have the education to prepare us for a career that suits our interests and talents. Then we hope for the opportunity to practice that career; and if the opportunity does not exist, we expect to fight for the opportunity. This is a personal journey, but to have children is in the majority of cases a shared experience, consented to by both parents. The fact that the mother is prepared to make an adequate living for herself but perhaps an inadequate living for herself and one or more children does not offer an excuse for the father to decamp.

Bloom's contention that most current family ills stem from the foregoing of feminine modesty is put into perspective by turning again to Wollstonecraft who looked from a woman's point of view at a generation of women whose only business was to please men within the formal eighteenth-century constrictions of feminine modesty. "The mighty business of female life is to please, and restrained from entering into more important concerns by political and civil oppression, sentiments become events, and reflection deepens what it should, and would have effaced, if the understanding had been allowed to take a wider range" (157). Wollstonecraft was fighting against the sacrifice of intelligence of the women of England to trivialities because of their exclusion from political and civil business outside of the home. Bloom has no concern for this sacrifice because he never acknowledges that there is anything to sacrifice.

Women Almost Worth Mentioning:

Only two women receive unmodified recognition for their work, Jane Austen and Ruth Benedict, described as an anthropologist influenced by Nietzsche (362). Hannah Arendt is recognized for her important ideas before the 1960s (322), but is given only passing credit for her acknowledgment of " 'the banality of evil' " (214). Bloom says that she perhaps bore "unconscious witness to my suggestion" that those who had docilely followed the philosophy of Weber had contributed to the rise of fascism in the 1930s (214).

Margaret Mead is first mentioned as a "sexual adventurer" who contributed to the evil of pluralism in America by telling us we needed to learn about and appreciate other cultures (33). Bloom's use of name-calling detracts from any evaluation of the worth of Mead's work. Later, as Bloom begins to show the legitimacy of anthropology as one of the best humanistic disciplines now existing in the American university, he identifies two progenitors, psychoanalysis and "the old understanding of philosophy as a way of life" (367). But then comes the zinger regarding Mead, the mother of the discipline of anthropology: "On a much less sophisticated level [than psychoanalysis or the former study of philosophy] but expressing something of the same ethos, Margaret Mead had a new science that took one to exotic places, brought back new understandings of society and also proved the legitimacy of one's repressed sexual desires" (367). Margaret Mead, thus, is given some credit for her "unsophisticated" work, but work which has contributed to our nation's sexual permissiveness. Because of Bloom's positive point about the discipline of anthropology, he is obliged to mention the seminal work of Mead, but it is not until he has diminished her status by pejorative language that he can address what anthropology has become: "the only social science discipline still exercising the charm of possible wholeness, with its idea of culture, which appears more really complete than does the economists' idea of the market" (368). Apparently, then, anthropology has been purified of its encouragement of pluralistic thinking and sexual permissiveness since the departure of Mead.

Bloom, in fact, assumes a general incompetence of women in the academy based on the fact that there is not a large pool of women scholars in the natural sciences and mathematics. Bloom uses as an example the faculty of Cornell advocating affirmative action in the 1960s:

...mathematicians wanted, for example, to see more blacks and women hired but could not find nearly enough competent ones—they in effect said that the humanists and social scientists should hire them. Believing that there are no real standards outside of the natural sciences, they assumed that adjustments could easily be made. (351)

Bloom's conclusion is that this accommodation of women and minorities in both the hiring of faculty and the admission of students has caused grade inflation and the debauching of the humanities and the social sciences, while the natural scientists have maintained their elitist position. To state such a cause and effect relationship is begging the question. No evidence is presented to show such a causal relationship. Even worse is the assumption that change constitutes a lowering of standards, a "debauching" of disciplines. The standards of a homogenous white male faculty and white male student body will be changed with the addition of heterogenous elements—women and minorities. I find this change to be an enrichment for those disciplines lucky enough to have substantial numbers of those of us Bloom deems to be spoilers.

Of course the absence of women, for the most part, from mathematics and science has nothing to do with female incompetence but with American acculturation. We have been taught that women are good with language and men with numbers. The current generation of educated young women is the first that has been encouraged through elementary school, high school, and college to undertake the study of science and mathematics.

Bloom's almost complete disregard for women of achievement of the past and his contempt for the entrance of women and minority faculty members into universities in the 1960s create a suspicion of the credibility of his writing on other subjects as well. I wish that he had been attentive throughout his statements on women to a good epigram he produced in one of the finer chapters of the book: "Reformers may often be intransigent or extreme in deed, but they are rarely intransigent in thought, for they have to be relevant" (279).

Language: An Exclusionary Weapon

Julia Penelope, a linguist, has written a feminist analysis of English, *Speaking Freely*, to show the way in which modern English was developed through the centuries by male grammarians. Their prescriptive grammar, particularly in gender-specific words, reinforces the cultural assumption of male dominance and female subservience. A semantic change from Old English is that in modern English "the male sex is the unmarked norm, the standard; the female sex must be marked as that which is non-male (other)" (102). Thus, when Bloom uses a male set of standards for what a university course should be, he is supported by the very semantics of his language.

Penelope further explains what happens in the writing of Bloom and many other men: "syntactic structures called 'impersonal' are used to describe the world as men perceive it and those descriptions are accepted as 'consensus reality' " (xxvii). Another problem implicit in our language, which I have mentioned earlier, is the use of "he," "him," or "his" as generic pronouns. Penelope agrees with the implication for women that I suggested: "Assuming that the male sex is normal and the female sex deviant also underlies the use of pseudo-generic *man*, and the use of *he* as though it encompassed women in its reference" (103).

Penelope calls language "an intangible, almost invisible weapon" (xx). Bloom's weapon is often the exclusion of women from his language, as he conforms to another statement by Penelope: "We have no words for aspects of the world we don't recognize, and a few for those features considered insignificant"

(90). A brief survey of Bloom's chronic use of generic male appellations or the use simply of exclusionary language shows what a piercing weapon the absence of reference can be for a woman reader:

"The teacher's standpoint is not arbitrary...nor is it imposed on him...." (19)

"...almost every student entering the university believes, or says he believes...." (25)

"Over the history of our republic, there have obviously been changes of opinion as to what kind of man is best for our regime." (26)

"This relation to man as man was the very definition of philosophy." (153)

"Freedom for man consists in ordering his life according to what he can see for himself through this most distinctive faculty...." (164)

"What is required is not brotherly love or faith, hope and charity, but self-interested rational labor. The man who contributes most to relieving human misery is the one who produces most, and the surest way of getting him to do so is not by exhorting him; but by rewarding him most handsomely...." (165)

"...man grows and grows into culture;...Man is a cultural being...What man has from nature is nothing compared to what he has acquired from culture." (190)

"...the new revolutions...are to be made by intellectually honest, committed, strong-willed, creative men." (202)

"And it [philosophic doubt] preserves the treasury of great deeds, great men and great thoughts required to nourish that doubt." (249)

"To enlighten is to bring light where there had previously been darkness...beginning from phenomena available to all men and ending in rational demonstration possible for all men." (256)

"...the science of man, meaning a political science that discerns the nature of man and the ends of government." (261)

"Freedom from the myths and their insistence that piety is best permits man to see that knowing is best...." (271)

"The tiny band of men who participate fully in this way of life are the soul of the university." (271)

"...the university is also informed by the spirit, which very few men can fully share, of men who are absent...." (272)

"He applies what he sees in nature to his own life." (277)

"The philosopher always thinks and acts as though he were immortal." (290)

"Together they represent what the university has to say about man and his education." (380)

And where am I and other women readers? We are absent. For all that Bloom attends to us, we appear still to be in the situation Wollstonecraft described, "restrained from entering into more important concerns" (183). Wollstonecraft also comments on this generic use of "mankind" by logically concluding that if women are to be regarded always as a part of "mankind" we should, therefore, be regarded as equal to men in every way (8). But at this point of time in our collective national consciousness, we must have linguistic equality, as well, so that women may always be recognized and significant.

A Contemporary Jonathan Swift

Bloom is a great admirer of Jonathan Swift, devoting a separate section to him in his history-of-philosophy chapter, "From Socrates' *Apology* to Heidegger's *Rektorastrede*." Swift is rightly esteemed for his satire in *Gulliver's Travels* of some of the results of the Enlightenment, particularly the neglect of the classical and the lack of attention to poetry (293). Bloom cites particularly Swift's creation of the Laputians—a society whose interests are reflected in their physiognomy. One of their eyes turns inward and one turns toward the sky. They lack any contact with the human dimension and have to be roused by a "flapper," a servant who hits them with a bag of peas on the ear or the mouth when they should listen to or speak with another person. The king and the nobles live on a floating island in the sky that descends only occasionally for contact with people outside the royal circle. Swift saw this lack of human concern in the philosophers and scientists of the British Royal Society, a society created in the atmosphere of the Enlightenment. The relevance of this for a feminist reader is the misogyny Swift displays in "A Voyage to Laputa" and throughout his other writings. When Swift satirizes the lack of human concern in the Enlightenment, he refers only to the concern of man for man. When Bloom summarizes "Laputa," he makes the following reference to women: "Their [the Laputians'] wives can commit adultery before their eyes without its being noticed" (294). This statement is, of course, from the male point of view because are not the women Laputians as well? They are discussed only as they relate to male Laputians.

Swift develops this adulterous aspect of the women by an anecdote about a noble wife who ran away to the land below the island. She was recovered from a relationship with a servant and reinstated in her island home, only to run away again to her abusive lover below. The lover is "an old deformed footman, who beat her every day, and in whose company she was taken much against her will" (Swift 187).

Gulliver's gloss on this story is this:

This may perhaps pass with the reader rather for an European or English story, than for one of a country so remote. But he may please to consider, that the caprices of womankind are not limited by any climate or nation, and that they are much more uniform than can be easily imagined (187).

The woman is, not surprisingly, entirely blamed for the adultery. Her preference for an ugly man who beats her, rather than for an attractive nobleman husband who is too abstracted to ever listen to her or speak to her, is described as capricious. This is the easiest explanation for the actions of a person whose point of view is not heard.

Bloom often displays this Swiftian disregard for women's points of view and sometimes makes completely false assumptions about the ways of life of women. For example, when he writes about the historical importance of spirituality in the American home, he shows only a patriarchal model, ignoring the fact that from at least the 1930s the women in Christian American homes have been the family leaders in religious practice (57-58, 60).

Women, as the poorest strata of American society, should also rightly take offense at Bloom's casual or blasé attitude about the disadvantaged people who haven't enough to eat or enough money to heat their home if they have a home: "To the extent that there is a project [in America], it is to put those who are said to be disadvantaged in a position to live as they please too" (85). Likewise, the "welfare state" is looked at not because state programs are essential to assist the poor but as a synonym for the errors in our natural capacity for psychological idealism: "Self-satisfaction, the desire to be adjusted, the comfortable solution to his problems, the whole program of the welfare state, are the signs of the incapacity to look up toward the heaven of man's possible perfection or self-overcoming" (198). There is no feeling expressed for people who require welfare services. When Wollstonecraft defined what education should be, she included the component missing from Bloom's writing: "...the most perfect education, in my opinion, is such an exercise of the understanding as is best calculated to strengthen the body and form the heart" (21). Any compassion that comes from the heart is anathema to Bloom. He makes a very male judgement call when he says that the university needs to be an "unpopular institution...that sets clarity above well-being or compassion" (252). Always being consistent to his Hobbesian view of human nature, Bloom goes so far as to say that compassion is only self-interest, enabling the "compassionate" to feel superior to those they assist (330). An enemy to psychiatry, Bloom berates the profession for using words relating to compassion and feeling, words that have no rational referent. Not surprisingly, the words he chooses as examples describe the singular strengths most women possess or desire: "There is a whole arsenal of terms for talking about nothing—caring, self-fulfillment, expanding consciousness, and so on, almost indefinitely" (155).

Bloom is not, however, without feelings from the heart. He regrets the absence of Eros from modern America. Nothing can substitute for the erotic feeling to stimulate imaginative creativity. He misses the nineteenth-century romantic novels such as *Madame Bovary* and *Anna Karenina* (132 ff.), interesting examples, indeed, for the feminist reader. The structure of the nineteenth-century romance by male authors required the dominance of the male protagonist. Women could only be happy in these romances if they were chosen by the proper, legitimate mate. Certainly, Emma Bovary and Anna Karenina did not fit this pattern.

In another literary reference Bloom shows himself an ageist in his discussion of Aristophanes' *The Assembly of Women*, echoing Aristophanes' description of "the old hags" (97), "older Athenian women, who because of their very repulsiveness, had a right to enjoy handsome young men..." (99). Each time the cultural equation of "old woman=repulsive" and "young=handsome or beautiful" is invoked, ageism is reinforced.

Bloom is also wrong about the status of younger women, the university students. He thinks that they are now completely accepted in all fields of study and that they have the same job opportunities as men do. Bloom's lack of recognition of females in the university throughout the book belies this assertion. The only students who may not be quite satisfied with their situation, according to Bloom, are homosexuals. The fact that homosexuals often have rights recognized by university authorities Bloom takes as evidence of the acceptability of everyone in a pluralistic university (107). The sexual harassment of women students and the increase in campus harassment of lesbians and gays in the last five years are not acknowledged.

Commenting on women beyond the university, Bloom states "that women have an instinctive attachment to children that cannot be explained as self-interest or calculation" (115). Such a sweeping generalization about all women is unacceptable. This belief gives credence to man's self-serving belief that childcare is always the mother's responsibility first.

When speaking of historical matters, Bloom continues his Swiftian omission of a woman's point of view. For instance, Socrates is probably the greatest hero of the book. Bloom describes Socrates's brilliant relations with statesmen, his students, and other philosophers (268), but no where does Bloom consider it important to mention that Socrates spoke and behaved as if he hated his wife—an encumbrance on greatness perhaps recognized by only female readers. Bloom also avows the universality of classical writings and of a classical education (305). A mystery for women readers of classical plays is not solved. How can there be a universal application of magnificent women characters, such as Agamemnon and Clytemnestra, in a society where women, in actuality, had only the freedom that their fathers and then their husbands gave them?

Far from the world of classical studies were the social studies that the evil 1960s pushed upon the universities. According to Bloom, students singled out serious scholars, who differed from the students' point of view on various subjects, to persecute. Bloom's conservatism is certainly present in the list he uses as examples: "These were scholars who seriously studied sexual differentiation or who raised questions about the educational value of busing or who considered the possibility of limited nuclear war" (355). "Sexual differentiation" immediately catches the eye of a woman reader. This has been a study used most self-righteously by male scholars to show women's incapacity to equal men in many areas where we have not reached positions of power.

As a modern Swiftian, Bloom's references to women show neglect of, distortions of, sweeping generalizations about, and plain unconsciousness of women's points of view.

As a feminist I could read Bloom only a little at a time, and I could write about *The Closing of the American Mind* only a little at a time because I am enraged by the single-sex culture Bloom longs for and by his assumption that only the purity of a single-sex culture can redeem the American future. "It is the hardest task of all to face the lack of cosmic support for what we care about" (Bloom 277).

Works Cited

Balenky, Mary Field, et al. *Women's Ways of Knowing.* New York: Basic Books, Inc., 1986.

Bloom, Allan. *The Closing of the American Mind.* New York: Simon and Schuster, 1987.

Penelope, Julia. *Speaking Freely.* New York: Pergamon P, 1990.

Rousseau, Jean-Jacques. *Émile* Trans. by Barbara Foxley. London: J. M. Dent & Sons Ltd., 1928.

Swift, Jonathan. *Gulliver's Travels.* New York: Random House, 1950.

Wollstonecraft, Mary. *A Vindication of the Rights of Women.* ed. Carol H. Poston. New York: W. W. Norton & Company, 1975.

A Bloom Amid the Reagan-Bushes

Margaret C. Jones

What's a Beautiful Soul Like Yours Doing in an Age Like This?

Since its publication in 1987, Allan Bloom's *The Closing of the American Mind* has enjoyed a popularity among the general public unusual for a work of its kind. This popularity may be attributed to a pervasive anxiety, within the academy and outside of it, about the future role of the humanities in an increasingly utilitarian sociocultural context; but also to the past ten years of social conservatism under Reagan and Bush.[1] Although in his book Professor Bloom is careful to distance himself from the vulgar banalities of Republican Party ideology, via disparaging references to specific Republican politicians, his cultural agenda is politically conservative in its implications, and has much in common with the celebration of "traditional" educational approaches of William Bennett, while Secretary of Education during Reagan's second term.[2] In these years of complacent neglect of basic educational and other social needs, accompanied by massive military expenditures and the ruthless pursuit of foreign policy by armed force,[3] a minority within the U.S. academy have quietly worked with local citizens' groups to retain a little sanity amid this madness. Their campaigns include work on civil rights, feminist and human rights issues. Bloom's chief complaints against the academy of this period seem to be (a) that the endeavors of students and faculty are informed by a liberal postmodernist skepticism, which Bloom tends to mistake for a lack of deep conviction; and (b) that they have brought their ideological perspectives (on feminism, for example) to bear not only on society at large, but on their reading of classic literary and philosophic texts.[4]

Before addressing each of these charges in detail, let me outline what seems to me the basic conviction at the heart of Bloom's project in *The Closing of the American Mind*. It has much in common with that outlined in a classic text of the late nineteenth century: Arnold's *Culture and Anarchy* (1867). Like Arnold, Bloom posits the existence of a literary-philosophic Western tradition, whose vitality must continue as the condition of society's retaining its moral and psychic health.[5] The corollary of this view is an essentialist belief in a changeless, universal human nature, capable of grasping eternal truths, for which, although faith in a personal God may no longer be possible, religious belief is regretfully contrasted with a reductive scientism. In Bloom's words, "The faith in God and the belief in miracles are closer to the truth than any scientific explanation which has to overlook or explain away the creative in man" (199). Bloom, although deeply pessimistic in his understanding of a post-Nietzschean philosophic universe, paradoxically moves further in this direction than Arnold, finding the highest formulation of the great ethical and spiritual questions in the thought of Plato.

In the light of these fundamental assumptions, then, Bloom considers that the highest function of the university is to inculcate in its students a thirst for knowledge of eternal and unchanging principles. Its goal should be to instigate exploration, not of the meaning of this or that ethical virtue in a particular social context, for example, but of the nature, in the absolute, of that virtue. The ideal is, like that of Socrates, investigation of "what justice is in the abstract, not its particular and partial manifestation in the historical moment" (312). This ideal, as the basis of an educational philosophy, raises as many questions as it resolves—a point to which I shall return shortly.

Much that Bloom has to say in *The Closing* is sharply perceptive, as when he points to the psychic isolation experienced by individuals in contemporary society as a function of altered sexual mores; or when he draws the reader's attention to the necessity of "alternative thoughts" for social freedom.[6] However, when it comes to his critique of the social ideals of the contemporary academy— I would like to say, "the social values," but "value" is one of those words, along with "lifestyle" and "ideology," from which Professor Bloom shrinks— as expressed by university students, Bloom's indictment is excessively sweeping, by any criteria. In his depiction of student community mores we find ourselves squarely confronted with Nietzsche's age of "the last man." The life of the youthful spirit, deprived of religious faith, finds itself sapped instead by the depredations of "culture leeches"—of professional pacifists, psychiatrists, advocates of the welfare state, the "Jesuits and bow unbenders of the spirit" (51, 198). These products of "egalitarian, rationalist, socialist atheism" entertain secular, relativistic, historicist notions, which the young—when and if they reflect critically at all—largely share. The souls of these young people are mirrors, not of "nature" but of "what is around" (apparently not the same thing at all) (197, 61). They have shallow ideals, or none, not even authentic prejudices; no heroes; an obsessive fixation on their personal concerns, to the exclusion of all else; and deplorable taste in music. As if all this were not bad enough, they yearn for a "class-less, prejudice-free, conflictless society," while exposing their vulnerable adolescent psyches to treacly renderings of "We Are the World" (74).

Leaving aside for the moment Bloom's general indictment of secular post-humanism for its relativism, atheism, egalitarianism, etc., it might be useful to examine more closely this portrait of the souls of the young, as Bloom observes them, on the campuses of what, in 1965, he called "the better" colleges and universities (49). Take, for instance, his curious idea that "the young" lack prejudices. "Show me a human being who does," might be the obvious (and glib) response. Yet the point is worth addressing for its relevance to Bloom's allegation that the young lack moral conviction. The very yearning for a classless society of which he accuses them would seem in itself to constitute a prejudice of some kind. Nor is it the case that today's students have no heroes. Admittedly, Bloom would not readily concede that Bruce Springsteen is much of a hero (although he is one to many teenagers); but it may also be the case that students do not want to shock Professor Bloom by confessing (as I have heard them say) that their hero is Nelson Mandela.[7] Their apparent responsiveness to the lyrics of "We Are the World"—not to mention student involvement, over the past five years, in work against apartheid in South Africa, homelessness in the U.S.A. and the destruction of the ecosystem (causes endorsed, incidentally by those rock idols Professor Bloom so despises)—would seem to suggest that the young are not wholly lacking in convictions or ideals.

One might inquire, furthermore, what is so wrong with pacifism, egalitarianism, or with a rational skepticism about natural phenomena, about society and one's own place in it? Bloom finds much of what he deplores about "modernity" represented by Flaubert in his character M. Homais, in *Madame Bovary*. Bloom, who faults Homais for his dispassionate rationalism, considers that in this character, "his greatest creation," Flaubert "encapsulated everything that modernity was and is to be" (205). If Homais is, in Bloom's words, a victim of his own "petty *amour-propre*," he is also a stimulating conversationalist, reasonable, tolerant, full of alert curiosity about his world, public-spirited.[8] His chief defect, for Bloom, is that Homais, unlike Emma Bovary, is incapable of the impossible dream of the beyond, of "a world of men who do not and cannot exist"(205). It may be an unfair question, but I will put it anyway. Which of the two, Homais, or Emma Bovary, would you prefer to educate your children?

If Bloom is troubled by what he regards as an unduly shallow and materialist ethos among students, he has even more serious allegations to make against the contemporary guardians of the academy's traditions, its teachers and scholars. He blames the academy's current spiritual "bankruptcy" on intellectual influences regarded as having reached their culmination in the campus radicalism of the 1960s. According to this view, Nietzschean and Heideggerian influences were diffused through the American academy, and thence into American popular culture, through the work of Weber, and later through Marcuse and others associated with the Frankfurt School in the 1950s. In Bloom's narrative, it was a largely "Nietzscheanized Heideggerianized Left," with an irrational and unthinking "hatred of bourgeois society"—one which shared with Heidegger a preference for "passion" over "reason"—which, with the blessing of adult members of the university community who ought to have known better, instigated student insurrection (314). The Heidegger connection would link the *trahison des clercs* of those American intellectuals who capitulated to collective opinion in the 1960s with that of the German scholars of the 1930s who acquiesced intellectually in the triumph of Nazism. Woodstock, for Bloom, is quite explicitly to be equated with Nuremberg; and in both cases, the adult teachers, more than the revolting young, are to blame (314-5).[9] However, whatever similarities may be found between the chaotically spontaneous musical event of 1969 and the mass political rally, carefully orchestrated by a ferociously authoritarian regime in the 1930s, Bloom will have difficulty persuading most readers that the inchoate student politics of the 1960s ever bore much resemblance to fascism. "Equality, freedom, peace, cosmopolitanism," hardly sound like a Nazi agenda (326). But the whole point about the Woodstock/Nuremberg analogy is not really to establish a connection, or even an analogy, between the Young Turks of the New Left and the Hitler Youth; rather to indict contemporary America, and the American academy, as corrupted by a spirit akin to that of the Weimar Republic: decadent and morally permissive. Their intellectuals, in Bloom's telling image, take a seaside vacation while Hitler's barbarian hordes pour into the Rhineland (329). It is the failure of America's spiritually flabby intellectuals that they have neglected to affirm those Lockean principles of reason and the rights of man on which the U.S. Constitution was founded, and, under the influence of their Heideggerianized mentors of the 1960s, gone chasing after such chimaeras as "commitment," "charisma," and "values" (238).

That for millions of people the "Sixties" did in fact offer a real liberation from the tyranny of old bigotries, prejudices, institutions and inhibitions, does not seem to occur to the author of *The Closing of the American Mind*. That the challenges mounted against entrenched ideas and established customs brought about an extension of civic rights, a questioning of unthinking obedience to governmental power, a new sense of possibility for women, blacks and members of other ethnic minorities, a challenge to the notion that America's greatness lay in the quest for global empire, are points Bloom either dismisses, or regards as (like the women's movement) having been mainly negative in their outcome.[10] The one development of the Sixties he does seem unconditionally to approve of—the civil rights movement—he chooses to regard as ideologically fueled by a lingering comprehension on Northern university campuses of the doctrine of the rights of man, as inculcated by an older academic generation who still believed in teaching such things. It is "doubtful," he considers, whether any such "decent political deeds" could arise from contemporary campuses, now presumably ideologically bankrupted by the anti-rational, anti-Lockean orgies of an earlier decade (335).

Bloom mentions the inevitable shallow posturing and sententiousness manifested when adolescents—and not only adolescents—engage in politics;[11] but he is surprisingly silent about the literally dozens of effective South African divestment protests the past five years have seen on campuses across the nation, about the small but substantial numbers of students who work for human rights organizations or for the homeless, or the thousands who have made at least token gestures toward combating wholesale destruction of the environment.[12]

In fact, whatever s/he does, neither the committed student nor the committed professional academic is able to win Bloom's approval. To dream, like students in the 1960s, of the extreme heroic posture, is dangerously conducive to histrionics, and leads to self-delusion. I agree. But to settle for more modest goals—to work quietly for nature conservation or the preservation of women's reproductive rights—is, to Bloom, merely "self-serving." The choice of these causes opens their advocates to wholly unsubstantiated charges of self-righteousness, presumably because Bloom disapproves of the causes themselves. Yet the workers on these issues, by and large, act upon a morality of everyday decencies, the "activity of a lifetime" of performing simple but necessary duties, which Bloom claims to find valuable (325).

We have still not arrived at the crux of Bloom's quarrel with activism in the academy. Bloom considers—mistakenly, in my view—that the engagement of academics with specific contemporary social issues is, at best, a distraction from the scholar's true vocation, and, at worst, leads to a total subversion of scholarly integrity. Such engagement tends to transform, not only the broader social context within which it is carried out, but scholarly theory and practice within the academy itself.[13]

Bloom correctly perceives that the commitment of academics to social change has exercised its effect on traditional humanities curricula in recent years—if not quite to the drastic extent he would have us believe, enough to have brought about substantial curricular change at the margins of humanities programs, particularly in history and literature. For Bloom such changes are especially disturbing as they affect reading of the "classic texts," as he calls them, of the Western tradition. Not only do such texts for Bloom embody unchanging human values, but, for the most part, socially conservative ones. Bloom's is an image of the Western cultural heritage in which the radically utopian implications of Plato's *Republic*, of Euripides, of the More of *Utopia*, of Milton's political writings, of Blake, Shelley, Wollstonecraft, Thoreau, simply go unacknowledged. To Bloom, the aim of a reader or teacher of Homer or Shakespeare should not be to "enrich" their "vision of the world" by discovering shared concerns in the classic texts, but rather to "learn to see the world as Homer or Shakespeare did" (374). The contemporary reader should respect the claims of classic texts "to be about the order of the whole of nature and man's place in it, to legislate for that whole and to tell the truth about it" (372). These formulations beg a number of questions—notably, whether an individual socialized in twentieth-century America *can* feel and think as did a Homeric Greek or a Renaissance Englishman. It also rests on naive notions of textual unity, in which fictional characters are assumed to express authorial viewpoints, without dramatic conflict or irony. One does not have to adopt an extreme deconstructionist position to find these assumptions problematic.

As a pedagogic ideal, Bloom's essentialism is not only wildly impractical, but overlooks the very real satisfactions that students find in the historicist exploration of texts, from the imaginative construction of the literature of earlier times from a contemporary perspective to—yes—even its appropriation for an interpretation of the modern context. This need not entail anything so crude as lambasting Homer for sexism, or turning Shakespeare's Brutus into an embryo marxist. But it can produce empowering readings that give credit to the utopian possibilities of many classic texts, while avoiding the pitfall of being obliged to develop apologies for the sexism, élitism and endorsement of various kinds of slavery that also form an integral part of the ethos of earlier traditions.

Bloom is mistaken if he really believes that young people have no appreciation of issues such as racism, sexism, or the conflict over women's reproductive rights, and that they find courses which address such issues irrelevant.[14] These issues form the stuff of their daily lives, in a society of which such conflicts constitute the very conditions of existence. Not surprisingly, members of ethnic minorities and women are particularly sensitive to such educational approaches, whether the African-American or Japanese-American student whose freshman compositions tell of racial harassment and cultural alienation, or the accomplished female graduate student who finds herself excluded from a "men's club" of the most able males in her class. To dismiss courses or textual approaches which attempt to deal with racism or sexism as merely "fancy packaging" is to show a real insensitivity to the importance of such concerns to students themselves.

The intellectual basis of Bloom's resistance to the ideological appropriation of classic texts is a conviction that the Platonic cave of illusion in which "the mass of men" dwell is "intractable," and that access to higher truth is possible only to a few finer spirits. By implication, he rejects the teaching of Enlightenment philosophers, that the cave could be changed by "a new kind of education"—let alone the possibility, not mentioned at all by Bloom, that it might even be subject to complete demolition by a new social order brought about by changes in technology or social organization (265).[15] Thus, for Bloom, the philosopher's "true" business (and, by implication, the business of the contemporary humanities scholar) has traditionally been, not to attempt aggressive engagement with society, in an effort to contribute to its transformation, but rather to accommodate to it, in order to guarantee the survival of philosophy in its purity. The initially corrupting influence in this context was, for Bloom, that of the Renaissance—of Machiavelli, Bacon and their Enlightenment admirers. Yet Bloom only makes his case for the social quietism of Classical philosophers by selectively appropriative readings, of Plato in particular. He de-emphasizes the clearly utopian social agenda of *The Republic*,[16] treating it as a mere *jeu d'esprit* without practical social implications. He ignores the abortive but apparently serious attempt of Plato as we learn of him in history, to guide the founding of a regime based on principles outlined in *The Republic*.[17] True, there never has been a "Platonic," or, for that matter, an "Aristotelean" form of government as such; but this point seems something of a red herring, designed to distract the reader from the observation that Bloom's Plato is as much a fictional construct as anyone else's. If one looks, for example, at an alternative representation of Socrates to Bloom's socially disengaged figure, he too may be found in Plato; an active participant in the military and political life of his society, who takes seriously a number of obligations to it, not omitting obedience to the laws that require his own death.[18]

Bloom fears that scholarly activism may endanger the integrity of the life of the mind, particularly where philosophy is concerned. In his words, "Intellectual honesty" and "commitment" get "in the way" of the philosopher's true pursuit, of "learning how to die" (261, 277). The proper place for such manifestations is not in philosophy, but in religious or political life. Commitment will only be an obstacle to the philosopher's vocation, opening it to "suspicion" and "criticism." Bloom idealizes those ancient philosophers who, as he represents them, ingratiated themselves with the aristocracy of their day through "An art of writing that appealed to the prevailing moral taste of the regimes in which they found themselves"; which sounds suspiciously like flattering the complacency of those regimes (283). One feels compelled to wonder how far this alleged position of the ancient philosophers really is from that of the Cornell professors who basely capitulated to their students' demands, in Bloom's account of the student unrest there during the Sixties. Of course, in the former case, the philosophers flattered "the gentlemen," in the latter, it was "the natives, in the guise of students" (an interesting post-colonial metaphor here), who "attacked" the campus institutions and faculty with insurrectionary intent (324). But I thought Professor Bloom believed in talking about the True in the absolute.

However much you may privilege the modern university as a special enclave, there is, in fact, in Bloom's own words, "no leaving civil society, no matter what Thoreau may have thought" (279). (The Thoreau of *Civil Disobedience* actually has moments of knowing better—and was never tempted to flatter the "prevailing moral taste" of anyone.)[19] You can, however, allow yourself the illusion—which nonetheless remains an illusion—of creating a privileged *mental* space on society's margin. Bloom's retrospective justification for the ancient philosophers' ethical and intellectual complicity with the aristocracy is that the aristocratic patrons might thereby have been lured out to an appreciation of the atmosphere of those "Elysian fields where the philosophers meet to talk" (283). The spatial image takes on additional significance in this context from its recurrence in Bloom's critique of those committed academics who feel morally uneasy (unnecessarily so in Bloom's opinion here) about their materially comfortable position, idling "in Epicurean gardens, asking questions that have already been answered and keeping a distance where commitment is demanded" (250). In privileging such metaphoric gardens, Bloom does, it seems, in the face of the undeniable implication of a certain relatedness even of philosophers with "civil society" wish to reclaim for the philosopher a special, marginal space (283).

Pace Bloom's insistence on the unquestionable influences of the Western philosophic heritage on the shaping of American thought, there is, it seems to me, something very American in this insistence on salvation via recourse to the margin. One is reminded of Emerson's response to Channing, when exhorted to involve himself actively in social causes: "Every one to his chosen work;/Foolish hands may mix and mar."[20] Bloom's Elysian region on the fringes of the polis, the scholar's Epicurean gardens, are the metaphoric equivalents of Hester Prynne's cottage on the forest edge, or of Huck Finn's raft—a space where the individual at odds with or isolated from society may recover the illusion of psychic wholeness. However, as the fictional Hester and Huck discover, it never remains a satisfactory refuge for very long.

In Bloom's images of spatial and psychic marginality may be found the key to his ideal for the contemporary academic's proper attitude to the urgent political and social questions of our time. He complains that contemporary scholars who feel uneasy with their comfortable and privileged social positions turn readily to the waging of a fight against social injustices, against "racism, sexism...elitism...as well as war" (314). This, according to Bloom, they do in the absence of any "other interest worthy of defending." It is a curious perception that regards such struggles, to which heroic natures within living memory have totally dedicated their lives, as merely a *faute de mieux*. In conclusion, then, let me suggest some reasons why the academic, far from being compromised by social and political commitment, is, rather, psychically and intellectually impoverished by the avoidance of such stands. The academic, like any other thinking social being, needs commitment, I would argue:

because in a world where university teachers are the targets of police and death squads hired and trained with our tax dollars, the intellectual and the political cannot be neatly separated;

because utopian social hopes are not always mere illusions, as the freeing of slaves and the toppling of dictators even in our own time amply demonstrate;

because, after all, Bloom is correct in believing that we owe something to a Western cultural heritage; and part of this heritage is the role played in the shaping and expression of utopian aspirations by Plato, by the More of *Utopia*, by Milton, Blake, Shelley, Sartre, Du Bois, de Beauvoir, Neruda and Havel;

because if Bloom's phrase "learning how to die" means anything, it means that we want to come to die having the satisfaction of knowing that we have lived.

Notes

[1]The interest and controversy inspired in academic circles by E.D. Hirsch's *Cultural Literacy* might seem, at first sight, to be indicative of similar concerns; but Hirsch's project is concerned with the establishment (or reestablishment) of a shared American cultural discourse, based on terms drawn from both the humanities *and* the natural sciences. The latter is also more egalitarian in intent than Bloom's, having among its expressed ideals the breaking of "the cycle of illiteracy for deprived children," and the achieving of "greater social justice" (145).

[2]See the report of the 1984 NEH Study Group chaired by Bennett, which calls for a traditional "core curriculum" in the humanities, and inveighs against "ideological" and/or relativistic textual approaches (11). Unlike Bloom, however, Bennett apparently takes for granted that religious faith continues to "infuse" American life with "a sense of transcendence" (*America's Schools* 179).

[3]This is not, of course, to exempt preceding administrations from their share in the use of violence for the securing of economic, military and political hegemony, which has been an intrinsic part of U.S. foreign policy throughout the century. It is merely that the Reagan administration was unusually triumphant about it, in a style that had been out of fashion for some decades. The administration's cultural spokespersons were not above such gloating; Bennett, for example boasted of the nation's military and political "successes" in El Salvador and Grenada (*America's Schools* 126).

[4]"The latest enemy of the vitality of the classic texts is feminism" (65).

[5]Arnold found in the world of late nineteenth-century Britain "a disquieting absence of sure authority." In *Culture and Anarchy* he suggested that, "Only in right reason can we get a source of sure authority; culture brings us towards right reason" (136). Arnold also entertains an idea not unlike that of Bloom, of the disinterested philosopher-mentor: "In his own breast does not every man carry about with him a possible Socrates, in that power of a disinterested play of consciousness upon his stock notions and habits...And he who leads men to call forth...this power...is at the present moment, perhaps...more in concert with the vital working of men's minds, and more effectually significant, than any House of Commons orator..." (176).

[6]See 113-118.

For Bloom, one condition of culture is "a vision of the cosmos that has a special place for one's people"; and an endorsement of "the West's universal or intellectually imperialist claims" which cultural relativism would destroy (37, 39). Not only does this ideal of Bloom's conflict with his spiritual essentialism, but it raises questions about the political implications of such a view. Too often in the past, Western intellectual imperialism has translated into a rationale for military conquest. This, Bloom is honest enough to concede, is inevitable while one holds to the concept of the competing separateness of different cultures (202).

[7]Mandela currently enjoys a position of honor and moral authority, even among those who called him a terrorist three or four years ago. In this respect, he is not so unlike certain heroic rebels in U.S. history much celebrated by Bloom, who, beginning with careers as terrorists and traitors, achieved metamorphosis into Founding Fathers, and a place in the history books.

[8]Homais closely resembles a historic figure of the Enlightenment in America, and one who played a crucial shaping role in the founding of the U.S. political system Bloom so greatly admires: Benjamin Franklin.

[9]"In both places the universities gave way under the pressure of mass movements, and did so in large measure because they thought those movements possessed a moral truth superior to any the university could provide" (314).

Marcuse is certainly a pivotal figure in the intellectual climate Bloom describes— if not the prophet of the irrational Bloom would make him out to be. Both in his Freudian exploration of the possibilities of social liberation (notably in *Eros and Civilization*) and in his analysis of blue-collar support for right-wing political extremism in the 1970s, Marcuse rivals and surpasses Bloom as an astute, cogently reasoning social critic.

[10]"...so far as universities are concerned, I know of nothing positive coming out of that period; it was an unmitigated disaster for them" (320).

[11]At least in Bloom's example, of the students at Brown who called for cyanide to be made available to the university community in case of nuclear attack, the intention behind the gesture was apparently to startle the community into reflection on the dangers of the armaments race. What comparable excuse can be made in favor of Michael Dukakis' posturing in an army tank, during the 1989 election campaign, or for Reagan's cowboy machismo, as he once playfully threatened, on national radio, to bomb the Soviet Union? No age group—nor political party—can claim a monopoly on "posturing."

[12]I am thinking not only of Amnesty International, but of student involvement in Witness for Peace, CISPES, the Nuclear Freeze campaign, the Free South Africa groups, Habitat for Humanity, the Hunger Task Force, Friends of the Earth, the various Public Interest Research Groups...Even this list is clearly not exhaustive.

[13]That social engagement/commitment *has* tended to transform cultural and pedagogic practice within the academy, whether in the application by Greenblatt and his followers of "new historicist" approaches to Renaissance texts, or in the feminist/marxist/deconstructionist readings of "subaltern" literature by Gayatri Spivak, is fairly clear. The effect of such changes has been, as Elizabeth Fox-Genovese suggested in a recent article on "The New Literary Studies of Race and Gender," to offer either "a welcome opening to pluralism" or "a modern Tower of Babel," depending on one's point of view (8-9). She puts most succinctly her case for rejecting the "American self of our tradition" in favor of a more skeptical understanding of this construct of white male cultural hegemony. I concur with her call for the acknowledgement of "diversity," but also with her sense of the need "forthrightly" to acknowledge a collective identity that simultaneously "transcends and encompasses our disparate identities and communities" (28-29). This ideal is, it seems to me, qualitatively different from, say, Bloom's endorsement of "intellectually imperialist claims" (See Note 6).

[14]Bloom complains that school "value-clarification" courses "are supposed to get children to talk about abortion, sexism or the arms race, issues the significance of which they cannot possibly understand" (61).

[15]In this connection, see Lyotard, *The Postmodern Condition*, for a suggestive discussion of alternatives for access to knowledge in "computerized societies"—either total control and regulation of the economy of knowledge by interested parties, or "the outline of a politics that would respect both the desire for justice and the desire for the unknown" (67).

[16]Plato's utopia is constructed on the premise that philosophers will play the key role in its direction. What didactic literature the young philosopher-candidates will be permitted to read is intended to help prepare them for their future executive responsibilities (327-8, 437).

[17]Plato's own account of his attempts to train Dionysius II in the duties of kingship suggests that even towards the end of his life he had not renounced the hope of intervening usefully in practical politics (*Epistle vii* 223-227).

[18]In the *Apology*, Socrates claims that his daemon has always debarred him from entering public life. Yet it is clear that he has, when called upon, served with honor and integrity as an elected member of the Council. His opposition to trying the naval commanders after Arginusae is based, not on the superior independent moral insight gained from private contemplation that Bloom alleges, but on an understanding that, under Athenian law, trial *"en bloc"* is unconstitutional (64).

[19]He would not, for instance, have exempted the philosopher from his dictum that, under a government which imprisons unjustly, "the true place for a just man is also a prison" (*Disobedience* 14); nor from his indictment of the average citizen's moral torpor in the face of the slave trade and the tragedy of John Brown (*A Plea* 8).

[20]Emerson's argument here, like Bloom's, may well owe something to the *Republic*. In Plato's utopia the citizens are required to operate in those occupational and political spheres for which they are qualified, "to perfect themselves in their own particular job" (187). Like Bloom, Emerson de-emphasizes the philosopher's politically active role in Plato. ("Ode Inscribed to W.H. Channing" *Selected Writings* 866).

Works Cited

Arnold, Matthew. *Culture and Anarchy: An Essay in Politics and Criticism.* Ed. Ian Gregor. Indianapolis: Bobbs-Merrill, 1971.

Bennett, William J. *Our Children and Our Country: Improving America's Schools and Affirming the Common Culture.* New York: Simon and Schuster, 1988.

———. *To Reclaim a Legacy: A Report on the Humanities in Higher Education.* Washington, D.C.: National Endowment for the Humanities, 1984.

Bloom, Allan. *The Closing of the American Mind.* New York: Simon and Schuster, 1987.

Emerson, Ralph W. *Selected Writings.* Ed. Donald McQuade. New York: The Modern Library, 1981.

Flaubert, Gustave. *Madame Bovary.* ed. Claudine Gothot-Mersch. Paris: Garnier Frères, 1971.

Fox-Genovese, Elizabeth. "Between Individualism and Fragmentation: American Culture and the New Literary Studies of Race and Gender" *American Quarterly* 42 (1990): 7-34.

Franklin, Benjamin. *The Autobiography.* Ed. Leonard W. Labaree, *et al.* New Haven: Yale UP, 1964.

Hawthorne, Nathaniel. *The Scarlet Letter.* Ed. Scully Bradley, *et al.* New York: Norton, 1978.

Hirsch, E.D. *Cultural Literacy: What Every American Needs to Know.* Boston: Houghton Mifflin, 1987.

Lyotard, Jean-François. *The Postmodern Condition: A Report on Knowledge.* Transl. Geoff Bennington and Brian Massumi. Minneapolis: U of Minnesota P, 1984.

Marcuse, Herbert. *Counterrevolution and Revolt.* Boston: Beacon P, 1972.

———. *Eros and Civilization: A Philosophical Inquiry into Freud.* Boston: Beacon P, 1966.

Plato. *The Epistles.* Ed. Glenn R. Morrow. Indianapolis: Bobbs-Merrill, 1962.

———. *The Last Days of Socrates: Euthyphro, The Apology, Crito, Phaedo.* Transl. Hugh Tredennick. Harmondsworth, England: Penguin, 1954.

———. *The Republic.* Transl. H.D.P. Lee. Harmondsworth, England: Penguin, 1955.

Thoreau, Henry D. *Civil Disobedience.* Boston: D. R. Godine, 1969.

———. *A Plea for Captain John Brown.* Boston: D. R. Godine, 1969.

Twain, Mark. *The Adventures of Huckleberry Finn.* Ed. Walter Blair and Victor Fischer. Berkeley: U of California P, 1985.

Permanent Questions, New Questions:
Opening American Minds to the Nuclear Age

Daniel Zins

Allan Bloom's *The Closing of the American Mind* has already engendered an extraordinary amount of commentary and discussion. A deeply flawed book, Bloom's polemic could nonetheless ultimately have a positive effect on American intellectual life by further invigorating the great canon debate on the role of the humanities in the academy and in our culture. But if this is to happen, the most serious shortcomings of Bloom's thinking, and their repercussions, must be accurately discerned and critiqued.

Still incensed by what happened in the United States during the 1960s, Bloom insists that this decade was nothing less than "an unmitigated disaster" for America's universities. At that time, Bloom recalls, he served on a number of committees at Cornell University, "and continuously voted against dropping one requirement after the next. The old core curriculum—according to which every student in the college had to take a smattering of courses in the major divisions of knowledge—was abandoned" (Bloom 320). Two decades later, students coming to universities find "a bewildering variety of departments and a bewildering variety of courses. And there is no official guidance, no university-wide agreement, about what he *should* study." In the absence of a required core curriculum, most students simply decide upon a career and begin preparing for it (338).

Our great universities, Bloom contends, seem unable to create a modest program of general education for their undergraduates (340). If in the eighties universities *are* attempting to restore requirements that were eliminated in the sixties, Bloom laments that reinstating such courses is a much more formidable task than dropping them. Nevertheless, for Bloom the only serious solution to the crisis in the humanities

is the one that is almost universally rejected: the good old Great Books approach, in which a liberal education means reading certain generally recognized classic texts, just reading them, letting them dictate what the questions are and the method of approaching them—not forcing them into categories we make up, not treating them as historical products, but trying to read them as their authors wished them to be read. (344)[1]

Bloom concedes, however, that even those who embrace his solution face a quandary:

The professors of humanities are in an impossible situation and do not really believe in themselves or what they do. Like it or not, they are essentially involved with interpreting and transmitting old books, preserving what we call tradition, in a democratic order where tradition is not privileged. They are partisans of the leisured and beautiful in a place where evident utility is the only passport.... After all, what do Shakespeare and Milton have to do with solving our problems? Particularly when one looks into them and finds that they are the repositories of the elitist, sexist, nationalist prejudice we are trying to overcome.

Not only did the thing in itself require a conviction and dedication not often really present in the professors, the clientele was disappearing. The students just were not persuaded that what was being offered to them was important. (353)

If more and more students in the past two decades have been deserting the humanities, perhaps at least part of the explanation is that there really *is* something seriously wanting in the way the humanities have been—and are still being—taught. Bloom writes that

The kinds of questions children ask: Is there a God? Is there freedom? Is there punishment for evil deeds? Is there certain knowledge? What is a good society? were once also the questions addressed by science and philosophy. But now the grownups are too busy at work, and the children are left in a day-care center called the humanities, in which the discussions have no echo in the adult world. Moreover, students whose nature draws them to such questions and to the books that appear to investigate them are very quickly rebuffed by the fact that their humanities teachers do not want or are unable to use the books to respond to their needs. (372)

I would like to suggest that there might be *other*, even more important, needs of students that are also being neglected, and that traditional approaches to the Great Books will perforce fail to meet these exigencies. In addition to his Great Books' nostrum, Bloom also believes that universities would do well to place less emphasis on computer literacy and begin accentuating "literacy literacy, inasmuch as most high school graduates nowadays have difficulty reading and writing" (341). But "literacy literacy," even if it includes the celebrated "cultural literacy" championed by E.D. Hirsch, cannot by itself effectively address either the malaise of our educational institutions or the most serious problems of the larger society. What today's students especially need is *critical* literacy, which must include both *nuclear* literacy and *ecological* literacy.[2]

According to Bloom, "True liberal education requires that the student's whole life be radically changed by it, that what he learns may affect his action, his tastes, his choices, that no previous attachment be immune to examination and hence re-evaluation. Liberal education puts everything at risk and requires students who are able to risk everything" (370). But in our time everything in fact *is* at risk. And it may indeed require that our whole lives "be radically changed" if we are to avert nuclear or environmental disaster. Liberal education, which has only recently begun to acknowledge these twin threats to our very survival, already appears to be once again ignoring one of them.

Even during periods of heightened cold-war tensions, most educators allocated very little of their teaching and research to the threat of nuclear war. Interest in this issue *did* increase during the first half of the 1980s, but with the Cold War now ending, there seems to be a widespread feeling that the nuclear problem itself has been resolved. But it is, of course, a possible *environmental* holocaust which is now being increasingly acknowledged as the cardinal threat to international security. The editor of *New Perspectives Quarterly*, devoting most of a recent issue to "A New Ecological Ethos," writes:

As the Cold War winds down and the atmosphere heats up, the environment is rising to the top of the global agenda. The number of refrigerators, not missiles, are what count now; the most urgent mission of the U2 spyplane is no longer detecting ICBMs on the ground in Russia, but ozone-depleting CFCs above the Arctic. Already, terms like "industrial disarmament" and "ecological security" are seeping into the mainstream political discourse. The Greening of *Realpolitick* has begun. In the past few months, nothing short of a revolution in awareness has overtaken world leaders once singularly fixated on balance-of-power politics. (Gardels 2)

Given the alarming condition of the planet's ecosystem, this "revolution in awareness" is, of course, long overdue. While we should all welcome an *environmental* decade in the 1990s, I submit that if we are to avoid once again abdicating one of our primary responsibilities as educators, we must not forget about the threat that until only quite recently seized the popular imagination: *nuclear* holocaust.

Few readers of *The Closing of the American Mind* are likely to conclude that nuclear weapons or environmental deterioration are particularly pressing concerns, or that educators should necessarily be addressing these issues. According to Bloom, "The imperative to promote equality, stamp out racism, sexism and elitism (the peculiar crimes of our democratic society), as well as war, is overriding for a man who can define no other interest worthy of defending" (Bloom 314). What Bloom cannot seem to imagine is that issues of class, race, and gender— as well as war, or even nuclear "war"—should be overriding concerns of *all* educators, including those who favor the Great Books approach and continue to revere "the tradition." To suggest that past and future *victims* of poverty, racism, and sexism—as well as war and militarism—might be "worthy of defending" would seem to be incontrovertible proof that one is still uncritically enamored of "the sixties." And to suggest that poverty, racism, sexism, and militarism might often be closely linked would undoubtedly constitute an even more egregious offense than "the peculiar crimes" themselves.

"Without recognition of important questions of common concern," Bloom writes, "there cannot be serious liberal education, and attempts to establish it will be but failed gestures" (343). Bloom does briefly point out that "composite," often team-taught interdisciplinary general education courses, such as "Man in Nature" or "War and Moral Responsibility," do occasionally attempt to redress the inadequacies of some approaches to core curricula. But after briefly noting the advantages of such courses, Bloom also points out their "dangers," and concludes that "they do not point beyond themselves and do not provide the student with independent means to pursue permanent questions independently, as, for example, the study of Aristotle or Kant as wholes once did" (343).

Throughout *The Closing of the American Mind* Bloom underscores the necessity of focusing on "permanent questions" and "permanent concerns." In his preface he observes that "What each generation [of the young] is can be best discovered in its relation to the permanent concerns of mankind" (19). He later maintains that the task of the university "is, in the first place, always to maintain the permanent questions front and center" (252). And near the end of his treatise Bloom writes: "Human nature, it seems, remains the same in our very altered circumstances because we still face the same problems, if in different guises, and have the distinctively human need to solve them, even though our awareness and forces have become enfeebled" (380).

But is it not conceivable that in "our very altered circumstances" we face not merely the same problems, but some entirely *new* ones?[3] In a 1986 *New York Times Magazine* article on the Yale critics, Colin Campbell observed that "critical thought has been rudely shaken since Matthew Arnold. It has had to deal with modernists and quantum physics and genocide" (Campbell 28). Perhaps a great deal more attention should be given to possible *connections* among critical thought, quantum physics, and mass death. As The American Council of Learned Societies report, *Speaking for the Humanities*, concludes: "One cannot proceed, in the humanities, by looking to past curricula, past conceptions of value and meaning, to provide the models that will allow us to meet current crises with which the humanities are now most profoundly concerned" (ACLS A22). Neither nuclear nor environmental holocaust, however, are ever mentioned in this report. And it is because of this failure (even in most of what I consider to be the most thoughtful writing on humanities education) to specifically discuss such dangers that we need not merely an expansion, but an *explosion*, of the canon debate.

"This is the American moment in world history," Bloom asseverates in his final paragraph,

the one for which we shall forever be judged. Just as in politics the responsibility for the fate of freedom in the world has devolved upon our regime, so the fate of philosophy in the world has devolved upon our universities, and the two are related as they have never been before. The gravity of our given task is great, and it is very much in doubt how the future will judge our stewardship. (382)

What Bloom seems unwilling to contemplate in his text is that it is *the future itself* which is now very much in doubt, which means that our fundamental responsibility as educators is to make a commitment to do what we can to ensure that our students *have* a future.[4] The gravity of our task, then, is certainly greater than Bloom indicates.

"It may well be that a society's greatest madness," Bloom declares, "seems normal to itself" (75). Bloom is commenting here not on the nuclear arms race, but on rock music! A penetrating new study of "the real history of the nuclear age" discloses that during the cold war the leaders of both superpowers repeatedly and intentionally risked nuclear war, not because they were seriously tempted to attack each other, but "to back up foreign intervention and the division of the world into superpower-dominated spheres" (Derber and Schwartz 81). How many of our students actually know about the many documented instances of this reckless and indefensible behavior, and about their nation's *real* (as opposed to the often very different *declaratory*) nuclear weapons policies? And how many educators are informed about these crucial issues? One is led to wonder why a book which contains a chapter-length diatribe against rock music does not allocate at least as much space to the history of the rather cavalier attitudes of many policymakers toward the possible use of nuclear weapons, and why its author fails to recognize—and thus vent at least as much spleen—over *this* madness?

Bloom, of course, is hardly alone in choosing to remain oblivious to this particular pathology. "Nietzsche's new beginning in philosophy," Bloom writes, "starts from the observation that a shared sense of the *sacred* is the surest way to recognize a culture, and the key to understanding it and all of its facets... What a people bows before tells us what it is" (204). What Bloom fails to point out is that for more than four decades now we have been paying obeisance to the *nuclear* deity.

We are only beginning to understand the underlying causes of our thralldom. In his thoughtful study of our "strange god," Ira Chernus underscores that

...no movement for nuclear disarmament can succeed with purely rational arguments and political methods. We shall never be able to turn away from our nuclear faith until we first understand it in its own symbolic terms. Above all, we must understand that, just as our ancestors found all religious meanings converging in one awesome beloved God, so we find all religious meanings converging in our strange yet alluring God— the Bomb. (Chernus 11)

But of course we rarely think of our terrifying idol even as we have allowed policymakers to make it the centerpiece of U.S. national security planning. And much less often, of course, do we contemplate its symbolic meanings or possible psychological reverberations.

Bloom relates a conversation he had with the wife of a high official of an Ivy League college, who informed Bloom that her son had a law degree but, like his friends, "had little ambition and moved from one thing to another." Asked for a possible explanation of this behavior, "She responded firmly, quietly and without hesitation, 'Fear of nuclear war'." When Bloom later asked his own students if they shared this fear,

The response was a universal, somewhat embarrassed giggle. They knew what their daily thoughts were about, and those thoughts had hardly anything to do with public questions. And they also knew that there are a great many right-thinking adults who expect them to use the nuclear threat as an excuse for demanding a transformation of the world political order and who also want to produce their maimed souls in evidence against our politicians' mad pursuit of the "arms race." (83)

It is, of course, extraordinarily difficult to determine precisely how, or in what particular ways, living with the threat of extinction affects the souls or psyches of either young people or adults. It may be unwise, however, to simply assume that the consequences of this unprecedented burden are insignificant. Moreover, even though the nuclear threat itself is surely reason enough "for demanding a transformation of the world political order," thoughtful, empathic individuals would also be aware of a number of additional, and equally compelling, reasons to work for the fundamental changes that will be indispensable if a just, stable, and enduring peace is to become a reality. Bloom writes that

> Students may indeed feel a sense of impotence, a sense that they have little or no influence over the collective life, but essentially they live comfortably within the administrative state that has replaced politics. Nuclear war is indeed a frightening prospect, but only when it appears imminent does it cross their minds. Even such a powerful, concerted effort as the nuclear freeze commotion, with its attendant entertainments like *The Day After*, has nothing to do with the lives students lead and is little more than a distraction. Very few of them are destined for a political life; and if they do actually enter politics, it is by accident, and does not follow from their early training or expectations. (85)

Even if students choose not to "actually enter politics," "politics" will nonetheless ineluctably "enter" their lives; however comfortable students are, or intend to become, it is no longer possible to insulate oneself from the (potentially apocalyptic) currents of the larger political world. Periodic promulgations to the contrary notwithstanding, neither ideology nor history nor politics has ended, and educators can perhaps do their solipsistic students no more important service than to help them to understand why, for most of the world's citizens, the notion that it is possible to separate the political and the personal into discrete realms is absurd. And it is a fantasy that even the planet's most privileged denizens may soon be forced to abandon. Bloom writes that

> Starvation in Ethiopia, mass murder in Cambodia, as well as nuclear war, are all real calamities worthy of attention. But they are not immediate, not organically connected to students' lives. The affairs of daily life rarely involve concern for a larger community in such a way as to make the public and private merge in one's thought. It is not merely that one is free to participate or not to participate, that there is no need to do so, but that everything militates against one's doing so. (84)

Including, Bloom might have added, most traditional humanities education. We need to begin asking why educators have not made a much more concerted effort to make issues such as world hunger, genocide, and militarism immediate to their comfortable students, or why they have failed to make explicit how their own nation's domestic and foreign policies have contributed to more than a modicum of the human suffering resulting from these evils.

Perhaps it is also time that we begin asking *why* our students "feel a sense of impotence," and why so many of them have convinced themselves that they are powerless to do anything to mitigate human suffering and misery now, or to reduce the likelihood of nuclear or environmental disaster in the future. Deriding a demand made by Brown University students a number of years ago— that their institution make cyanide available in case of nuclear war—Bloom concludes that "Survivalism has taken the place of heroism as the admired quality" (84). But one might also view the demand by the Brown students as a quite understandable (if, unfortunately, despairing) reaction to the reckless rhetoric and irresponsible nuclear weapons policies of the Reagan Administration. Bloom, however, would obviously prefer to scoff at the not unreasonable fears of thoughtful young people than to decry the thoughtless discourse and unreasonable policies which spawn such fears and resignation.

But for Bloom the pervasive nihilism in America is really a "nihilism without the abyss." Nihilism, Bloom writes, "is the announcement that all the alternatives or correctives—for example, idealism, romanticism, historicism, and Marxism—have failed. Americans on the other hand, have generally believed that the modern democratic project is being fulfilled in their country, can be fulfilled elsewhere, and that that project is good" (158). Bloom also contends that

Our condition of doubt makes us aware of alternatives but has not until recently given us the means to resolve our doubt about the primacy of any of the alternatives. A serious life means being fully aware of the alternatives, thinking about them with all the intensity one brings to bear on life-and-death questions, in full recognition that every choice is a great risk with necessary consequences that are hard to bear. (227)

But what Bloom fails to point out is that on the great life-and-death questions of our time, Americans have *not* been made aware of the alternatives, which has contributed in no small measure to a pervasive cynicism. In his incisive analysis of this phenomenon, Peter Sloterdyjk writes that

In societies where there is no effective moral alternative and where potential oppositional powers are to a large extent entangled in the apparatuses of power, there is no longer anybody in a position to be outraged about the cynicism of hegemonic power. The more a modern society appears to be without alternatives, the more it will allow itself to be cynical. (112)

What makes this cynicism particularly insidious is that while it has long suffused our intellectual life and now pervades our entire culture we have failed to acknowledge it or call it by its proper name. What has long passed for "realism" in our political debates might actually be a profound cynicism, or a largely unreflective conviction that we are helpless either to significantly reduce the injustices in our world, or to avert its collapse. The narrow, bipartisan, cold-war consensus which dominated American political discourse throughout the Cold War consistently disparaged alternative proposals for dealing with nuclear technology or the Soviet Union as naive, utopian, irresponsible, or "soft on communism."

What has passed for debate on the most important issues of our time, then, has often been really no debate at all. Bloom himself concedes that "In the heat of our political squabbles we tend to lose sight of the fact that our differences of principle are very small, compared to those over which men used to fight. The only quarrel in our history that really involved fundamental differences about fundamental principles was over slavery" (248). And Bloom also appreciates that

Freedom of the mind requires not only, or not even especially, the absence of legal constraints but the presence of alternative thoughts. The most successful tyranny is not the one that uses force to assure uniformity but the one that removes the awareness of other possibilities, that makes it seem inconceivable that other ways are viable, that removes the sense that there is an outside. (249)

What Bloom is unwittingly but accurately describing here is the tyranny of the American nuclear national security state. For in a very important sense even the nation which continually and proudly proclaims itself to be the freest in the world is, at the same time, a profoundly *unfree* country. Viewing the "Soviet threat" as a permanent emergency—a dogma that even now a number of policymakers seem loath to relinquish—the nuclear national security state has demanded constraints on the flow of information and levels of secrecy incompatible with the ideals of a democracy or an open society.

What official national security discourse has consistently concealed from ordinary citizens is that any "defense" system which relies on genocidal "weapons" for its ultimate surety is incapable of providing either real freedom or genuine security. And ever since Hiroshima, for both policymakers and the mass media, any suggestion that there might be viable, nonnuclear, alternative defense systems really *has* been inconceivable. If the "alternative thoughts" that Bloom ostensibly champions are ever to gain a hearing in the nation's nuclear debate, it is imperative that we appreciate *why* the voices which articulate them have been effectively silenced for so long. What is especially needed, then, is some insight into both the origins, and persistence, of the remarkable uniformity of thought on America's nuclear weapons and national security policies.

The etiology of this enduring bipartisan consensus, which still shackles foreign policy debates in the United States, must be traced back at least to World War II and to the political repression which followed the war. In their widely discussed book *What Do Our 17-Year-Olds Know?*, Diane Ravitch and Chester E. Finn, Jr., report that "only 42.6% associate Senator Joseph R. McCarthy with anticommunist investigations; many think he was the Senator McCarthy who led the protest movement against the war in Vietnam. Thus we are raising a generation for whom the term 'McCarthyism' has little meaning." (83)

Unfortunately, it appear that some of the *educators* of this generation also have little understanding of this disturbing phenomenon, or of its still baleful legacy. Claiming that "we need constant reflection of the broadest deepest kind," Bloom also maintains that "The most important function of the university in an age of reason is to protect reason from itself, by being the model of true openness" (252, 253). Attempting to expose a number of what he calls the "myths" of "McCarthyism" and of the 1950s, Bloom defends this decade as "one of the great periods of the American university, taking into account, of course, the eternal disproportion between the ideal and the real" (322). In his peculiar reading of this period Bloom also contends that

Another aspect of the mythology is that McCarthyism had an extremely negative impact on the universities. Actually the McCarthy period was the last time the university had any sense of community, defined by a common enemy. McCarthy, those like him, and those who followed them, were clearly nonacademic and antiacademic, the barbarians at the gates. In major universities they had no effect whatsoever on curriculum or appointments. The range of thought and speech that took place within them was unaffected. Academic freedom had for that last moment more than an abstract meaning, a content with respect to research and publication about which there was general agreement. The rhetoric about the protection of unpopular ideas meant something, partly because the publicly unpopular ideas were not so unpopular in universities. Today there are many more things unthinkable and unspeakable in universities than there were then, and little disposition to protect those who have earned the ire of the radical movements. The old liberalism—belief in progress and the free market of ideas—had its last moment of vigor at that time. In the sixties, when things seemed to be going in the right direction, the old liberalism was understood more and more to be a part of bourgeois ideology, favoring and protecting the voices of reaction as opposed to those of progress. In the fifties the campuses were calm, most professors were against McCarthy (although, as one would expect in a democracy, some were for him; and, as one would also expect, human nature and professors being what they are, some who were against him were too timid to speak out). Professors were not fired, and they taught what they pleased in their classrooms. For that moment at least, there was a heightened awareness of the university's special status as a preserve against public opinion. That was a very healthy thing. (324)

About a hundred pages earlier in *The Closing of the American Mind* Bloom had observed that "Forgetting, in a variety of subtle forms, is one of our primary modes of problem-solving" (230). As a nation we have indeed forgotten about "McCarthyism," but Bloom's tract suggests that perhaps even more insidious than collective repression of this shameful era are attempts to rewrite the period in ways that consistently violate the historical record.

If we really do need "constant reflection of the broadest and deepest kind," and if the university's most important purpose is to be a "model of true openness," then the McCarthy era surely *did* have "an extremely negative impact on the universities." To suggest that the "range of thought and speech" in America's universities was "unaffected" at this time is absurd. To maintain that "Professors were not fired, and they taught what they pleased in their classrooms," is also more than a little disingenuous. On the contrary, it was a time of enormous fear and self-censorship, with deleterious effects on both universities and on the larger culture. The truth is that the real closing of the American mind occurred during the very decade which Bloom now so uncritically extols.

A much more veracious account of what really happened in America's colleges and universities can be found in Ellen W. Schrecker's *No Ivory Tower: McCarthyism and the Universities*, published a year before Bloom's best-seller. "The academy," Schrecker writes in the concluding paragraph of her assiduously researched study,

did not fight McCarthyism. It contributed to it. The dismissals, the blacklists, and above all the almost universal acceptance of the legitimacy of what the congressional committees and other official investigators were doing conferred respectability upon the most repressive elements of the anti-Communist crusade. In its collaboration with McCarthyism, the academic community behaved just like every other major institution in American life. Such a discovery is demoralizing, for the nation's colleges and universalities have traditionally encouraged higher expectations. Here, if anywhere, there should have been a rational assessment of the nature of American Communism and a refusal to overreact to the demands for its eradication. Here, if anywhere, dissent should have found a sanctuary. Yet it did not. Instead, for almost a decade until the civil rights movement and the Vietnam war inspired a new wave of activism, there was no real challenge to political orthodoxy on the nation's campuses. The academy's enforcement of McCarthyism had silenced an entire generation of radical intellectuals and snuffed out all meaningful opposition to the official version of the Cold War. When, by the late fifties, the hearings and dismissals tapered off, it was not because they encountered resistance but because they were no longer necessary. All was quiet on the academic front. (340)

In the early years of the nuclear age, when nothing was more important than exploring every reasonable option for dealing with a profoundly changed and potentially much more dangerous world, an anxious America permitted only that most narrow spectrum of ideas to be voiced. Perhaps the most pernicious effects of the McCarthy era have been on the Democratic Party and on the U.S. foreign policy. Failing to counter the ludicrous Republican claim that they had "lost China," and haunted by the fear that someday they might also be charged with "losing Indochina," Democrats became obsessed with making their foreign policy invulnerable to the charge that it is "soft on communism" or "weak on defense."[5] For more than four decades now, very few members of the Democratic Party have dared to challenge this *idee fixe*.

Postwar conflict with the USSR was inevitable, and perhaps the nuclear arms race itself could not have been prevented. But even as they formulated their very narrow range of options for dealing with the Soviet Union, and with the bomb, policymakers were in fact considerably less constrained by circumstances than is commonly believed. Other alternatives were available, and, had they been pursued, the Cold War might not have become nearly so intense and protracted, or the arms race nearly so costly and dangerous. But throughout the postwar era those who have envisioned more sensible policies have rarely been able to make their voices heard, and today, more than three decades *after* the "fabulous fifties," we still have not had a meaningful national debate on how to best achieve real security. Teachers and scholars in the humanities must accept part of the responsibility for this failure.

On the most pressing issues of our time, the American mind remains closed. Allan Bloom, in a book which purports to decry this phenomenon, has, unfortunately, only exacerbated it.

Notes

[1]Those who still believe that we can "just read" books and allow the texts themselves to "dictate what the questions are and the method of approaching them" would perhaps benefit most from an exploration of some of the more recent theories of knowledge, and of the humanities.

[2]For a thoughtful discussion of why colleges should ensure that all of their students confront the possibility of environmental holocaust, see William Heyen, "The Host: Address to the Faculty at SUNY College at Brockport," *American Poetry Review* 18:4 (July/August, 1989), 19-21.

[3]Which is not to say, of course, that many canonical writers cannot help us to answer them. They obviously can, particularly if we give innovative readings to various canonical texts. For example, I can think of no book more relevant to our current dilemmas than Thoreau's *Walden*.

[4]See Robert Jay Lifton, *The Broken Connection: On Death and the Continuity of Life* (New York: Simon and Schuster, 1979).

[5]See Godfrey Hodgson, *America in Our Time* (New York: Random House, 1976).

Works Cited

American Council of Learned Societies. *Speaking for the Humanities. The Chronicle of Higher Education.* January 11, 1989. A11-A22.

Bloom, Allan. *The Closing of the American Mind.* New York: Touchstone Books, 1988.

Campbell, Colin. "The Tyranny of the Yale Critics." *The New York Times Magazine.* 9 February 1986.

Chernus, Ira. *Dr. Strangegod: On the Symbolic Meaning of Nuclear Weapons.* Columbia: U of South Carolina P, 1986.

Derber, Charles, and William A. Schwartz. *The Nuclear Seduction: Why the Arms Race Doesn't Matter and What Does.* Berkeley: U of California P, 1990.

Gardels, Nathan. "Comment: A New Ecological Ethos." *New Perspectives Quarterly.* 6:1 (1989).

Schrecker, Ellen W. *No Ivory Tower: McCarthyism and the Universities.* New York: Oxford UP, 1986.

Sloterdyjk, Peter. *Critique of Cynical Reason.* Trans. Michael Eldred. Minneapolis: U of Minnesota P, 1987.

The Great Books vs. America:
Reassessing *The Closing of the American Mind*

Kenneth Alan Hovey

The light which we have gained, was given us, not to be ever staring on, but by it to discover onward things more remote from our knowledge....They are the troublers, they are the dividers of unity, who neglect and permit no others to unite those dissevered pieces which are yet wanting to the body of Truth.

Milton, *Areopagitica* (742)

Against the dark background of contemporary American higher education, Allan Bloom paints a bright image of former teacher/student excellence—Socrates and his disciples outside the Areopagus of ancient Athens. This model, Bloom makes clear, is approachable in America today, since he saw it approximated in his own classroom at Cornell in the sixties. The best occupants of that classroom are the heroes of his book. In the first third of *The Closing of the American Mind*, titled simply "Students," Bloom excoriates most students today but praises his own, at least those who had studied under him by 1965. He speaks fondly of the time when he "first started teaching and lived in a house for gifted students," Telluride house at Cornell, and found "at that moment a spiritual yearning, a powerful tension of the soul that made the university atmosphere electric" (49, 70). This moment ended, he makes clear in the last third of his work, "The University," when Cornell capitulated to the demands of Black Power activists in 1969. In this crisis, however, a group of his students remained heroically separate, "contemptuous of what was going on, because it got in the way of what they thought it important to do" (332). This principled assertion of difference has evidently stayed with his best students, at least with the ten whom he acclaims individually in his preface as "old students, now very independent thinkers" (23).

Producing independent thinkers should certainly be the goal of democratic education and, according to Bloom, his own old students are the proof that that goal is attainable. Though not one of the select ten nor a member of the group of separatists of 1969, I was a student of Bloom's during his banner years. I came to Cornell in 1965 as a junior, lived among Bloom's most ardent disciples at Telluride House, took the two best classes of my undergraduate career from him, and left Cornell in 1967 indelibly marked by his Socratic questioning of the values of modern America. Provoked by his teaching, I expanded my classical language training from Latin to Greek and Hebrew, spent a year in Europe after supplementing my French with German, and went on to become a professor in the humanities with a Ph.D. in English and a penchant for intellectual history. More than anything else, however, it seems that I have spent the past twenty years seeking out, as Milton describes it, "those dissevered pieces which are yet wanting to the body of Truth" (742) for which Bloom supplied the skeleton. Between the few masterworks he then taught and still emphasizes, Bloom left large gaps which I have been seeking persistently to fill.

Since Bloom values his students pre-eminently for their independent minds, he boasts that his mention of ten of them "in no way implies that they endorse [his] views" (23). Having followed the light that I gained from Bloom, I find that in reading his book I cannot endorse them. I agree with him that in moral and political matters the time-honored wisdom of our fathers needs to be taken more seriously than the shifting trends of the present and, therefore, that humanistic studies should be rooted in "the old Great Books conviction" rather than in "devotion to the emergent" (51, 352). But not all the fathers and not all their greatest books agree. By focusing entirely on a single line of tradition within our tradition, Bloom creates the illusion, however, that they do. From this super-canon he derives a single set of transcendent principles by which he condemns American higher education during the past twenty years. It is this set of principles, rather than the Great Tradition itself, that is truly revered in *The Closing of the American Mind*, and it is with those principles that I disagree. They stand not just against the post-sixties American university but against the very idea of America, both as it was originally conceived and as it has been passed down to us in American tradition.

Bloom's principles, while comprehensively applied in *The Closing of the American Mind*, are more straightforwardly stated in the work acclaimed in Saul Bellow's "Foreword" as "an excellent book on Shakespeare's politics" (11). Despite the gap of years between them, Bloom's most recent book was clearly written as a sequel to his first one, *Shakespeare's Politics* (1964). As the second is dedicated "To My Students," the first is dedicated by Bloom and Harry V. Jaffa, the author of its last chapter, "To Leo Strauss, Our Teacher." As the one opens by claiming that "there is one thing a professor can be absolutely certain of: almost every student entering the university believes, or says he believes, that truth is relative" (25), its predecessor opens with the related assertion that "the most striking fact about contemporary university students is that there is no longer any canon of books which forms their taste and their imagination" (1). The avowed object of *The Closing of the American Mind* is to reveal the baneful effect of the relativizing of accepted principles, chief among them the authority of the canon of Great Books, while the object of *Shakespeare's Politics* is to explain the most important of the principles as found in one author of the lost canon, Shakespeare. These principles deal with four issues handled separately in the four chapters written by Bloom: national character, racial diversity, religious diversity, and the role of the philosopher.

Bloom's first principle is stated forcefully in the opening chapter of *Shakespeare's Politics*, on the setting of Shakespeare's plays: "Various nations encourage various virtues in men; one cannot find every kind of man in any particular time and place" (11). In *The Closing of the American Mind* Bloom laments that "sensitivity to national character, sometimes known as stereotyping, has disappeared" (91) and attempts to revive it. His book offers a new characterization of America and begins, as his principle implies it should, by explaining "Our Virtue," which he identifies as "openness" (41). To set off America's virtue Bloom offers briefer characterizations of four other Western nations: England, Italy, France, and, especially, Germany. In contrast to the land of Shakespeare, the land of Dante and Machiavelli, the land of Descartes and Pascal, and the land of Goethe, America has, according to Bloom, no central national thinkers and has needed, therefore, in its uncivilized modernity to depend on Western Europe (52). This means that the best American students in Bloom's view have always gone or longed to go to Europe with the "openness [of] the quest for knowledge and certitudes" (41).

Unfortunately, according to Bloom, Europe has come in the last two centuries to be increasingly dominated by the culture of modern Germany, and Germany, having transferred its allegiance from Goethe to Nietzsche, has turned on Western civilization altogether. The result is the barbarism of the Nazis which, in Bloom's view, definitively characterizes the German mind today. Consequently, Americans who imbibed European culture in the first half of this century were poisoned by "The German Connection" (141), which Bloom traces through the long and tortuous middle third of his book, "Nihilism, American Style." As a result, contemporary American students, educated by Germanized intellectuals, no longer turn to traditional European thought for anything and thus have transformed "Our Virtue" into "Our Ignorance," as the conclusion to the middle third makes clear. American openness has become the "openness of indifference" and in consequence "the longing for Europe has been all but extinguished in the young" (41, 320).

Bloom's generalizations about the character of European countries are based so largely on anecdote and unsupported assertion that they seem hardly more than personal prejudices, the chief of which are marked Francophilia and severe Germanophobia. But his definition of American national character, though much fuller, is not more fair. Having denied that America has any "national authors" in the sense that England, Italy, France, and Germany do (52), Bloom declines to examine any non-contemporary American author at all. The Founding Fathers are touted repeatedly throughout the book as a "race of heroes" (55), but none are given more than a sentence of individual attention. The whole nineteenth century in America is passed over with only two disparaging remarks on Thoreau, and even the Americans with whom Bloom agrees most, Henry Adams and H.L. Mencken, are noted only in passing. While anything that an American has said since, or even before, the Declaration of Independence and *The Federalist* is easily dismissed as derivative, the "very French" De Tocqueville is regarded as authoritative on all things American (52, cf. 227). So frequently and admiringly is de Tocqueville cited throughout *The Closing of the American Mind*, that Bloom's book might appropriately be regarded as an elaborate update of *Democracy in America*, particularly of its chapter on "The Intellectual Life of the Americans" (246).

Despite the undoubted excellence of de Tocqueville's book, it is a clearly dated and highly partisan work. It belongs to a long series of anti-egalitarian critiques of democratic America written before the Civil War by European visitors, including Dickens and Mrs. Trollope, as well as by Europe-minded Americans like Crevecoeur, Irving, Cooper, and Calhoun. Crevecoeur rejected the American

Revolution, Irving Jeffersonian democracy, Cooper Jacksonian democracy, and Calhoun and his Southern followers the federal Union. First-rate as all these authors are, de Tocqueville among them, to read them without reading the more egalitarian but equally classic works of Franklin, Paine, Emerson, Whitman, and Twain is to abuse the canon and seriously misjudge America. The latter authors, who are more commonly thought to represent the American mind, considered leaving Europe more important than going there and established a tradition of intellectual independence that was thoroughly rooted on this side of the Atlantic, though open to foreign influences, long before Nietzsche and the crypto-Nietzscheans that Bloom exposes corrupted Europe.

Bloom implicitly admits that de Tocqueville, as a post-Rousseauian, is not a classic author of the highest order, but, instead of considering any opposing classics of similar stature, justifies his anti-egalitarian preference by aligning this "rarest flower of the old French aristocracy" (227) with older and undoubtedly higher authorities. One of these is Shakespeare. In *Shakespeare's Politics, Othello* and *The Merchant of Venice* become the joint prototypes of *Democracy in America*, for Bloom treats Venice as the model for the United States as it was originally conceived and reads Shakespeare's plays as studies of republicanism in Venice. Venice, like the United States, was a "tolerant, bourgeois, and republican" nation which sought to establish "an interracial, interfaith society" on the basis of "human brotherhood" (16-17, 36). Shakespeare's Venetian plays, which Bloom considers "the profoundest recorded analysis of the relation of Jew and Christian, of white man and black man," prove Bloom's next major principle, that "the brotherhood of man can only come into being on the basis of the lowest common denominator" or, in other words, "the difficulties that stand in the way of human brotherhood" are all but insuperable (17, 23, 36; cf. 38).

On the basis of this principle Bloom turns Desdemona and Jessica into the real villains of the Venetian plays. Rebelling against their fathers who reject brotherhood with a different race or religion, they seek to join black and white, Christian and Jew, but only succeed in bringing degradation to themselves and tragedy to Brabantio and Shylock. These false daughters are clearly the models for the American students in *The Closing of the American Mind* who sing "We Are the World," which Bloom characterizes as "a pubescent version of *Alle Menschen werden Brüder*, the fulfillment of which has been inhibited by the political equivalents of Mom and Dad" (74).

Bloom's prior reading of *Othello* as a pessimistic study of miscegenation leads naturally to his major statements on racial issues in *The Closing of the American Mind*, offering him the opportunity to attack not just American character in general but the individual regional characters of both the North and the South. Northern liberals are, of course, blamed for the excesses of integration *de jure*, which Bloom portrays as a failure *de facto*. But Bloom blames Southern conservatives even more. Southerners initially adopted a "'different strokes for different folks' philosophy," Bloom maintains, to safeguard their "peculiar institution," slavery (32, 35). When this philosophy eventually caught on among Northern liberals, it transformed the quest for integration into the cult of Black separatism and Black power, like that which promoted the seizure of Cornell. Thus the "Nietzscheanization of the Left" is matched by the

Southernization of the North, and Bloom shows himself as eager to expose the Southern connection, "which has not been sufficiently noted," as he is the German one (32, 217).

In attacking the "Jim Crow South" (95), as in attacking Nietzscheanized Germany, Bloom is clearly trying to show that the classics upon which he stands do not simply authorize all Right wing movements. Consequently, he is careful to distinguish Southern racism and slavery from ancient racism and slavery: "Racial prejudice did not exist in the modern sense [before the seventeenth century] nor as it does in America with its special political history" (*Shakespeare* 41); "Even the proponents of slavery [in the South] hardly dared assert that some human beings are made by nature to serve other human beings, as did Aristotle; they had to deny the humanity of the blacks" (*Closing* 248).

But this distinction is entirely imaginary, for Antebellum Southerners turned to the Great Books, not to any modern philosophy of "different strokes for different folks," to lend authority to their views. Genesis 9, in which God ordained that the descendants of Ham—including all Africans—should serve the rest of mankind, was the chief of many biblical texts used to support black slavery (Faust 10-11, 136-67). Furthermore, far from denying the humanity of blacks, leading defenders of Southern slavery rested heavily on Aristotle:

Such is the theory of Aristotle, promulged more than two thousand years ago, generally considered true for two thousand years, and destined, we hope, soon again to be accepted as the only true theory of government and society. (Fitzhugh 71)

The South knew that its institution seemed peculiar only in the nineteenth century and consequently turned for a model to "the glory that was Greece/And the grandeur that was Rome," as Poe, the greatest Southern poet, put it (Gottesman 1212; cf. Faust 12). Slaves were named for classical heroes, mansions were built with Greek revival facades, and the whole confederacy was patterned on the ancient Greek amphictyony. Bloom could hardly have found truer believers in the "good old Great Books" or truer supporters of Desdemona's father.

Jessica's father is similarly supported in *The Closing of the American Mind*, at least in his adherence to Jewish religious tradition. Bloom's personal models are his own grandparents in whose home everything "found its origin in the Bible's commandments...Their simple faith and practices linked them to great scholars and thinkers who dealt with the same material" (60). Their opposite is Woody Allen, whom Bloom attacks "for playing with his Jewishness, which apparently has no inner dignity for him" when he portrays Zelig as coming from a "family of silly, dancing rabbinic Jews" (145). Unlike in Europe, Bloom claims, "a Jew in America...is as American as anyone" (53), but Allen illustrates the religious dangers to which such national inclusiveness leads. In general Bloom admires "real religion and knowledge of the Bible" as opposed to "respect for the Sacred—the latest fad" and despises modern courses which "teach 'The Bible as Literature,' as opposed to 'as Revelation,' which it claims to be" (56, 375). Consequently, he insists that one must take seriously the spiritual claims of great religious figures and, in particular, that "Calvin might actually have had a revelation from God" (210).

Woody Allen may well have derived his views from Riesman, Riesman from Fromm, Fromm from Heidegger, and Heidegger from Nietzsche, as Bloom supposes, but Allen's disrespect for the traditional faith of his fathers is nothing new in America. It belongs, in fact, to a tradition whose fountainhead is the eldest of the Founding Fathers, Benjamin Franklin. Franklin caricatured his own family's traditional Presbyterianism in the portrait he offered in his *Autobiography* of the Presbyterian divine who turned a biblical text of the most broad-minded humanity into a narrow sectarian polemic (Gottesman 351). Rejecting this faith as dangerous folly, Franklin created his own famous schedule of virtues and became as much of an inner-directed value-positer as Zelig. Neither he nor any of the "race of heroes" that sat at his feet regarded the Bible as Revelation, and, consequently, they devised a government in which church and state were strictly separated. One group of earlier Americans did, of course, take the Bible very seriously indeed, the theocratic Puritans of New England, and, authorized both by it and by Calvin, punished witches, Quakers, Indians, and other deviants with deadly rigor. Bloom claims that Right and Left meet in Nietzsche, but history itself shows that both Northern Puritan and Southern slave-owner meet in the most generally revered of the Great Books, the Bible.

They do not, however, meet in Shakespeare, as Bloom's reading of the Venetian plays might suggest. Bloom himself admits that Desdemona is not the only villain in *Othello* and, declaring that "Shakespeare does not understand Judaism," criticizes him for not making Jessica "pay the penalty for [her] crimes" (30-31). Furthermore, the overwhelming failure in both plays of the attempt to overcome racial and religious differences are countered, according to Bloom, by the limited successes of two individuals actively devoted to "common sense," Emilia and Portia (24, 61). As the wisest characters in their plays they point the way to even wiser characters in *Julius Caesar*, the self-proclaimed philosophers Brutus and Cassius.

Philosophy is the one distinction that is able in Bloom's view to raise one above the other distinctions of nationality, race, and religion and establish a common human bond on the highest level, that of timeless reason. The timelessness of philosophy is what Bloom especially seeks to show in his examination of the model Shakespearian philosophers. Brutus and Cassius grew up in Rome when it was a republic and thus a prototype like Venice of modern America. When Caesar "destroyed the Republic which was the seed bed of great Romans" (78), these philosophers foresaw the tyranny that would follow and rose above their Romanness to resist the trend of their own time and place. "Their seemingly futile gesture helped, not Rome, but humanity," Bloom writes, and it verified his last principle, that elevated by philosophy "men need not give way before the spirit of the times" (105).

The modern heir to the philosophic role, Bloom makes clear in *The Closing of the American Mind*, is the university. But the university, rather than philosophically resisting the spirit of the times, has bowed obsequiously before it, as the faculty of Cornell signally showed when they yielded to the demands of the Black Power activists in 1969. "Simply," Bloom concludes, "the university is not distinctive" (337). Ironically, the Cornell of the 1960s, Bloom's chief example of modern academic "servility, vanity, and lack of conviction" (313), seems to have been striving for nothing so much as distinction. Seeking, as Bloom admits, to be "in advance of its time," it established a "six-year Ph.D. program" and "was in the forefront of certain trends in the humanities...from Sartre, through Goldmann, to Foucault and Derrida...to give new life to old books" (341, 352). But Bloom sees nothing distinctive in being new. To rise above the times one must go back, not forward, and restore to the old books their original life and luster.

Bloom's view clearly echoes that of the Renaissance, which turned to classical antiquity in order to overcome the ignorance and superstition of the Middle Ages. Of the Great Books revived by the Renaissance none was more revered than the one Bloom places first in his canon, Plato's *Republic*. America, first settled by Europeans in the Renaissance, was initially regarded as the great opportunity to remake civilization according to Platonic principles. Sir Walter Raleigh, the establisher of the first British colony in the South, was a practical Platonist, and the Pilgrim colony in the North was an experiment in Platonism as well as Christianity. Yet Platonism failed to catch on in either place. William Bradford, writing in the earliest American classic, *Of Plymouth Plantation*, reflected on the Pilgrims' attempt to run their colony on the model of Plato's republic:

The experience that was had in this common course and condition, tried sundry years and that amongst godly and sober men, may well evince the vanity of that conceit of Plato's and other ancients applauded by some of later times. (120)

The Pilgrims, probably more than any other Americans since them, took the Great Books of antiquity seriously and ardently sought to live by the principles contained in them. But refusing to let the past they so highly revered tyrannize over the present and the future, they adopted as their highest principle the covenant that "as the Lord's free people [they would] walk in all His ways made known, *or to be made known unto them*, according to their best endeavors" (9; my italics). This notion of progressive revelation was reaffirmed by Franklin when he acclaimed the decision of a later but similar protestant sect, the Dunkers, to refrain from publishing any "Articles of their Belief" on the grounds that

some Doctrines which we once esteemed Truths were Errors, and the others which we had esteemed Errors were real Truths. From time to time [God] has been pleased to afford us farther Light,...and we fear that if we should once print our Confession of Faith, we should feel ourselves as if bound and confin'd by it, and perhaps be unwilling to receive farther Improvement. (Gottesman 378)

The farther improvement that Franklin and the other Founding Fathers sought was political rather than religious. Freeing themselves from the admired ideal of Plato's Great Book no less than from the revered tradition of European rank and royalty, they determined to establish something quite new, a nation founded on the principle that "all men are created equal."

The guiding axiom upon which all of Bloom's principles rely is stated succinctly in *Shakespeare's Politics*: "Men's separateness is an act of divine providence" (24). To Bloom men are not created equal, they are created separate. As a result, they are sharply divided into nation, race, and religion. Nothing can bridge these divisions but philosophy, yet in bridging them it establishes an even more important division, that between the philosopher—a rare being in Bloom's view—and the ordinary mortal. Consequently, human writings are divided between Great Books and mere literary ephemera. But who is to draw the line between the two? It is not the philosopher rising above time, but the times themselves looking back and declaring who is and who is not timeless. Bloom, no less than Calvin, Jesus, Moses, and Socrates, may well have had a revelation, but only through the events of time can divine providence, if it exists, be recognized by those who have not had one. Truth is not simply fixed and known but always further "to be made known." In the light of this creed, the creed of America since its beginning, all the heroes of the past are reduced to human proportions and "the Great Books" are only "books" in the lower case.

Being the works of men who, like us, are necessarily limited, books of the past may well be of great but never of transcendent value. The best of them reveal the sins of our fathers no less than their virtues. These settlers and founders of America, while recognizing the need for authority, saw its dangers as well and rejected the authority of a canon of books as much as they did a state church and a hereditary king. As a result, in America all books as well as all men are created equal. As some men, nonetheless, show themselves to be worthy of higher offices, some books in time gain higher respect. Philosophers and their books may claim to resist the times but are, in fact, part of their times too and will be judged by the times to come. This is not to say that they should not resist what they consider to be the evils of their day, but when they claim for themselves eternity or God they fall into a greater evil. "The almost universal historicism prevailing in the humanities," Bloom declares near the end of his book, has "prepared the soul for devotion to the emergent" (352). Evil as that may be, devotion to a few principles from a narrow canon within the canon of the European past is no better, and to such idolatry the American mind has always been wisely closed. The canon deserves respect, but, as the canon itself teaches, there are "dissevered pieces...yet wanting to the body of Truth" (Milton 742) which only the virtue of openness can hope to discover.

Works Cited

Bloom, Allan. *The Closing of the American Mind*. New York: Simon and Schuster, 1987.

Bloom, Allan, with Harry V. Jaffa. *Shakespeare's Politics*. New York: Basic Books, 1964.

Bradford, William. *Of Plymouth Plantation, 1620-1647*. Ed. Samuel Eliot Morison. New York: Random House, 1952.

Faust, Drew Gilpin. *The Ideology of Slavery: Proslavery Thought in the Antebellum South, 1830-1860*. Baton Rouge: Louisiana State UP, 1981.

Fitzhugh, George. *Cannibals All! or, Slaves Without Masters*. Ed. C. Vann Woodward. Cambridge: Harvard UP, 1982.

Gottesman, Ronald, et al., eds. *The Norton Anthology of American Literature*. 1st ed. Vol. 1. New York: Norton, 1979.

Milton, John. *Complete Poems and Major Prose*. Ed. Merritt Y. Hughes. Indianapolis: Bobbs-Merrill, 1984.

Socrates-Bloom:
An American Tale

Bonnie A. Hain

The Plot

Human beings require stories to give meaning to the facts of their existence. I am not talking here about those specialized stories that we call novels, plays, and epic poems. I am talking about the more profound stories that people, nations, religions, and disciplines unfold in order to make sense out of the world.... If our stories are coherent and plausible and have continuity, they will help us to understand why we are here, and what we need to pay attention to and what we may ignore. A story provides a structure for our perceptions; only through stories do facts assume any meaning whatsoever.... Without air our cells die. Without a story, our selves die.

—Neil Postman

Plato's mythical dialogues stand as a testament to the power of an author to order the universe with well-told tales; Platonic plots permeate Western thought. One of the most recent, popular texts to incorporate Platonic elements into its story is *The Closing of the American Mind* by Allan Bloom. In the conclusion to this book, Bloom writes:

Throughout this book I have referred to Plato's *Republic*, which is for me *the* book on education, because it really explains to me what I experience as a man and a teacher, and I have almost always used it to point out what we should not hope for, as a teaching of moderation and resignation. But all its impossibilities act as a filter to leave the residue of the highest and non-illusory possibility (381).

The story of education told by *The Republic* centers on the philosophy of forensics. Socrates, through a series of dialogues, teaches the elite young men of Athens to distinguish justice from injustice, the democratic leader from the tyrant. By the end of the dialogue, the youth are persuaded to pursue the philosophical and the just and to forego mercantilism and the unjust. Thus the implication is that they will not be tyrants, but that they will be ready now to lead as forthright citizens. Bloom's *The Closing of the American Mind* teaches through similar dichotomies (philosophy/mercantilism, just/unjust, democracy/tyranny), but the form of the two plots is different. Plato's story is one of dialectic, where one term is opposed to its antonym and then to itself slightly changed, until an ideal definition of the term is arrived upon by the participants in the dialogue. Bloom's story is one of rhetoric; the dialectic is assumed, since Bloom defines the terms in his book.[1] His tale focuses on the elements of persuasion that have been used and abused to create a university of mercantilism, injustice, and tyranny.

His story is meant to demonstrate rhetorically that the university can use alternate means of persuasion to create a more ideal university, one which fosters philosophy, justice, and democracy.[2] If we read Bloom's text as one of rhetoric, then we can best understand it if we oppose it to Plato's best known text of rhetoric, *Phaedrus*, rather than the dialectical text, *The Republic*.

Phaedrus tells the story of a young man's education concerning the nature of love and rhetoric. The dialogue begins when Phaedrus visits his older friend and mentor, Socrates, and relates a speech by the popular rhetorician, Lysias. The purpose of Lysias's speech is to persuade a young boy to grant his love more readily to a non-lover than to one who loves truly. Socrates gives two speeches to teach Phaedrus the art of speech-making; the first is a better rendition of Lysias' speech, and the second one argues most persuasively the opposite premise of the first talk. The three speeches act as a protracted allegory on the significance of belief and the art of rhetoric. Socrates' culminating speech demonstrates that a non-lover, like a person who does not believe the argument which he/she attempts to put forth, can never be logically suitable for a young boy. Socrates shows Phaedrus that lovers, rhetoricians, and teachers need to know the truth and believe it completely before they can help a youth develop fully as a person.

By the end of the "dialogue" Socrates persuades Phaedrus to forego the faddish teachings of the young, dynamic instructor, Lysias, and to pursue instead serious, long-term study like his master-teacher. Socrates ends his lecture with this prayer:

'Dear Pan and ye other gods who inhabit here, grant that I may become fair within, and that my external circumstances may be such as to further my inward health. May I esteem the wise man rich, and allow me no more wealth than a man of moderation can bear and manage' (103).

With this speech, Socrates shows Phaedrus that the monetarily lucrative "knack" of rhetoric is morally inferior to the morally correct, but economically unsound, study of philosophy. In the end, Phaedrus learns that the captivating, youthful, and monetarily successful Lysias cannot provide Phaedrus with love, for Lysias, like the non-lover, knows no philosophy. Instead, Phaedrus comes to desire his teacher, Socrates, the one who knows, the one who believes in knowledge.

The Closing of the American Mind recasts the story of Plato's *Phaedrus*, with Bloom as Socrates, the new literary theorists as Lysias, and the reader as Phaedrus. In Bloom's rendition of Plato's myth, the young student reader comes to Bloom persuaded that the non-believer is preferable to he who believes. According to Bloom, students say:

The true believer is the real danger. The study of history and of culture teaches that all the world was mad in the past; men always thought they were right, and that led to wars, persecutions, slavery, xenophobia, racism, and chauvinism. The point is not to correct the mistakes and really be right; rather it is not to think you are right at all (26).

Too, the naive reader thinks that the non-lover is preferable to he who truly loves.

Perhaps young people do not say "I love you" because they are honest. They do not experience love—too familiar with sex to confuse it with love, too preoccupied with their own fates to be victimized by love's mad self-forgetting, the last of the genuine fanaticisms. Then there is distaste for love's fatal historical baggage—sex roles, making women into possessions and objects without respect for self-determination. Young people today are afraid of making commitments, and the point is that love *is* commitment, and much more (122).

The Socratic Bloom must teach his students to believe and to love. He tells a story to demonstrate this point:

When I was a young teacher at Cornell, I once had a debate about education with a professor of psychology. He said that it was his function to get rid of prejudices in his students. He knocked them down like tenpins... I found myself responding to the professor of psychology that I personally tried to teach my students prejudices, since nowadays—with the general success of his method—they had learned to doubt beliefs even before they believed in anything. Without people like me, he would be out of business...So I proposed a division of labor in which I would help to grow the flowers in the field and he could mow them down (42-43).

Like his hero, Socrates, Bloom knows that he must vie for the respect and love of his students with those who do not believe. Socrates persuades Phaedrus to disregard the teachings of Lysias by demonstrating that the rhetoric of Lysias is immoral because it focuses on the gain of temporary, monetary wealth, rather than on the acquisition of a more permanent wealth, knowledge. Bloom attempts to persuade his reader with the same argument.

Because there is no tradition and men need guidance, general theories that are produced in a day and not properly grounded in experience, but seem to explain things and are useful crutches for finding one's way in a complicated world have currency. Marxism, Freudianism, economism, behaviorism, etc. are examples of this tendency, and there are great rewards for those who purvey them (254).

The "general theories" that fall into the "etc." category include deconstruction, feminist theory, and cultural criticism. Bloom wants the reader to believe that teachers who purvey these theories do so only to reap economic "rewards." Just as Socrates never makes explicit the financial details of the transaction among Lysias and Phaedrus, Bloom never specifies concrete details of the source of the funds, the dollar amounts involved, or the specific, immoral activities which the modern theorists engage in to garner their monies. Instead, through allusion and insinuation, a Socratic Bloom attempts to persuade the reader to beware the Lysias-like-theorist who hawks attractive, but worthless baubles.

The danger of the mercantilism of the modern rhetorician in both Plato and Bloom is the same; the student who follows the teachings of the modern rhetoricians weakens his/her soul. Thus Bloom writes: "The active presence of a tradition in a man's soul gives him a resource against the ephemeral, the kind of resource that only the wise can find simply within themselves" (247). The non-traditional approach to education, like the rhetoric of Lysias, is religiously heretical, since it promotes the pursuit of physical, rather than spiritual gain. To study the classic texts, Plato, Chaucer, Shakespeare, Milton, and Donne, is to ennoble the soul.[3] The reader allured by Plato's and Bloom's argument comes to believe that the tradition is ordained by God, while the modern theories are man-made.

In the end, Bloom hopes that his reader, like Phaedrus, will choose to love and desire the Socratic philosophic endeavor and the instructor who teaches it, that the reader will reject the alluring, faddish, blasphemous teachings of those who do not believe (i.e. the Marxists, Freudians, and Deconstructionists). He concludes:

The real community of man, in the midst of all the self-contradictory simulacra of community, is the community of those who seek the truth, of the potential knowers, that is, in principle, of all men to the extent they desire to know. But in fact this includes only a few, the true friends, as Plato was to Aristotle at the very moment they were disagreeing about the nature of the good (381).

The reader who fails to be persuaded by Bloom's arguments, like Lysias whom Socrates fails to befriend,[4] must necessarily be excluded from the community because he/she is not wise enough, nor moral enough, to enrich the community.[5]

The story of Lysias, Phaedrus, and Socrates is compelling, and Bloom's version of the tale captures all the essential elements of the original (love, sex, music, religion, friendship). Bloom's mistake, and the error of many who read his work, is to fail to recognize that Plato's dialogues were fictional, that an author named Plato created plot, characters, discourse, and setting to instruct and delight a reader. Though there was a man named Socrates who lived in ancient Athens, Plato's stories of this man and his pursuits don't necessarily capture actual history. Thus, Plato's fictional dialogues do not translate as models for "real" situations as easily as Bloom would have us believe. An analysis of the theoretical and pedagogical principles at play in the myth reveals the ludicrous nature of Bloom's attempt to make the fiction "real."

The Characters
Against the dark background of contemporary American higher education, Allan Bloom paints a bright image of former teacher-student excellence—Socrates and his disciples outside the Areopagus of ancient Athens. This model, Bloom makes clear, is not unapproachable in America today, since he saw it approximated in his own classroom at Cornell in the sixties. The best occupants of that classroom are the heroes of his book.

—Allan Hovey

Though Plato terms *Phaedrus* a dialogue, the student-learner, Phaedrus, could hardly be said to contribute to the conversation. His most lengthy contribution comes when he recites the words of another, the speech of Lysias. After this recitation, he speaks only to encourage lectures from the teacher, Socrates. This encouragement takes the form of leading questions and statements. Phaedrus is a passive learner who never demonstrates critical thinking. As a character, his role as a student is to listen carefully to the authoritative words of his teacher and to prompt the teacher to continue the lecture whenever the words of Socrates lapse.[6] In the text, Phaedrus does not act, but is acted upon, thereby allowing the dialectic to move along swiftly, efficiently. Since he always asks the right questions, he always receives the right answers.

The character of Lysias in the *Phaedrus* too fails to fully contribute to the "dialogue," and thus helps the dialectic to move along swiftly. Socrates manipulates the words of the voiceless Lysias to persuade his student to forego the teachings of the false teacher.[7] In providing close analytical readings of Lysias's text, in defining what Lysias has said without giving Lysias a chance to define for himself what he meant, Socrates uses rhetorical dexterity to define himself as protagonist and Lysias as antagonist. In *The Closing of the American Mind*, Bloom attempts to manipulate voiceless modern literary theorists for the same purpose. He alludes to the evils of Marxism, Freudianism, Deconstruction, Feminist Theory, and Cultural Criticism. Like Socrates, Bloom defines the concepts these modern theorists use to his own purpose, without allowing the critics to speak for themselves; he does this by writing about the general notions of the critics, without quoting specific words or texts.[8] Thus, the teacher, Bloom, controls the dialogue of his book efficiently and the argument moves along swiftly to serve his purpose (to define the ideal relationship of educators and students in an ideal learning environment).

Seen in this light, *The Closing of the American Mind* allows us to read Bloom's desire to play Socrates to his students' Phaedrus as a desire to control the dialectic. As Socrates-Bloom, an author character, Bloom can define and redefine the truth.[9] He can write and revise the questions and answers to rhetorical perfection, and thereby more easily persuade the passive student/reader to disregard the teachings of others and to believe in and respect him as teacher. He can constrain the "meaning" of other teacher's texts by never allowing the texts to "mean" outside his world of discourse. Unlike real teachers, Socrates-Bloom doesn't need to earn his students' respect and admiration through a logical dialogue with students or other teachers, for his teacher characters are drawn as unintelligible, unintelligent beings and his student characters are made too "nice," "silent," and well crafted to ever disagree with him.

Bloom's need to control the discourse to gain the students' respect and admiration is especially significant when one realizes the import both Plato and Bloom place on a student's feelings for the teacher. In both author's texts, the teacher-student relationship is characterized by the feelings each has for the other. Plato's text makes explicit the implicit sexual nature of teacher-student relations, by likening the rhetoric a teacher uses to persuade his student to a rhetoric of flirtation. The allegory defines the three terms, "teacher," "rhetorician," and "lover," as one and the same, wherein the needs of young boys (as students, rhetoricians, and lovers) are best fulfilled through love relationships where those whom they love also love them truly. Within the realm of the allegory, Socrates, as Phaedrus's teacher and rhetorician, is also his lover. In the text, the physical desire which Phaedrus and Socrates might share as lovers transmogrifies to spiritual desire; the student takes on the beliefs and values of the teacher, and spiritually, rather than physically, they become one. So Socrates prays at the end of his speech to the God of Love, Eros:

If in the beginning Phaedrus and I uttered aught that offended thy ears, lay it to the account of Lysias the true begetter of that speech and make him cease from such words; turn his heart to the love of wisdom, even as the heart of Polemarchus his brother is turned, so that this his loving disciple [Phaedrus] may no longer be in two minds, as he is now, but may employ his life in philosophic discussion directed towards love in singleness of heart (66).

If the God of Love answers Socrates's prayer, Phaedrus will no longer pursue both physical and spiritual desire, the love of Lysias and the love of Socrates, instead Phaedrus will love only the spiritual, only Socrates.

Similarly, Bloom's text establishes a metaphor of desire to describe the relationship of teacher to student in its ideal and base forms.

A significant number of students used to arrive at the university physically and spiritually virginal, expecting to lose their innocence there. Their lust was mixed into everything they thought and did. They were painfully aware that they wanted something but were not quite sure exactly what it was, what form it would take and what it all meant. The range of satisfactions intimated by their desire moved from prostitutes to Plato, and back, from the criminal to the sublime. Above all they looked for instruction. Practically everything they read in the humanities and social sciences might be a source of learning about their pain, and a path to its healing. This powerful tension, this literal lust for knowledge, was what a teacher could see in the eyes of those who flattered him by giving such evidence of their need for him. His own satisfaction was promised by having something with which to feed their hunger, an overflow to bestow on their emptiness. His joy was in hearing the ecstatic "Oh, yes!" as he dished up Shakespeare and Hegel to minister to their need. Pimp and midwife really described him well. The itch for what appeared to be only sexual intercourse was the material manifestation of the Delphic oracles' command, which is but a reminder of the most fundamental human desire, to 'know thyself.' Sated with easy, clinical and sterile satisfactions of body and soul, the students arriving at the university of today hardly walk on the enchanted ground they once did (136).

For Bloom and Plato, the ideal student desires his teacher sexually. The ideal teacher converts this desire for physical satisfaction into a desire for the spiritual. Just as mercantilism (the pursuit of worldly goods) must be replaced with philosophy (the pursuit of spiritual goods), sexuality (the pursuit of worldly pleasures) must be replaced with philosophy (the pursuit of spiritual pleasures). So, Bloom's desire to control the discourse is an attempt to control student desires. He believes that if he can control these desires, he can persuade his students to value the spiritual more than the physical.

The absurdity of this scenario of a Platonic teacher-student relationship for modern America, where students desire philosophy and their teachers and not sexuality, monetary wealth, and their lovers, becomes clear with a minimum of analysis. In Plato's story, a state of philosopher kings is possible, since the literary characters can live on forever with no physical sustenance. The characters, Socrates and Phaedrus, can live only on philosophy. Modern American students, however, even those who pursue the study of philosophy like Bloom, must have physical goods to survive (i.e. food, clothing, shelter). Literary characters can multiply with the stroke of the pen; the human race cannot survive without intercourse. The myth of a world based solely on spirituality delights us as readers, which may account for the popularity of Plato's and Bloom's fiction, but the world we live in has a physical component and no realistic solution to the problems faced by higher education can ignore the physical realm.

Furthermore, we may assume that the state needs philosophers (otherwise none would exist), but the philosophers too need the state. The state could not function if all its people were philosophers. Even if Bloom's ideal teacher could persuade all his students to study philosophy and not business, given the current lack of jobs for Ph.D.'s in philosophy, it seems unlikely that Bloom's model for education would be ideal.

In addition, Plato's teacher-student relationship fails to translate into a reasonable model for American higher education because it rests on an assumption antithetical to the most basic American law, as stated in the constitution, that all people are created equal. For Plato, not all people are equal; the bricklayer and the shepherd are of less value as "souls" than the philosopher. For example, in *Phaedrus*, he explains the hierarchy in this way:

In its first incarnation no soul is born in the likeness of a beast; the soul that has seen the most enters into a human infant who is destined to become a seeker after wisdom or beauty or a follower of the Muses and a lover; the next most perceptive is born as a law-abiding monarch or as a warrior and commander; the third as a man of affairs or the manager of a household or a financier; the fourth is a lover of physical activity or a trainer or physician; the fifth is given the life of a soothsayer or an official of the mysteries; the sixth will make a poet or a practitioner of some other imitative art; the seventh an artisan; the eighth a popular teacher or a demogogue; the ninth a tyrant (54).

Bloom adopts Plato's hierarchy of "souls" and makes it his own. For example, just as Plato's text assumes a male student population, so too Bloom categorically defines women out of the American education system, and into a lesser realm. Throughout his text, Bloom uses the pronoun "he" when the gender of a person is generic. One might excuse this as ignorance of the academic social standard of non-sexist language, were it not for Bloom's insistence on the "natural" place of women. Women in his text are relegated to the traditional roles of wife and mother. For example, he writes:

"Locke believed, and the events of our own time seem to confirm his belief, that women have an instinctive attachment to children that cannot be explained as self-interest or calculation. The attachment of mother and child is perhaps the only undeniable natural social bond. It is not always effective, and it can, with effort, be suppressed, but it is always a force. And this is what we see today. But what about the father? Maybe he loves imagining his own eternity through the generations stemming from him. But this is only an act of imagination, one that can be attenuated by other concerns and calculations, as well as by his losing faith in the continuation of his name for very long in the shifting conditions of democracy. Of necessity, therefore, it was understood to be the woman's job to get and hold the man by her charms and wiles because, by nature, nothing else would induce him to give up his freedom in favor of the heavy duties of family (115).

The natural domain for women is the home, for men it is the world of knowledge/scholarship. In direct opposition to the equal opportunity laws which define for many what it means to be "American," Bloom negates the rights of women to attend the university by claiming a higher law, "natural law" ("Nature should be the standard by which we judge our own lives and the lives of peoples" [38]). Bloom similarly dismisses the rights of other minorities protected by equal opportunity legislation when he writes:

Franklin Roosevelt declared that we want 'a society which leaves no one out.' Although the natural rights inherent in our regime are perfectly adequate to the solution of this problem, provided these outsiders [minority peoples] adhere to them (i.e., they become insiders by adhering to them), this did not satisfy the thinkers who influenced our educators (30).

For the minority to have "natural" access to the rights of our nation, i.e. education, they must become a part of the majority. The tyranny of such a vision of "nature" and the lack of logic in the belief that the Black man can naturally become white, or the Jew a Christian seems to escape Bloom, but no careful nor moral reader could find Bloom's position possible, much less desirable. The hierarchy of "souls" so beautifully written in Plato's myth, when translated into Bloom's "practical" model for American education, is distasteful, ugly, and fundamentally, anti-American.

To make this elitism palpable to the American public, Bloom attempts to redefine what it means to be "American," such that one can be both "American" and "Elitist."[10] Bloom wants to return to an "old view" of "American," and to define the concept as "a recognition of and acceptance of man's natural rights, where men have a fundamental basis of unity and sameness. Class, race, religion, national origin or culture all disappear or become dim when bathed in the light of natural rights... there is a tendency, if not a necessity, to homogenize nature itself" (27). However, elitism, as a concept, relies on the idea that things are not the same, that we can determine the relative value of particular objects in relation to an ideal object. So, "American" and "Elitism" are contradictory terms, as Bloom defines them, since "American" works toward unity and "Elitism" works toward disunity. This fundamental contradiction in terms, along with the impossible task of defining a heterogeneous American student population, also makes Bloom's theory of education highly unrealistic.

In an alternate vision of this contradiction, we could note too that Bloom's text defends elitism and the heterogeneity of student abilities,[11] but his fictional utopia simultaneously rests on the assumption that if the teacher controls the text competently, every student can learn in exactly the same fashion, exactly the same things, an assumption that depends on the homogeneity of student abilities. Even with the control of the texts and the discourse of the teacher, and with limits placed on the students admitted to the university, Bloom's model of education cannot "control" the environment enough to produce the perfected fiction of Plato's dialogues.

In Bloom's real classrooms and in those of you and I, no such control exists. Students, unlike Phaedrus, do not passively await our words of wisdom. They refuse to speak only to prompt long-winded lectures from the teacher. Instead, they speak to express their wants, needs, and desires. In a real classroom, students are never merely acted upon. Even the silent student, with his/her presence and non-verbal gestures, acts. As Helene Moglen points out, "education is "a collaborative project" where "authority is derived from depth of insight, where breadth of learning and experience are shared and where directionality is changed in a process that strives to be fundamentally interactive" (Moglen, p. 63). Teachers and students alike speak, act, and react. The dialectic necessarily moves slowly; students and teachers ask digressive questions and make digressive statements; together they discover what they wish to say. Teaching and learning occurs, but not in the neat, efficient manner expressed in Plato's and Bloom's myths, because the living discourse of teachers and students is inherently different from that of fictional characters.

The Discourse

Plato's dialogues are written and classroom exchanges are oral. The two modes of speech are distinct. Written sentences in each dialogue move logically from idea "A" to idea "B" to prove some larger idea, "C." Since Plato presumably had time to revise the discourse of each dialogue, the logic and rhetoric of the speech are flawless. In oral exchanges among live beings, there is no revision.[12] Oral speech is characterized not by perfect logic and rhetoric, but by interruptions, pauses, breaks in the discourse. Bloom's utopic vision seeks to "fix" oral speech, to make living language die. Since real teachers and real students can't revise their speech in the same way that Plato can revise Socrates' language, the teacher who attempts to play "Socrates" may find himself/herself quite frustrated. Even if the teacher lectures and refuses to allow student interruptions (in the form of questions or comments), unless the instructor reads carefully, crafted prose, the teacher's own spoken discourse will be imperfect, and he/she will fail to live up to the "Socratic ideal."

This ideal, with its emphasis on authoritative teachers who know and believe the truths they teach to passive students who are willing to be persuaded and who wish to become their teacher, speaks too of issues of reading and writing discourse. We can surmise that Bloom assumes that for the master-teacher to know and believe the truths of the master-texts, and for the teacher to be able to instruct the students on how to gather these truths, the truths must be inherent in the texts. The writers of the master-texts must have intended to put these truths down for posterity, and the purpose of reading must necessarily be to help the reader to understand and to make one's own these beliefs. The reader, like the learner, passively removes from the lecture of the teacher, the writer, the inherent values and truths of the master-texts. Thus, the Socratic method is consistent for the critic who sees the reader-writer relationship as does Bloom, but his pedagogy poses serious problems for teachers who do not share his belief that reading is a passive activity where a message is conveyed objectively through a text.

The attack on the concept of the passive reader is a relatively old one and has been argued persuasively by many, including the phenomenologists, reading theorists, composition theorists, semioticians, and deconstructionists, not surprisingly the very critics Bloom makes the antagonists of his text. Any theorist who denies the validity of "the passive reader," if his/her logic is consistent, must also find Bloom's educational model implausible.

The Setting

Our world has become infinitely large and each of its corners is richer in gifts and dangers than the world of the Greeks, but such wealth cancels out the positive meaning—the totality—upon which their life was based. For totality as the formative prime reality of every individual phenomenon implies that something closed within itself can be completed; completed because everything occurs within it, nothing is excluded from it; and nothing points at a higher reality outside it; completed because everything within it ripens to its own perfection and, by attaining itself, submits to limitation. Totality of being is possible only where everything is already homogeneous before it has been contained by forms; where forms are not a constraint but only the becoming conscious, the coming to the surface of everything that had been lying dormant as a vague longing in the innermost depths of that which had to be given form; where knowledge is virtue and virtue is happiness, where beauty is the meaning of the world made visible. That is the world of Greek philosophy.

—Georg Lukacs

Modernism speaks of the wasteland our society has become due to the replacement of a totalized world view with a fragmented one. Eliot, Pound, Joyce, and Woolf all yearn for a lost civilization, for a simple, uncomplicated time and place, a world where the inhabitants knew everything. Bloom, as a modernist, writes of a lost "classroom." In this special place, all the inhabitants knew why they were there, the ground to be traversed, and the order of the world. Like Lukács and other, modernist authors, he laments the loss of "the" place and the totalized world view, and he decries the new world, with its fragmentation and its relativistic notions of knowledge. Lukács and most other modernists recognize that a complete, totalized world view is not plausible today, given the complex nature of human endeavors, but Bloom fails to render up his ideal world.

After a reading of the *Symposium* a serious student came with deep melancholy and said it was impossible to imagine that magic Athenian atmosphere reproduced, in which friendly men, educated, lively, on a footing of equality, civilized but natural, came together and told wonderful stories about the meaning of their longing. But such experiences are always accessible (381).

Yet, Bloom's world is not accessible. Teacher and student are never "on a footing of equality." There is "an inescapable power relationship in any institutionalized teaching.... Trying to pretend that the power and weapons are not there...only gets the power more permanently and insidiously into the air." (Elbow, p. 79). Teachers and students are seldom "friends." They do tell wonderful stories, but in most classrooms, the elements of the fictions told are constrained by the politics of the classroom. Moreover, in most American universities, classes are not homogenous in terms of culture or gender. The racial and sexual politics of the classroom, an element not present in Bloom's Platonic model, also determines the stories told. The political complexity of the modern American classroom makes the idyllic "totalized" world that Bloom believes we can and should institute implausible.

The Moral

Every English teacher acts on the basis of theory. Unless teaching is a random series of lessons, drills, and readings chosen willy-nilly, the English class is guided by theories of language, literature, and pedagogy. That is, insofar as teachers choose readings and plan instruction, they are implementing a theory. The question, of course, is whether or not teachers understand the theory that guides their instruction.

—W. Ross Winterowd

The "Socratic Method" and "The Great Books Approach" to education that Allan Bloom proposes has no basis in reality. His story, like the myths he bases it on, Plato's dialogues, is full of interesting, but implausible notions. We cannot make Bloom's fiction real, just as we cannot create Plato's cave or Plato's republic. All human beings need to tell and to hear stories, and teachers have a great deal of control over the fictions to be told and heard. The repugnance of Bloom's particular fiction, with its open call for racism, sexism, and elitism, its illogical and implausible description of teacher-student relations, and the popularity of the text, suggest the real problem facing American educators today. We need to replace now popular tales which work to undermine who we are and what we desire to be, as Allan Bloom's story does, with more finely crafted, more responsible stories, ones which will save our selves.

Notes

[1]His definitions are often incompatible with those one might find in a dictionary, which explains in part the controversial nature of his text. For example, he writes: "Prejudices, strong prejudices, are visions about the way things are. They are divinations of the order of the whole of things" (43). This definition with the positive connotations of the terms "visions" and "divinations" works to build a positive connotation for the term prejudice, a term that few of us would normally find positive.

[2]Many have argued that Bloom is an elitist who despises democracy. For example, Benjamin Barber writes of *The Closing of the American Mind*: "It is a new Book of Truth for an era after God. Its only rival is democracy, which Bloom, with those he comforts, can only despise" (Barber, 65). If one opposes elitism with democracy, that is, if one uses the common, American definition of the term, then certainly Bloom is anti-democratic. Yet, one needs to be cautious here, because Bloom isn't using that common term, but the Platonic one, where democracy is defined as an equality of voices among the already chosen or elite. Within Bloom's own dialectic, the opposite of democracy is not elitism, but as in Plato, "tyranny."

[3]In Plato's *Phaedrus*, Socrates demonstrates the blasphemy of Lysias's speech, and of his own first speech which speaks of non-belief and physical love in grandiose terms, when he notes that "I might be 'purchasing honour with men at the price of offending the gods' "(44).

[4]Socrates: Nature, my dear Phaedrus, has not left the man [Isocrates] devoid of a certain love of wisdom. That is the message that I am taking from the divinities here to Isocrates, who is my favourite, and you must take the other [that Lysias, as a poet/speech-writer/ maker of laws is devoid of wisdom] to Lysias, who is yours. (Plato, 103)

[5]Helene Moglen offers an insightful analysis of Bloom's exclusions. She names his theory of education "unabashed prejudice" (Moglen, 62), and traces his bias to a deep-seated "machismo." " 'Machismo' is indeed revealed to be the defensive and insecure inventor—not the essential counterpart—of female modesty, as it is the inventor of all

the qualities that mark the threatened 'other' as inferior. It is fundamentally his 'machismo,' then, that Bloom wishes to affirm at any cost, with the Western tradition that is, in his judgment, its expression and justification. He has written his book in its defense" (Moglen, 62).

⁶In Plato's dialogues, the illocutionary speech acts of the participants (e.g. Phaedrus and Socrates) prompt interaction and perlocution between the reader and the text, thus the reader derives education from Plato's words.

⁷Lysias may be said to be voiceless because he never speaks in the dialogue himself; his words come solely through the voice of Phaedrus who recites Lysias's speech.

⁸For the non-critical or careless reader, Bloom may successfully demonstrate that Bloom is the protagonist and the new rhetoricians are antagonists. The critical reader is more likely to note the trick and to come away confused as to the why Bloom fails to provide the close readings of his antagonists' texts, as Socrates did for Lysias.

⁹As Moglen points out, Bloom sets himself as the "high priest to whom the function of revelation appropriately belongs" (Moglen, 62).

¹⁰His attempt to conflate the two terms, in claiming that there is or once was a homogeneous "American population" is tasteless and ludicrous in light of historical records, as most of the reviewers of *The Closing of the American Mind* have pointed out (i.e. see Moglen or Postman); however, I think it is important to do more than just point to the prejudice present. An analysis of Bloom's words, even when we grant Bloom the right to his own dialectic definition of terms, proves the lack of logic of his argument, and thus the illogical nature of the prejudicial statements.

¹¹In an interview in *Time* (see Works Cited list), Bloom stated his theory of elitism frankly: "One of the most important things to human beings is the capacity to recognize rank order or decent people or moral people, or intelligent and wiser people. Without those kind of elites, we don't have leaders" (74).

¹²Speakers often recast words already spoken to refine the expression of idea, but the original phrases, once spoken, remain present in the mind of the listener. Readers, however, seldom see the original phrases of a writer.

Works Cited

Barber, Benjamin. "The Philosopher Despot: Allan Bloom's elitist agenda." *Harper's Magazine* 276 (1988): 61-65.

Bloom, Allan. *The Closing of the American Mind: How Higher Education Has Failed Democracy and Impoverished the Souls of Today's Students*. Simon and Schuster, 1987.

———. Interview with William McWhirter. *Time* 17 October 1988. 74-76.

Elbow, Peter. *Embracing Contraries: Explorations in Learning and Teaching*. New York: Oxford, 1986.

Hovey, Kenneth Alan. "The Great Books versus America: Reassessing *The Closing of the American Mind*." *Profession 88* (1988): 40-45.

Lukács, Georg. *The Theory of the Novel: A historicophilosophical essay on the forms of great epic literature*. Trans. Anna Bostock. Cambridge, MA: MIT Press, 1985.

Moglen, Hélene. "Allan Bloom and E.D. Hirsch: Educational Reform as Tragedy and Farce." *Profession 88* (1988): 59-62.

Plato. *Phaedrus and The Seventh and Eighth Letters*. Walter Hamilton, tr. London: Penguin, 1988.

Postman, Neil. "Learning by Story." *The Atlantic* 264 (1989): 119-124.
Winterowd, W. Ross. Introduction. *A Teacher's Introduction to Deconstruction* by Sharon Crowley. Illinois: NCTE, 1989.

Mysteries and Jeremiads:
Narrative Elements in
The Closing of the American Mind

John Peacock

Published in the April 1989 *New Art Examiner*, Vol. 16, No. 8. Reprinted with permission.

What Hayden White argues in *Metahistory* about historical theories being plotted as comedies, tragedies, or satires—what Stanley Edgar Hyman in *The Tangled Bank* argues about Darwin, Marx, Frazer, and Freud as imaginative writers—is true in a more general sense of many other works of nonfiction as well: they "sometimes turn out to be dramatic compositions to a truly terrifying degree."[1]

A prime example is Allan Bloom's best seller *The Closing of the American Mind* the success of which, I would argue, partly depends on the book being very subtly narrativized along two popular storylines: the jeremiad and detective story—both of which typically feature uncompromising detectors of personal and institutional corruption, who, by reasserting traditional discipline, resist the forces of crime, apocalypse, revolution, or declension. Even readers who disagree with Bloom's evidence may still feel compelled by his hidden plot, and therefore accept his solutions to the problems besetting American education.

Reviewer Martha Nussbaum, in the *New York Review of Books*, succinctly and fairly summarizes what, according to Bloom, the central problem is:

As Bloom sees it, the central problem in higher education today, and in American society more generally, is widespread relativism. Both teachers and students have been taught that all conceptions of the good human life are equally valid, and that it is not possible to find an objective viewpoint from which to make rational criticism of any tradition. ("Undemocratic Vistas," *NYRB*, 5 Nov. '87, p. 20)

From his own teaching experience, Bloom recounts that to criticize this relativism is to invite the question "Are you an absolutist?" (25), as if there were no other alternative. His students insist that relativism is one of those "things you don't think about" (25). To them, according to Bloom, it is "not a theoretical insight but a moral postulate" (25). To Bloom, relativism has perverted our fundamental political and social ideals. For example, the Constitution, he complains, is now generally thought of as protecting subcultures rather than citizens—the difference he sees is that citizens have agreed to forgo some of their

111

individuality to join the social contract, whereas minorities that resist cultural assimilation make such a contract impossible to fulfill.

Bloom focuses on how this longstanding problem in American culture applies to schools, colleges, and universities. In his view, relativism—or "keeping an open mind"—has become synonymous with a closed mind about the classics of Euro-American culture.

The irony Bloom sees is that the tradition these classics uphold invites criticism of itself and contemplation of other traditions. "Only in the Western nations," he writes, "i.e., those influenced by Greek philosophy, is there some willingness to doubt the identification of the good with one's own way." Bloom makes a convoluted argument that, nonwestern cultures being closed, in teaching openness to them, "Openness to closedness is what we teach" (*Closing* 39).

Returning to reviewer Martha Nussbaum, herself the author of an article entitled "Internal Criticism and Indian Rationalist Traditions," Bloom's premise that nonwestern cultures are closed-minded

shows a startling ignorance of the critical and rationalist tradition in classical Indian thought, of the arguments of classic Chinese thinkers, and, beyond this, of countless examples of philosophical and nonphilosophical self-criticism from many parts of the world. . . . It shows as well a most un-Socratic unwillingness to suspect one's own ignorance. I have rarely seen such a cogent, though inadvertent, argument for making the study of non-Western civilizations an important part of the university curriculum. ("Undemocratic Vistas" 22)

But it is not just the inaccuracy of Bloom's characterization of nonwestern cultures that concerns us here. By praising as unique the West's willingness to doubt its own identification with the good, Bloom in fact identifies the West, beyond a shadow of a doubt, with the good that comes from self doubt. A perfect paradox—to assert one's superiority over others by virtue of one's ability to criticize oneself—places Bloom's book squarely in the tradition of the American jeremiad, a genre in which self-criticism figures as a source of pride for regenerating one's own group.

In the logic of the genre, to achieve regeneration through self-criticism requires scapegoats, from inside and outside the group, upon whom to project the very sins that Jeremiah fears in himself and his own.

It should not be surprising therefore that, in his role as Jeremiah, Bloom himself commits venial versions of the mortal sins he condemns. If he blames cultural relativists for historical reductionism, never mind that he himself skews history to suit his argument, equating 1960s student radicals with 1930s Nazi Youth, for example. "The fact that in Germany the politics were of the Right and in the United States of the Left should not mislead us," he says (314).

Among Bloom's favorite scapegoats are feminism, black studies, and the French left, particularly those he calls Parisian Heideggerians such as Jacques Derrida, Roland Barthes, and Michel Foucault. Bloom blames black, feminist, and French cross-cultural comparison and criticism for fabricating the great problem, as described by Richard Rorty in "Philosophy and Pragmatism," that it is difficult "to step outside our own skins—the traditions, linguistic and other, within which we do our thinking and self-criticism—and compare ourselves with something absolute" (Rorty 32). Fixated as African-Americanists, feminists, and the French may, for various reasons, be on this problem, they certainly did not invent it. Bloom skirts their critiques of the myth (in the negative sense of ideology) of Western objectivity in order to advocate Western objectivity as a myth in the positive sense of one of the "truths" people need (as they once needed God) in order to survive as a culture. A Grand Inquisitor in the Dostoyevskian sense rather than a crude essentialist, Bloom warns of the hazards of historicism and cultural relativism. This is his jeremiad.

More seductive than Bloom's negative scapegoating is another kind of positive mythmaking in which he engages at the beginning of his book, so as to set himself up as Jeremiah in the first place. He needs to reinvent the image of Jeremiah precisely because that austere prophet's traditional image is one Bloom explicitly rejects—"I no more want to be Jeremiah than Pollyanna," he writes (22). By assuming the more contemporary trappings of a mythic figure other than Jeremiah, Bloom solves the problem of what rhetorical stance his jeremiad is going to take.

As narratives, jeremiads are comparable to contemporary detective stories in criticizing institutional backsliding and attempting to restore order before (and maybe even after) it is too late. The main similarity is the assumption that regeneration may come after violence, upheaval, revolution, or apocalypse, but only if we play our cards right. Unless and until we do, Jeremiah feels a sense of doom. The detective's equivalent state of mind is visualized, in movie versions of that genre, by *film noir* conventions of dark, brooding urban streets.

Another similarity is that detective stories, like jeremiads, function the way Lévi-Strauss said myths do: to contain, without really resolving, paradoxes such as the one we have already examined between self-criticism and a sense of superiority over others. One way to contain without resolving this paradox is by projecting qualities (such as closed-mindedness) that one criticizes in oneself onto others, who are then seen to share these negative qualities, only to a much worse degree. This is the tendency to scapegoat that has already been discussed, and it functions in the relation between hero and bad guy in the detective genre just as it does in the jeremiad.[2]

If these are the similarities, the obvious difference between jeremiads and detective stories is that the latter are much more modern in terms of setting and character—the character of victim and especially that of hero. As I learned once at a convention of detective writers and publishers, what keeps the genre current is a constant updating of the old triad of inept cops, criminal masterminds, and private eyes. Lately, the first two of these—old-style cops and underworld criminals—have often been replaced by more or less inept professionals, often working together in the same institutions: hospitals, law firms, nursing homes, day care centers, art museums, churches, schools. If evil has become more institutional in post-war mysteries, the victims of evil are often those the institution serves; the crime is sometimes so seductive its victims may not realize what happened and instead even feel that they benefited. Victims are not always just killed—as Bloom's subtitle puts it in the case of students, their souls are "impoverished."

Enter the hero. Unlike Jeremiah, he does not stand above but rather rubs elbows with the fallen and the damned. Not always a professional detective, the hero of contemporary mysteries is sometimes a whistle blower from inside the same corrupt institution run by his adversary—a detector rather than detective per se. Conservative detectors want to restore things to their original purpose; subversive ones show that things were never right to begin with.

Following are some typical quotations used to introduce this hero. I will identify the source in a moment:

"[He] has his own way of doing things..."
"He often flashes out provocatively and wickedly."
"...he can hit, with the best (or I should say the worst) of them, very hard."
"...a front-line fighter in the mental wars of our times..."

Molding the character of the hero are the mean streets of, for example,

"...Chicago, that center of brutal materialism...the slaughterhouses, the steel mills, the freight yards, the primitive bungalows of the industrial villages that comprised the city, the gloom of the financial district, the ballparks and prizefights, the machine politicians, the prohibition gang wars...the free-for-all U.S.A...."

The detective uses graphic expressions to define his conflict:

"The soul has to find and hold its ground against hostile forces."
"In this regard I find myself...between a rock and a hard place."

Part of this conflict stems from ambivalence about intellectuality and/or spirituality:

"I might easily have gone on to the rabbinate if the great world, the world of the streets, had not been so seductive."

"To rest my book-stained eyes I played pool and Ping-Pong at the men's club."

"I enjoy making fun of...pedantry!...I myself, in reading Montaigne as I sometimes do, am tempted to skip his long citations from the classics, which put my high school Latin under some strain, and it is not amusing to send oneself back to high school."

The above-quoted descriptions of the hero, his city, language, and conflict were all written by a novelist introducing a character with whom he obviously identifies as narrator. Not Dashiell Hammett introducing Sam Spade nor Ross MacDonald introducing Lew Archer, but Saul Bellow introducing Allan Bloom in the foreward to Bloom's book (11-17).

Rhetorically speaking, then, a major novelist is drawing on his considerable talents to characterize Professor Bloom as a kind of hard-boiled detector of—in the words of the book's subtitle—"How Higher Education Has Failed Democracy." To what extent, does Bloom himself measure up to Bellow's characterization?

Certainly he knows how to talk tough. Twice in his own Preface, Bloom cites his thirty years experience that have produced a book he calls "a report from the front" (22)—one of the metaphors of post-war hard boiled fiction. And he portrays himself—using the third person pronoun—as a teacher whose "task is to assist his pupil to fulfill human nature against all the deforming forces of convention and prejudice" (20). But this mission presents Bloom with a conflict: "teaching can be a threat to philosophy because philosophizing is a solitary quest, and he who pursues it must never look to an audience" (20).

But, when you think about it, how representative a depiction of philosophers is this? Socrates didn't separate teaching and philosophy. Rousseau and Marx always looked to an audience. Bloom's conflict between being a private seer and yet fighting all the antidemocratic forces of convention and prejudice does not describe the philosopher/teacher as well as it does the contemporary private eye—a detective who, unlike teachers and cops, is not a public servant and in fact is often reluctant to become one. Bloom's rhetorical strategy is evidently to borrow from popular images of this detective so as to redefine, as a conflict between public and private selves, the contemporary philosopher's loss of traditional, objective grounds for judgment.

The loss of grounds for judgment and the conflict between public and private selves may be related issues, but they are not the same. Bloom conflates them in order to make a hero—in contemporary detective stories, this means an underdog, specifically someone sucked into public life against his better private instincts—to make this kind of contemporary antihero of the philosopher whose essentialist grounds for judgment have been deconstructed by women, blacks, and the French. The final question, of course, is: Could borrowing from popular stereotypes of the detective hero in this way really give the declining image of the philosopher a shot in the arm?

It is too early to tell whether Bloom's book will finally be perceived to have done so, but if we look to the related effects of a better established trend in recent *political* rhetoric, we may get a clue. I am referring to the unprecedented way Ronald Reagan brought back the once tarnished office of the Presidency by talking like western-detective cross-over hero Clint Eastwood when Reagan delivered his most memorable sound bite: "Make My Day." In a multi-ethic America, struggling to reach consensus, the one thing we all have in common are the images and rhetoric of mass entertainment. They serve, as all myths do, in lieu of real solutions to our problems. Sometimes, believing them almost makes them so.

Returning to Bloom, we can at least conclude at this time that, in resorting to a rhetorical strategy that subtly capitalizes on mythic persuasion rather than real argument, he implicitly engages in the vulgar popularization of teaching and philosophy that he so explicitly condemns. His preface, together with Bellow's forward, sets the scene, portrays the hero, and draws the conflict—all in ten brief pages (not too much for readers to skim standing in a bookstore)—ten pages that would be any publisher's dream. The deceits and pleasures of this rhetorical strategy may tell us more than Bloom's ostensible thesis about how higher education has failed democracy and impoverished the souls of today's students. One thing is for sure, Allan Bloom has successfully re-packaged the traditional, austere figure of the American Jeremiah as a best-selling contemporary detective hero.

Notes

[1]The words are Harold Rosenberg's, from *The New York Times Book Review*, quoted on the back cover of Hyman's book.

[2]For the cultural function and perennial nature of the jeremiad, see Sacvan Bercovitch, *The American Jeremiad*; for the theory of *Regeneration Through Violence*, see Richard Slotkin's book by that name; for the role of intellectuals as scapegoats in American society, see Richard Hofstadter's *Anti-Intellectualism in American Life*; and for elements of projection and scapegoating in detective fiction, see Barbara Rader and Howard Zettler (eds.), *The Sleuth and The Scholar: Origins, Evolution, and Current Trends in Detective Fiction*.

Works Cited

Bercovitch, Sacvan. *The American Jeremiad*. Madison: U of Wisconsin P, 1978.

Bloom, Allan. *The Closing of the American Mind: How Higher Education Has Failed Democracy and Impoverished the Souls of Today's Students*. NY: Simon and Schuster, 1987.

Hofstadter, Richard. *Anti-Intellectualism in American Life*. New York: Knopf, 1963.

Hyman, Stanley Edgar. *The Tangled Bank: Darwin, Marx, Frazer, and Freud as Imaginative Writers*. NY: Atheneum, 1974.

Nussbaum, Martha. "Undemocratic Vistas: Allan Bloom's American Mind." *New York Review of Books*. Nov. 5, 1987.

Nussbaum, Martha and Amartya K. Sen. "Internal Criticism and Indian Rationalist Traditions." In *Relativism*. Ed. M. Krauz. Notre Dame UP, 1988.

Rader, Barbara A. and Howard G. Zettler (eds). *The Sleuth and The Scholar: Origins, Evolution, and Current Trends in Detective Fiction*. Westport, CT: Greenwood P, 1988.

Rorty, Richard. "Pragmatism and Philosophy." In *After Philosophy: End or Transformation?* Ed. Kenneth Baynes et al. Cambridge, MA: MIT Press, 1987. 26-66.

Slotkin, Richard. *Regeneration Through Violence: The Mythology of the American Frontier, 1600-1860*. Middletown, CT: Wesleyan UP, 1973.

White, Hayden. *Metahistory: The Historical Imagination in Nineteenth-Century Europe*. Baltimore: Johns Hopkins UP, 1973.

Allan Bloom's *Closing*:
On Re-Opening the American Mind
to Heteroglossic Discourse

Patricia Lorimer Lundberg

Myth

Long afterward, Oedipus, old and blinded, walked the roads. He smelled a familiar smell. It was the Sphinx. Oedipus said, "I want to ask you one question. Why didn't I recognize my mother?" "You gave the wrong answer," said the Sphinx. "But that was what made everything possible," said Oedipus. "No," she said. "When I asked, what walks on four legs in the morning, two at noon, and three in the evening, you answered Man. You didn't say anything about women." "When you say Man," said Oedipus, "you include women too. Everyone knows that." She said, "That's what you think."

Muriel Rukeyser

Three years ago, while recovering from surgery, I attempted a return to intellectual consciousness and renewed membership in my social and academic communities by reading Allan Bloom's *The Closing of the American Mind: How Higher Education Has Failed Democracy and Impoverished the Souls of Today's Students.* Perhaps only half conscious then, I did not fully realize until recently while revisiting the Bloomland of Bloom's text just why I resisted joining its cast of characters—and how deliciously ironic that my malady during my first experience of *Closing* was a Female Complaint. Like Muriel Rukeyser's Oedipus, Bloom too seems not to be saying much about women that women like me can embrace as the reality of our own lives.

Three years ago, trying to understand the reasons for the town-and-gown clamor surrounding this unlikely best-seller, I read quickly for the argument without annotating the text, contrary to my usual practice. Then, leaving Bloomland behind was easy and, I thought, final: I didn't seem to fit into the Bloomian community on the other side of *this* mirror. Only now as I revisit Bloom's text for this rebuttal, my pen slashing in the text and at its margins, do I recognize how dangerously exclusive Bloomland is, and yet *Closing*'s agonistic rhetoric has apparently persuaded an enormous audience of believers brought before its distorting mirror.

The Bloomland in *Closing* seems a place my Alice has never experienced: neither as a student in the sixties, nor as a student and a teacher in the eighties. As an Alice, I find myself lost and alien in Bloomland. My Alice has never played on Bloomland's comic—or tragic—stage. Indeed, Bloomland seems a

117

masculinist hell, and, as both Virgil and Milton have reminded us, this work, this work (of extricating ourselves from its seductive rhetoric) is hard.[1]

Bloomland's music and lyrics throb with moral energy and indignation, as well as relentless confidence. Although *Closing* targets many social and ethical ills warranting frontal attack, in its pretense as a totalizing American community Bloomland risks generalizing some of us right out of reality, right beyond the mirror. And in turning our backs on its distorting mirror we unfortunately then reject what good thinking it does offer. Jerry Ward puts it succinctly:

> Devoted to reason of a peculiarly instituted Western type, Bloom gives himself over to the absolute language of aristocratic pathology, effectively isolating himself and his sympathizers from those "other" Americans who must labor for the necessities of life and who have the slightest chance of being born again into the magic circles of philosophic community. (22)

We need to reassert the polyglossia of the American Dialogue, re-open it to the many voices that are not heard from the monologic Bloomland stage.[2]

Closing's Bloomland conflates the personal and the political into polemic. In a departure from most mainstream academic practice, but curiously like some feminist writing, Bloom dares to be personal in *Closing*: he describes himself as an American Jewish academic, alluding to his childhood, his formation, and his adherence to a worthy set of values and belief structures. His academic credentials are impeccable: Cornell, Yale, Tel Aviv University, the Universities of Toronto, Paris, and Chicago. His stance seems both moral and ethical. Courageously, Bloom dares to bare his prejudices. He insists we must clothe ourselves in our prejudices, else how shall we ever know and overcome them while retaining our true, traditional values? For Bloom these values are universal, tested over time and transmitted through the family. Yet his values, worthy though they indeed are, are not necessarily universal. Some of us may not even have a family structure capable of transmitting worthy values; we must discover them elsewhere or not at all. My own trouble in re-visiting Bloomland is that I find I must costume myself as for the stage, not dress in my ordinary clothes. And I must speak the Bloomland monologue.

Let me too describe some of my ordinary clothes, my labels, my signifiers, my prejudices. Let me too be personal: I am, in no order of significance, a WASP woman raised a Catholic—a middle-class, heterosexual, feminist daughter, wife, mother of two, stepmother of three, mother-in-law to two Isei Japanese women and a Persian-American man, grandmother to four Nisei grandchildren, housekeeper, student, teacher, academic, corporate spouse, and retired editor/ publisher. I dress for all of these roles in my life's play. Yet many of the roles I know best seem absent or misplayed on the Bloomland stage. I'm not sure I'm even in the audience of Bloom's *Closing*, although I well may be offstage in the Chorus. Here follow my reflections on why the Bloomland of *Closing* seems so alien to me.

As early as the Preface—let me liken it to the Prologue of the play—I feel excluded from Bloomland's audience. I'm not at all sure Bloom is talking to me from the stage. The first paragraph of the Preface, describing *Closing* as a "meditation on the state of our souls, particularly those of the young and their education" (19) from a teacher's perspective, labels the teacher's pupils as "his students," albeit only once, a forgivable single lapse into sexist language. But paragraph two of the Preface brandishes that masculine pronoun like a weapon against female readers—no less than fifteen times—it masculinizes teacher, student, and child.

In the same paragraph of the Preface, the term "midwifery" becomes a metaphor for the delivery system of teaching in which nature births the child independent of the midwife/teacher:

Midwifery—i.e., the delivery of real babies of which not the midwife but nature is the cause—describes teaching more adequately than does the word socialization. The birth of a robust child, independent of the midwife, is the teacher's true joy, a pleasure far more effective in motivating him than any disinterested moral duty would be, his primary experience of a contemplation more satisfying than any action. (20)

No feminine pronouns find a home here in Bloomian Teaching/Midwifery Land. Curious that Bloom, in choosing midwifery for his analogy, chooses a profession dominated by women for eons until appropriated and mystified by the doctors in Patriarchyland and only recently re-femininized as more women become obstetricians and more mothers opt for home delivery with midwives. Off the Bloomland stage, beyond Bloomland, delivery "independent of the midwife" of whatever credentials and sex is difficult at best, of this I can assure you in my role as a mother. Yet Bloom's midwife/teacher takes a masculine pronoun for companion. Curious. And, as Alice and her companions would say, things in Bloomland get curiouser and curiouser.

How is it that even in 1987 such annoying—if not destructive—sexist language can find its way into print or even onto the Bloomland stage? Even if Bloom, in exercising his first-amendment rights, holds to the archaism of the generic masculine pronoun, editors and publishers do not choose deliberately to alienate a significant segment of a book's audience. Of this I am certain from my own experience as an editor and publisher. Indeed, most of *Closing* beyond the Preface, with only occasional lapses, seems to have been recast in gender-neutral terms. Did Bloom tone down the sexist language throughout the better (pun intended) part of the book at the urging of editors sensitive to its readership only to reinsert it at the most damaging place, the very beginning of his Preface? Does the Preface represent an inviolate place, written last as a last bastion for that not-so-long-lost community of male teachers and male students? Imagine for a moment the scene in the Bloomland play in which the hapless editor strives valiantly to eradicate the script of sexist language only to have the playwright feature it in a prologue somehow beyond the reach of the editor's pen.

More serious than the annoying use of the non-generic personal pronoun in *Closing* are the other ways Bloomland seems contrary to my own life experience, seems to exclude the experience of women like me. Indeed, of many minority perspectives. If, as Bloom insists, the "liberally educated person is one who is able to resist the easy and preferred answers, not because he is obstinate but because he knows others worthy of consideration" (21), then Bloomland must afford its people, male and female, other answers "worthy of consideration." Too often Bloom's *Closing* generalizes what might better be presented as particularized experience from a limited and atypical sample of Americans. Bloom, an erudite and accomplished academic, portrays students and teachers primarily situated in the rarified air of the most elite schools in the United States. The experience gained in this milieu cannot automatically be universalized to all American campuses, let alone across the entire range of social strata that comprise the American melting pot of recent immigrants and descendents of less recent, willing and unwilling, immigrants. As a nation of immigrants, we have much to learn from each other, and limiting ourselves to the values we learned individually at our mother's and father's knees, were we fortunate enough to have such knees, does not necessarily afford us other "answers...worthy of consideration."

Generalizations abound in Bloomland. Take, for example, middle-class life in Bloomland. Says Bloom, "Almost everyone in the middle-class has a college degree, and most have an advanced degree of some kind.... [T]he country is largely middle-class now, and scholarship aid is easily available for those unable to pay" (59, 90). Not in the middle-class communities I know. In my own middle-class family, some of my generation are still struggling, well into their adulthood, to get through college. Cultural and financial restraints kept me from completing my bachelor's degree for more than twenty years. When I began graduate school, my own father told me to stop the nonsense and stay home to take care of my husband. The only aid available to me was financial and emotional support from a generous husband who disagreed with my father's advice. My sister and two of my sisters-in-law all have advanced degrees, just like the inhabitants of Bloomland, but they fought against familial and social resistance unknown in Bloomland. Does it really need mentioning that the women in my family with graduate degrees earn less than the men in my family without them?

Every semester I meet others like me, often but not always returning women students; often they are Black or Hispanic. The middle-class students I know, young and not so young, male and female, often are the first generation in their families to go to college. Funding usually is scarce. Some students I know work from six in the morning until noon in order to afford the full courseload they take in the afternoons and evenings. They throw up their hands in despair when told they should work fewer hours to do better in their coursework. These students often lack the luxury of parents and scholarships to finance their education. As Peter Passell wittily puts the dilemma of the middle-class student,

tuition subsidies for all but the poorest students have become scarcer than Taittinger in Teheran. Loans at market-rate interest are generally available.... But not surprisingly, the children of financially pressed parents are loath to begin their working lives burdened with tens of thousands of dollars in education debts. (22)

I don't even include here those poor students struggling to get *into* the middle-class by working their way through college, some of them parents, trying desperately to get off welfare. To them, a liberal education is indeed a luxury they cannot afford. Yet they often luxuriate in the few liberal arts courses afforded them as part of their general education before going on to technical majors.

Sometimes I hear of students' spouses who have refused to support financially and emotionally their mates who have returned to college. And I shudder to think what will become of the few veiled Islamic women I see in college now that eighty Islamic clerics in Pakistan have condemned education for women. The clerics have called for the closing of women's schools and their confinement to their homes, unless they have their husband's permission to go out and can then take care not to wear perfume or clothing that rustles or laugh when speaking or, God help them, look at a man with "'a sexual sense'." The edict condemns teaching women liberal arts and insists they learn only Islamic roles and texts ("Moslem Clerics..." 12). Only far from Bloomland and far from the United States do such controls over women occur? Doubtful. The same day I read this news, I was sitting in a hospital surgical waiting area watching as two veiled and gowned women, one old and one young, bid goodbye to a young man on his way to surgery, then sat quietly reading small casebound texts in Arabic, turning the well-worn pages from back to front. Eerily, I watched and imagined the news made flesh, only a few miles as the Chicago pigeons fly from Bloomland.

Meanwhile, back in Bloomland, we are told that students, though free to read what they wish, have nevertheless "lost the practice of and the taste for reading. They have not learned how to read, nor do they have the expectation of delight or improvement from reading" (62). I know a lot of students like these in Bloomland, weaned on television and teething biscuits. But avid readers still abound. My own children, taught by excellent teachers to read well and living in a household where television represented a last resort, read voraciously. Students who take my Western Literature survey courses thrill to encounter ancient, medieval and Renaissance literature that can still speak to them, that incites them to confront their biases, that underscores their own personal victimizations. Returning women students, especially those who have had personal experience in the perils of patriarchy, respond dramatically on discovering their troubles anticipated by Penelope, the Wife of Bath, Criseyde, Cordelia, Clarissa, Jane Eyre, Dorothea Brooke, and other great female literary characters. Students are still gripped by good literature, and they keep coming back for more. A significant number refuse to live in Bloomland.

Just as students still turn on to good literature, so too do they turn on to good music. But not in Bloomland: "Classical music is dead among the young [except, possibly, for] not more than 5 to 10 percent of the students" (69). Instead, the young have rock music, which "ruins the imagination of young people and makes it very difficult for them to have a passionate relationship to the art and thought that are the substance of liberal education" (79). Outside Bloomland, however, some students, my own children as well, lose themselves in rock and in the classics, in Elton John and Sinead O'Connor, Pink Floyd and the Beatles, Beethoven and Bach, Philip Glass and Mick Jagger. The music is ubiquitous, often annoying—I certainly claim to be no authority on music. But an obsession only of today's students? Hardly. Maria Rosa Menocal labels this assertion "almost perversely skewed" (56). Rock music may temporarily ruin the imaginations of some young people just as earlier musical styles favored by the young must have done. Pubescent youths must find ways to channel their feelings of frustration and alienation, and music seems one of the classical and least destructive ways in which to find release and relief. Many survive such pubescent escapes from the emotional highs and lows of their lives to have that "passionate relationship to the art and thought that are the substance of liberal education" (79). Some actually thrive.

The scenario Bloom paints in broad aggressive strokes of the thirteen-year-old, pubescent boy working a math assignment in Walkman headphones, "whose body throbs with orgasmic rhythms...[whose] life is made into a nonstop, commercially prepackaged masturbational fantasy" (75), reminds me very much of the recent Italian film *Cinema Paradiso*. In it, a scene set in the forties depicts young boys masturbating while watching romance films from which the kissing frames have been cut by the village priest. Young boys pulsate to whatever music they have at hand or can imagine. I suspect they always have.

What I find most disturbing about students in Bloomland is the way they feel about Important Things in Life:

Religion and national origin have almost no noticeable effect on their social life or their career prospects. Although few really believe in "the system," they do not have any burning sentiment that injustice is being done to them.... A few radical feminists still feel the old-time religion, but most of the women are comfortably assured that not much stands in the way of their careers. (82)

This utopic Bloomland little reflects the Dystopia beyond it. If even a slim majority of American students escape discrimination based on religion, national origin, race, class, or sex, I would be amazed. Among my own multi-national, bi-racial, and multi-religioned family, I have witnessed all five of these forms of discrimination, some of it more subtle than others. I can attest to overt prejudices of all kinds on the American college campuses I've seen and in the communities that surround them.

Feminism fares poorly in Bloomland. The term, like so much in Bloomland, represents some kind of totalizing entity, in which feminists reject modesty, men whenever biologically possible, and fathers always. Yet feminism is a complex set of diverse beliefs, theories, and practices, not a monolithic monster. In its most basic sense, feminism is the belief that all women should be free from discrimination solely on the basis of their sex. A woman who avows she is not feminist but believes she should have the same educational opportunities as her brothers and receive equal pay for work equal to that a man performs is indeed a feminist. Those men who believe the same are also feminists. These closet feminists just don't like to be associated with "women's libbers" and all that this phrase negatively implies in some quarters. Beyond this crucial belief in the equality of women, feminism branches into many feminisms, only a few of them separatist, in that such feminists reject the need for men in their lives and insist on living separately. In *Closing*'s Bloomland, however, a feminist is of only one ilk and inherently destructive to the good old American family:

The fact that there is today a more affirmative disposition toward child-bearing does not imply that there is any natural impulse or compulsion to establish anything like a traditional fatherhood to complement motherhood. The children are to be had on the female's terms, with or without fathers, who are not to get in the way of the mother's free development.... The return to motherhood as a feminist ideal is only possible because feminism has triumphed over the family as it was once known, and women's freedom will not be limited by it. (105)

Motherhood has always been a feminist ideal. The issue is that women be free to choose motherhood or not, as they feel best for themselves and their families. Further, I can attest that parenting is difficult at best and would be even more strenuous if good fathers were discouraged from helping in the struggle! And of course freedom in democracy is always limited. Hyperbolic energy runs high in the above-quoted passage.

My own experience suggests that young female American college students in the sixties awakened to a feminist consciousness in the face of overt sex discrimination, just as the civil rights movement sustained awakening black consciousness and overturned institutionalized racial prejudices. Actual prejudices remain little changed—even entrenched—through the eighties, although less formalized and institutionalized. If the students in Bloomland don't feel prejudice, then they haven't been on the other side of the distorting mirror yet. As for feminists, they are born when they discover that sex discrimination thrives, usually as a personal experience. So the young female students of Bloomland and beyond may simply be oblivious of what awaits them in the American corporate, academic, and professional worlds out there. What awaits them is, roughly, sixty cents on the dollar. Older female students in my experience do not suffer from this utopic vision of equality out there. They've already been to Dystopia and are back in school to find ways to beat the discrimination they've suffered. They hope education is the key toward equality.

Not all students I know are like these in Bloomland:

Whatever their politics, they believe that all men—and women—are created equal and have equal rights.... These kids just do not have prejudices against anyone...[S]tudents take women's equality in education, their legitimate pursuit of exactly the same careers as men and their equal and often superior performance in them, completely in stride.... The one eccentric element in this portrait, the one failure...is the relation between blacks and whites. White and black students do not in general become real friends. (82-83, 90-91)

I agree that Black and White students do not easily become friends. I'm not sure that male and female students, Black or White, really do either. I wish they would. But outside Bloomland we still have a long way to go, baby.

I'm also not at all sure that Bloomland students are as blameless for the segregated student bodies on American campuses as Bloom suggests:

I do not believe this somber situation is the fault of the white students.... These students have made the adjustment, without missing a beat, to a variety of religions and nationalities, the integration of Orientals and the change in women's aspirations and roles. It would require a great deal of proof to persuade me that they remain subtly racist. (92)

Outside Bloomland, campuses reflect communities, and racism is more or less overt in some than in others. But that all of us, black, white, yellow, and brown, have managed to overcome all smidgens of *subtle* as well as overt racism—let's just say the assertion is unsupportable, let alone generalizable. The proof is in the fear and anxiety of anyone who is afraid to walk or ride anywhere because of their particular skin color. Bensonhurst is only the latest disastrous example. Right-thinking people fight their prejudices all the time. Our prejudices are deeply ingrained and difficult to eradicate. I doubt that all students, even in Bloomland, have succeeded. Affirmative action [quotas] takes a beating in Bloomland for the deterioration of race relations in America (92-97); but surely the polarization of the races long antedates such programs in academe and stems from ongoing racism—black and white. Affirmative action may be no panacea, but the main culprit? No.

But let me return to feminism as Bloomland plays it. Now this I know a lot about, and the margins of my copy of *Closing* are heavily annotated indeed under the section somewhat self-consciously labelled "Sex." The feminist project, according to Bloom, is "overcoming what is variously called male dominance, machismo, phallocracy, patriarchy, etc. . . ." (101). One of the adverse consequences of this project, at least as it is played out in Bloomland, is that

Male sexual passion has become sinful again because it culminates in sexism. Women are made into objects, they are raped by their husbands as well as by strangers, they are sexually harassed by professors and employers at school and at work, and their children, whom they leave in day-care centers in order to pursue their careers, are sexually abused by teachers. All these crimes must be legislated against and punished. What sensitive male can avoid realizing how dangerous his sexual passion is? (101)

This passage is a rhetorical *tour de force*. It rings true enough, except the first and the last sentences anointing its center. As a heterosexual woman, I sincerely would wish that any lover of mine be both sensitive and sexually passionate. It takes a great—an impossible—leap of logic to go from the horrors of sexual violence against women and children (and sometimes men) to the casting of all male sexual passion as sin. Feminism cannot be blamed for such a distortion! Sexual passion doesn't necessarily spill over into the sin of sexual violence and in fact has little to do with passion and everything to do with control and power aberrations.

In Bloomland, "central to the feminist project is the suppression of modesty," which "extends sexual differentiation from the sexual act to the whole of life" (101). Here, modesty is a "voice constantly repeating that a man and a woman have work to do together that is far different from that found in the marketplace, and of a far greater importance" (101). Here, feminists oppose pornography, not because of its violence against women and children, but because "it is a reminiscence of the old love relationship, which involved differentiated sexual roles—roles now interpreted as bondage and domination" (103). Bloomland artificially constructs a hierarchical opposition, love and sex/bondage and domination, that is readily deconstructed on the other side of the distorting mirror. Most feminisms, and there are many, value love and sex while they reject bondage and domination. Heterosexual relationships require a differentiation of sexual roles, but such acceptance of sexual difference doesn't automatically condemn its adherents to bondage or domination. Some feminists even find some pornography, if they can find any that does not exploit women or children, erotic.

In Bloomland,

[m]en and women are now used to living in exactly the same way and studying exactly the same things and having exactly the same career expectations. No man would think of ridiculing a female premed or prelaw student, or believe that these are fields not proper for women, or assert that a woman should put family before career.... There is very little ideology or militant feminism in most of the women, because they do not need it.... [T]he battle here has been won. Women students do not generally feel discriminated against or despised for their professional aspirations....(107)

This doctrine, no matter how many times chanted in Bloomland, cannot be made true. There are data everywhere refuting these claims. Bloom seems a willing victim of gross selection bias. His data are valid as observed over time, but valid only in their limited setting, the rarified air of Bloomland U. They are utterly invalid as generalized to the polycultural American mind, although an agonistic presentation of them appeals to many. That *The Closing of the American Mind* has appealed to so many is an unsettling reflection on the need for many Americans to suppress or silence the voices of those who are not like them and whom they do not like because they are "other." But the future of Americans relies on opening ourselves to all the voices that make up our polyglot nation. Let me conclude with some advice from Mikhail Bakhtin, who understood well the nature of both language and its speakers that comprise cultures:

A sealed-off interest group, caste or class, existing within an internally unitary and unchanging core of its own, cannot serve as socially productive soil...unless it becomes riddled with decay or shifted somehow from its state of internal balance and self-sufficiency.... The heteroglossia that rages beyond the boundaries of such a sealed-off cultural universe, a universe having its own literary language, is capable of sending only purely reified, unintentional speech images, word-things.... It is necessary that heteroglossia wash over a culture's awareness of itself and its language, penetrate to its core, relativize the primary language system underlying its ideology and literature and deprive it of its naive absence of conflict. (*Dialogic Imagination* 368)

Embracing the dialogic discourse of a polyglossic culture transforms "one's own and another's word" into "one's own/another's" (Bakhtin, "Toward a Methodology..." 168) without losing the distinctive quality of either voice.[3]

Notes

[1]See *Paradise Lost* ("Long is the way/ And hard, that out of Hell leads up to light" [2.432-33]]), itself echoing Virgil's *Aeneid* ("*Facilis discensus averno/ Sed revocare/ Hoc opus hic labor est*" [6.145-47] [literally translated, "Easy is the descent to Hell, But to go back up, this work, this work is"]).

[2]Among other voices responding to *Closing*, see William K. Buckley, who finds, "Sometimes the book is the leisured and cranky lament, characteristic of the small-town editorial page; in other places it is the thick treatise" (4). Helene Moglen reads *Closing* as "conservative critique...written as personal tragedy" (63).

[3]For a lengthy discussion of Bakhtinian dialogical discourse empowering social communities to broaden their perspectives, see "Dialogically Feminized Reading: A Critique of Reader-Response Criticism."

Works Cited

Bakhtin, Mikhail. *The Dialogic Imagination: Four Essays by M. M. Bakhtin.* Trans. Caryl Emerson and Michael Holquist. Ed. Michael Holquist. Austin: U of Texas P, 1981.

———. "Toward a Methodology for the Human Sciences." *Speech Genres and Other Late Essays.* Trans. Vern W. McGee. Ed. Caryl Emerson and Michael Holquist. Austin: U of Texas P, 1986. 159-72.

Bloom, Allan. *The Closing of the American Mind: How Higher Education Has Failed Democracy and Impoverished the Souls of Today's Students.* New York: Simon and Schuster, 1987.

Buckley, William K. "The Good, the Bad, and The Ugly in Amerika's Akademia." *Profession 88*: 46-52.

Lorimer Lundberg, Patricia. "Dialogically Feminized Reading: A Critique of Reader Response Criticism." *Reader: Essays in Reader-Oriented Theory, Criticism and Pedagogy* 22 (Fall 1989): 9-37.

Menocal, Maria Rosa. " 'We can't dance together.' " *Profession 88*. 53-58.

Moglen, Heléne. "Allan Bloom and E. D. Hirsch: Educational Reform as Tragedy and Farce." *Profession 88*: 58-64.

"Moslem Clerics: Shut Schools for Women." *Chicago Tribune* (June 26, 1990) 1:12.

Passell, Peter. "Economic Scene." *New York Times* (July 4, 1990): 1:22.

Rukeyser, Muriel. "Myth" (1973). *The Norton Anthology of Literature by Women: The Tradition in English.* Ed. Sandra M. Gilbert and Susan Gubar. New York: Norton, 1985. 1787-88.

Ward, Jerry W., Jr. "Hirsch, Bloom, and the Proper Ends of Education." *ADE Bulletin* 94 (Winter 1989): 21-22.

Arbiters of Culture

Peter Siedlecki

L'Academie Française began rather privately and casually. The intention of its members in 1629 was to serve as a kind of editorial board evaluating each other's literary efforts. However, the secrecy of their experiment was poorly kept; and by 1635, with the assistance of his littérateur-crony Boisrobert, Cardinal Richelieu had become aware of the secret meetings and had seen to it that the body became a public entity by arranging for its official incorporation. Soon he would use the Academy as an instrument through which the romantic excesses of writers like Pierre Corneille could be formally censured, and it would continue to "school and correct" the literature as well as the cultural climate of France, well into the eighteenth century. The revolution would deal its ultimate blow to the celebrated French orderliness more than a century and half later.

Defending the actions of those who instituted the Reign of Terror requires much practice in rationalization, but there is little doubt that the revolution itself occurred because of a propensity, especially on the part of the ruling class, to limit the parameters of truth. History is witness to the fact that those who establish inflexible standards often invite their own demise.

One can easily identify, however, if not sympathize, with the concerns of the Academy and its sponsors as it attempted to impose restrictions upon the likes of Corneille. His was a renaissance spirit, a practitioner of the baroque, born out of time and often unable to function comfortably within the constraints of neoclassicism. Wary of the monstrous excesses of sixteenth-century decadence, of the Spaniards, of the exuberance of Rabelais, the Academy assumed under Richelieu's sponsorship the position of arbiter of good taste in the production of an art that would contribute to the maintenance of the existing societal order. Artists were expected

...to place authority above personal freedom and discipline above insubordination. They built their lives according to a set of rules, of a method, which corresponded to the view of the common weal conceived by all-powerful minister (Burckhardt 377)

Some of the Academy members' insistence upon transforming Aristotle's observations regarding poetics into absolute requirements frustrated Corneille, who submitted to the authority of the Academy and imposed temporary exile upon himself from the French theater. Subsequent audiences would acknowledge *Le Cid* as deserving of the label master-piece, but the Academy proclaimed that the work violated orderly dramatic principles.

It is only useless conjecture to suggest that Pierre Corneille might have been a different artist, and even more successful playwright, had he not been confronted with the task of squeezing his heart into an area declared permissible by the Academy's guidelines. And the fact that he yielded to the will of the academy indicates that despite his romantic spirit, politically, he was a true child of his time. Much of his work, in fact, corroborates this. As an artist, he has survived both neoclassicism and the French academy. So too did literature; for that matter, a genius such as that possessed by Moliere flourished to near perfection within its restrictions. Neoclassicism and its Academy did not last however, except as memories. The very existence of their strictures invited upheaval, not only in art but in the French society as well. The upheaval rendered the Academy's concerns meaningless, and the newly constituted Academy established after 1735 was an agency significantly different from its predecessor.

The upheaval created the climate in which Rousseau's contradictions were acceptable, and in which the encyclopedists' cunning use of the cross-reference would undermine elitism; and, despite ensuing abuses of power in the hands of the populace, positive ramifications of the revolution were felt throughout Europe and the western world. The need to assert the rights of man had replaced the imposition of a designed universe whose abusive restrictions had been arrogantly promoted as reflective of the mind of God. Finally, the path was cleared for new ideas, some of which were expounded by men who would eventually be discredited by Allan Bloom for having contributed to the dissolution of culture in America.

This romantic celebration of the mind's liberation was demonstrated never more emphatically than it was among the intellectuals of the German principalities. In a passage in which Allan Bloom displays his own capacity for cultural relativism, he employs one of those Germans so directly responsible for the changing aesthetic to support his own call for the traditional classical education. He cites Gotthold Ephraim von Lessing's statement, "Beautiful men made beautiful statues, and the city had beautiful statues in part to thank for beautiful citizens." Out of the context of chapter two of *Laokoon* such a statement indeed suggests something of the neoclassical predilection for standardized behavior. However, Lessing's study of artistic criteria—as his *Hamburgische Dramaturgie* did with drama a year later, in 1767—celebrated the more fluid aspect of classicism and an understanding that different circumstances, different genres, and different time periods demand the application of a diversity of artistic standards. It was Lessing, with his emphasis upon the substance of classicism, rather than its accidents, who—even more so than Klopstock or Wieland—made young Germans in the 18th century receptive to *Sturm und Drang*. It was Lessing's influence as well, his acknowledgement of relative values and fluidity, that spurred the movement's culmination when Goethe finally rejected its romantic "sickness" in a section of Part II of Faust that displays yet another example of situational relativism: in "Arcadia," Faust realizes that his attempt to marry Helen of Troy (and to achieve a union between Nordic vitality and classical tradition) served only to force an unnatural synthesis. He reluctantly accepts Helen's disappearance from his embrace as a sign that one cannot repossess the past, that everything is motion and change, and that fluidity is the only permanence. While one may touch the richness of the classical period and be affected by it, he must move beyond it to effect his own time and his own eternity in his own way. This is a lesson that will be as true for Nietzsche and for Mick Jagger as it is for Faust and for Goethe and for any innovator. It is also this same fluidity that is responsible for the accursed atmosphere of newness that Allan Bloom finds so reprehensible.

What remains then for the advocate of fluidity is to systematically refute Bloom's arguments that favor time-tested values and simply to subvert the reactionary posture of *The Closing of the American Mind*. This, however, is not so easily accomplished for two reasons. The first is that many of those values remain cogent. Certainly one could not argue with the validity of studying the achievement of the Greek philosophers; in fact, such a study undertaken objectively and liberated from the Scholastic straight-jacket might serve to reassess the position of pre-Socratics like Heraclites, whose teachings seem much more in tune with the findings of quantum physics and current research into chaos than are the inflexible doctrines of Aristotle and the transcendent hierarchies of Plato.

The second reason Bloom's arguments are difficult to contend with is their rhetorical method, particularly the use of the *ad hominem* attack upon all those with whom Bloom disagrees. Fully exploiting the authority of the printed word, he proceeds within his text to attach derogatory labels so effectively to those he accuses of negatively affecting Western culture that, subsequently, the mere mention of a name like Nietzsche or Heidegger serves to connote a plethora of negative implications. Those whom Bloom opposes become villains in a self-serving fiction but one that is completely lacking in self-reflexiveness. To counter Bloom, then, one must engage in the concoction of apologies for each of an entire cast of characters whom the author has managed to associate with insidious evil and the degeneration of culture. Such a task is not only tedious but also seems trivial and invites Shakespeare's charge of excessive protest. By the time one is finished defending the author's colleagues at Cornell, Heidegger, Jane Fonda, Mick Jagger, et cetera, he begins to feel as absurd and frantic as is the text of *The Closing of the American Mind*. The task is as hopeless as Corneille's attempt to resist the judgment of the French Academy.

Richelieu had his way because he was authoring the text in which Corneille and even most of the Academy's members were playing their parts. In the end however the persistence of fluidity made a mockery of Richelieu's inane inflexibility while preserving the truly noble achievements of the Academy such as the valuable publication of the French dictionary.

Allan Bloom and Cardinal Richelieu share a common tendency. They disguise their aristocratic argument for the preservation of what one might term *the comfortable familiar*—in which their position remains secure—as a reference for an indisputable paradigm. And in the latter portion of the 1980s the reference contrived by Allan Bloom attained an almost biblical authority for a society that had languished in the comfort of the bumbling fatherliness of Reaganism and which maintains its suspicion and fear of all that is new and different. E.D. Hirsch's list of requisites for a properly informed culture, Robert Richman's call for a revival of good old-fashioned rhyming poetry, William Bennett's demand for a return to the basics of education are all symptoms of a last-stand, a tightening of the circle of wagons against the attack by the primitives upon the comfortable familiar. And unless the cavalry bugle were to sound in the form of Jesse-Helms type proscriptions from the federal government, those of us who observe the desperation of this aristocratic effort at rescuing the effete might even entertain a few moments of sympathy before welcoming the inevitable.

What this inevitability *is* is alluded to in a brief phrase from Edmund Wilson's monumental study of the influence of the symbolist movement on literature between 1870 and 1930, *Axel's Castle*. In his first chapter Wilson offers the significant observation that

> The Symbolist Movement broke those rules of French metrics which the Romantics had left intact, and it finally succeeded in throwing overboard completely the clarity and logic of the French classical tradition, which the Romantics had still to a great extent respected (Wilson, 16).

Similarly, the romantics had broken rules left intact by their renaissance progenitors. The examples are many. Byron could take *his* Don Juan farther than Tirso De Molina had been willing to take the prototype. Goethe allowed Faust more latitude than Marlowe had allowed his Dr. Faustus nearly two-hundred years earlier. In each romantic era, as rules are being broken, a certain amount of respect and credibility is granted to many of the existing standards—often because the artist having been nurtured within the climate of those standards regards them virtually as a part of nature and has difficulty imagining an artistic life without them. James Russell Lowell, for example, spoke of not having considered as a young man that poetry could be written in any manner different from that of Alexander Pope. And Ralph Waldo Emerson could advocate organic form in poetry, but when it came to writing *his* poetry, his concept of a more natural line involved something no more innovative than the use of the iambic tetrameter rather than the more traditional iambic pentameter. It was only after Whitman's publication of *Leaves of Grass* that Emerson realized what he had been looking for.

Whitman's poetry, of course, was greeted with the predictable charges of immorality by those unprepared for his apparent disdain for standardized metrics, poetic language, and acceptable content. Yet, in 1855, what Walt Whitman really represented was the inevitable subversion of *the comfortable familiar*. Also in the mid-nineteenth century, the German music critic Eduard Hanslick repudiated the new music of Wagner, Berlioz, Schumann, and Bruckner (Johnston, 132-140). In 1876, art critic Albert Woolf called impressionists Degas, Renoir, Pissaro, and Morisot a company of lunatics for what they were calling painting (Denvir, 100-101). In our own time, Allan Bloom tells us that the "sixties were the period of dogmatic answers and trivial tracts. Not a single book of lasting importance was produced in or around the movement." The movement to which Bloom refers of course is that period of campus unrest during which so many of his own idols were smashed by "a few students" who had "discovered that pompous teachers who catechized them about academic freedom could, with a little shove, be made into dancing bears."

The books that were produced during this period as well as the books that were written during preceding years and which had a direct influence upon what Bloom refers to as the "movement" are very likely those that Bloom would place into the category of "no lasting importance." As he obliquely decries the effect of modern literature upon the human psyche, he makes no mention, for example, of William Carlos Williams whose poetic intentions were inspiration for great numbers of young poets who were abandoning the dark modernism of T.S. Eliot. It was Williams who remarked that every age produces its standards of perfection and for the artist not to oppose those standards was "morally reprehensible" (Allen and Tallman, 140). And it was Williams who, when it came time in his autobiography to state his own poetic theory, chose instead to include the 1950 essay by Charles Olson, "Projective Verse," a work which once again annihilates the acknowledged rules of poetic composition and which has been cited as the hallmark work in establishing a postmodernist poetics. Certainly, Allan Bloom would consider the works of the postmodernists and the abstract expressionists (the school of painters and sculptors so closely connected with Olson and Black Mountain College) of no lasting value, but it would be difficult to deny the stature of Allen Ginsberg, Robert Duncan, or Robert Creeley in the world of letters today. Each of these disciples of Williams and Olson has attained a prominence that might even associate them with setting the standard for literary art in the late twentieth century—certainly a precarious position in Williams' view. The thirtieth anniversary of the publication of Ginsberg's "Howl," a work that was once considered anathema by the traditionalists and immoral by the American courts was recently celebrated by so reputable an organization as the Modern Language Association. Creeley, whose poetry bewildered so many keepers of tradition for so many years, was cited in 1989 as the official poet of New York State.

These developments, of course, might simply stand as evidence for Bloom that America's cultural development has been impaired but if it has, the popularity of Ginsberg and Creeley in Europe, especially in Eastern European countries, might indicate that by Bloom's criteria, America is closing the mind of the rest of the world as well as its own. Rather than impaired, however, it would seem as though consciousness has been expanded. When Creeley lectured on poetics and read from his work in Berlin in 1960, his words and ideas were appreciated by the Germans as a thoroughly American product reflecting the kind of freedom in poetry that the German—because of his attachment to poetic and linguistic restrictions—could not write. The recent German translations of Creeley indicate that significant changes in German poetics have occurred over the past thirty years. And that these changes have been largely the result of an American cultural influence.

Kurt Vonnegut's novel *Slaughterhouse Five* was another piece that grew not only out of the author's own personal response to the bombing of Dresden but also out of the kind of consciousness that was rising in the sixties. To call it a work of no lasting value would be as pointless as it would be to insist upon the permanent significance of his entire corpus. Only time will determine which view is valid; but by all indications, Vonnegut's work continues to grow in value and in critical estimation.

Choosing names like Ginsberg, Creeley, and Vonnegut is not a random grasping for data that will support an anti-Bloom perspective. They are connected. Vonnegut is generally regarded, especially by critics like Jerome Klinkowitz and Brian McHale as virtually the guiding light of the new American fiction—an

American fiction that had its beginnings in the sixties, a fiction that includes the names Abish, Apple, Elkin, Katz, Barthelme, Federman, Kosinski, Sukennick, Majors, Reed, and others whose work has been considered immoral by John Gardner because of its self-reflexiveness and its refusal to directly concern itself with how man should live his life in the world. It is ostensibly a non-judgmental fiction that accepts the lack of order in the universe. "So it goes," says Vonnegut as his variety of worlds fall apart. These *connoisseurs of chaos* to use Wallace Stevens' phrase, depict a reality that critics like Gardner and Gerald Graff would prefer to deny, a confused reality that is a far more accurate delineation of quotidian existence than are the illusions of reality devised by the modernists of the 1930s and 40s. And they are more valuable too than those illusory visions of some mythical classical past in which everyone was possessed of some uncanny inclination toward a proper order. At times members of this new breed of writers have gone to extremes—as with Ronald Sukennick's proposal for the "Bossa Nova" novel with no plot, no character, no meaning, etc., or with Federman's comments contained in *Surfiction*, proposing the end of representation in fiction (Federman, 5-15 & 43). Such extremes are frightening to those attempting to preserve a comfortably familiar situation; and upon many occasions the death knell has been sounded for the movement these authors represent. Too disruptive, too disconnected, the critics have said. Verging on inhumanity is another charge.

Much of the criticism has a certain foundation but the material upon which that foundation is built has an intention: the disruption and disconnection has been purposeful. The method employed by these writers is not unlike the method of randomness employed by Allan Ginsberg in "Wichita Vortex Sutra." It owes some of its character specifically to the ideas of Charles Olson which have been carried on in the work of Robert Creeley. Sukennick has suggested that the method of his work is indebted to Olson's ideas of kinetics, principle and process as delineated in "Projective Verse." The purpose of the approach adopted by the creators of the new fiction is to depict the chaotic nature of human existence, that life is not neatly plotted, nor is its line of action an orderly rise to a climax. It is filled with tangents, dead-ends, non-sequiturs, and apparently meaningless events.

Books such as James Glieck's *Chaos* and Nick Herbert's *Quantum Reality* have popularized a notion that underlies this existence—life on earth is not as orderly as we would prefer to believe; or at least, its order is not what we have assumed it is. The fiction which took much of its nourishment from the hectic sixties and which is variously called surfiction, postmodernism, meta-fiction, or simply new fiction is representative of a conviction expressed by Emerson in his essay "The Poet" in which he proclaims that the poet shows the way to the scientist:

...science always goes abreast with the just elevation of the man, keeping step with religion and metaphysics; or the state of science is an index of our self knowledge. Since every thing in nature answers to a moral power, if any phenomenon remains brute and dark it is because the corresponding faculty in the observer is not yet active. (In Perkins, 100-101)

It is the poet, according to Emerson, who activates in us these faculties. He is the animal whose instincts we trust to find the road when we have lost the way. He is the "Namer" and the "Language Maker" and his is the "activity which repairs the decays of things." To use Ezra Pound's phrase, he "makes it new." How pertinent these words are when considered alongside the efforts of so many of today's writers, especially those whom so many of the critics want to chase away because of their violation of *the comfortable familiar*. And among these writers, it is very likely that there is one, who, having been liberated by the words of Williams, or Olson, or Vonnegut, or Federman, or Sukennick, will be quoted one day as having said, "When I was growing up it never occurred to me that one could write in any way other than the way Robert Frost or Saul Bellow wrote."

This is the author who Bloom and the other members of *l'Academe Americaine* fear. He is the one whose inevitability is disruptive to their perception of how the world ought to be. And even as many try to convince themselves that his "experimentation" has become exhausted, he is the one who will remain a force in the world of art and in the world of culture until something newer and better comes along. As Hegelian as it may sound, it is the protest against him and his disconnection with the past and its comfortable familiarity that is serving to make his position more secure. And so it goes.

Works Cited

Allen, Donald, and Warren Tallman. *The Poetics of The New American Poetry.* New York: Grove P, 1973.

Burckhardt, Carl J. *Richelieu and His Age*, vol. III. New York: Harcourt, Brace, Jovanovich, Inc., 1970.

Denvir, Bernard. *The Impressionists at First Hand.* London: Thames and Hudson, Ltd., 1987.

Emerson, Ralph Waldo. "The Poet." *American Poetic Theory.* Ed. George Perkins. New York: Holt, Rinehart, and Winston, 1972.

Federman, Raymond. *Surfiction: Fiction Now and Tomorrow.* Chicago: Swallow P, 1981.

Johnston, William M. *The Austrian Mind.* Berkeley: The U of California P, 1972.

Lessing, Gotthold Ephraim. *Laocoon.* Trans. Edward A. McCormick. Baltimore: The Johns Hopkins UP, 1984.

Wilson, Edmund. *Axel's Castle.* New York: Charles Scribner's Sons, 1931.

In Defense of Universal Norms:
Reflections on Allan Bloom's Critics

Mark W. Roche

My disagreements with Allan Bloom's *The Closing of the American Mind* are many, ranging from his critique of affirmative action to his misinterpretation of Woody Allen's masterpiece *Zelig*. Though Bloom's book bothers me, I am bothered even more by the academic community's widespread dismissal of the book, evident, for example, in *Profession 88*. A major organ of the Modern Language Association, *Profession* contains in its 1988 edition evaluations of Bloom's *The Closing of the American Mind* and E. D. Hirsch's *Cultural Literacy*; not a single contribution defends Bloom. If we are to take seriously the postmodern elevation of the marginal and if programs at recent conventions such as those of the Modern Language Association or the International Association for Philosophy and Literature reflect the regnant position of historicist and poststructuralist theorizing, then the only consequential stance would seem to be to become truly marginal and speak out on behalf of norms and with that on behalf of Bloom's book.

In doing so, one runs the risk of being perceived as immodest—projecting one's own positions or those of Bloom as universally valid. But first, I'm not convinced that the refrain one hears against Bloom—He believes in transcendent truths. I am modest and recognize my finitude—is cogent.[1] Modesty is the fact of not drawing attention to one's virtues; so as soon as one points to one's modesty, one is no longer modest. One is allowed to draw attention to one's modesty only when one refrains from doing so. There is, moreover, a hidden arrogance in an age that discards the argumentative figures of thinkers from Plato to Hegel as naive miscalculations or sophistic ploys. In addition, our current inability to solve certain problems need not imply that these problems are in principle unsolvable. Finally, if finitude is our most privileged category, I don't quite understand why finitude is viewed as absolute and not as finite. If everything is finite, then so too the statement that everything is finite. If the finitude of the finite is recognized, such that finitude passes over into another, but not, however, another form of the finite (for that would mean a self-contradictory absolutization of the finite), but rather that which is not finite, we are again in the realm of absolutes or of norms.

As soon as one speaks of norms, one also apparently runs the risk of being no longer open. It is said that one should not embrace Western values over others. But if one really wanted to overcome the Western view, one would not be open to other cultures (openness, after all, is a Western trait, and there is nothing more Western than the view that West and East are each individually valid). Instead, one would take seriously the predominant Eastern view that East and West cannot both be right. Cultural relativism is a Western view and as such its expansion into other cultures is a form of Western imperialism. To be truly non-Western, one would have to be normative, albeit at times arbitrarily normative, but certainly not relativistic.

Viewing marginality, modesty, and openness somewhat irreligiously, if, I believe, consistently, I am suggesting that these categories, when made absolute, suffer dialectical contradictions and cancel themselves. Critics frequently attack Bloom for believing in normative values per se and not a particular set of normative values; yet these same critics measure Bloom's text with normative values of their own, demanding logical coherence and consistency, the fairness of listening to other models, the equality of viewpoints. Though one will want to disagree with many of Bloom's norms, other norms are shared—necessarily—by anyone who enters into dialogue with him; to cite a simple example, the very tenets of dialogue are embraced: fairness, consistency, communicability. And not only by Bloom, these values would be embraced even by the thinker wanting to *argue* against the validity of rational norms.

These shared values did indeed arise from a variety of contingent historical factors, but their origins in history do not undermine their normative validity. The historical and psychological conditions under which a theory is discovered are to be separated from the logical conditions under which a theory is valid or invalid. The argument that every position is historically conditioned and therefore illusory must itself be historically conditioned and illusory: it is self-canceling.[2] If it can be shown that a proposition cannot be refuted without self-contradiction and without also necessarily presupposing the proposition to be refuted, then that proposition is necessarily true. If the statement "All truth is in flux" is true, then this insight into the passage of truth must itself be in flux, such that " 'Truth is in flux' is in flux" or "At least some truth is not in flux." If all our truths are to be revised, as critics of Bloom suggest,[3] it is only consistent that one revise the theory that all our truths are to be revised.

Not only do I think that some truths are not in flux and not in need of revision (they can be deduced *a priori* by way of the self-cancellation of their negation, that is, they are deduced rationally, they do not derive from nature).[4] And not only do I think that Bloom's critics adhere to some truths that are more than mere conventions, I also think that this is a good thing, and that Bloom's insight into the need for recognizing universal norms needs more supporters. Global problems demand universal solutions. Instead of focusing on universals (as does a great political leader such as Gorbachev),[5] many contemporary philosophers and literary theorists are overly busy stressing their particularities and differences.

Critics of Bloom do not hesitate to call him reactionary, even fascist,[6] but fascism is perhaps best understood—at least on its metalevel—in the context of antinormative thinking.[7] Though national Socialism is often viewed as an absolute, we must recognize that it is an *arbitrary* absolute and therefore arises not from an absolute philosophy (there are universal truths) but from a relativistic position that has passed over into power positivism (because there are no universal truths, one subject or group of subjects has the right to assert its irrational truths over others). If one relativizes the absolute, one is free to absolutize the relative—and that, not absolute philosophy, is what National Socialism was: an absolutization of the relative, namely power and race, as a result of the undermining of the absolute. This is clearly demonstrated in the major work of National Socialist philosophy, Alfred Rosenberg's *Myth of the Twentieth Century*. In this book, which sold over a million copies by 1943, Rosenberg rebukes those systematic thinkers who assert the viability of *a priori* or absolute truths and base values on logic and the law of noncontradiction. Much like the contemporary postmodernist, Rosenberg mocks the philosophical search for absolute truth: "Like the hopeful thinkers of antiquity, all of today's practicing philosophers are seriously and eagerly searching or hunting for the so-called one, eternal truth. They seek this truth in a purely logical manner by continually making inferences from axioms of the intellect" (681-82).[8] According to Rosenberg, any philosophy that teaches logically deduced transcendent values errs (127). Values are to be created by the individual race or will; they cannot be discovered, nor can they be refuted, by logical analysis. Socrates, who spoke of " 'the Good' in itself" and claimed that virtue was universal, destroyed Greek culture (285); in recognizing only individuals and universals, he failed to understand the significance of race (286). Even German philosophers have been prone to this mistake; Hegel's well-grounded assertion, "logic is the science of God,"[9] is for Rosenberg "a blow in the face of every genuine Nordic religion, every genuine Germanic...science" (287).

Any claim to universal truth is for Rosenberg by its very nature untenable (125). The philosopher of National Socialism opposes knowledge of race to all universal philosophies: "This knowledge...places us...in the sharpest opposition to all 'absolute' and 'universal' systems, which, from the standpoint of an alleged humanity, once again desire a unification of all souls in the future" (136). Rosenberg contrasts empty, universal, logical truth with the organic truths of blood and race: "Thereby, however, an entirely different conception of 'the truth' is alluded to: that for us truth does not mean a *logical* right or wrong, but rather that an *organic* answer be demanded of the question: fruitful or unfruitful, autonomous or constrained?" (690). In another passage he asserts: "That is the other—'truer'—current of genuine (organic) truth-seeking as opposed to the scholastic-logical-mechanical struggle for 'absolute knowledge' " (691). Humanity, dissolved of racial origins and considerations, is a meaningless fiction (22), yet humanity must be countered insofar as the concept dissolves racial identities and leads to valuelessness: "raceless valuelessness" (120). Rosenberg's fear of this raceless universality is softened by his claim that no real communication occurs among races. Rosenberg likens race to Leibniz's monads: "the monad opposite a personality of entirely alien blood again becomes 'windowless' " (694). Having abandoned universal, coherent, and positive categories, Rosenberg absolutizes the negative figures of difference and otherness.

Within academic circles Rosenberg's critique of reason and of universals found great resonance.[10] Ernst Krieck, for example, includes as a recurring theme in his three volume *Racial-political Anthropology* an attack on logic as artificial, abstract, and opposed to intuition. (See esp. 1:38-39; 2:7-10; and 3:11-12.) He speaks disparagingly of the "dogma of reason," which teaches that all human beings—independently of race, nation, and history—have in principle a common faculty that enables them to reach universally valid insights and norms (2:8; cf. 3:14 and 3:123). Truth derives from character as well as social and historical factors, not the so-called laws of reason (3:125). For Krieck, as for Rosenberg, truth is always culturally relative; "natural" right exists only insofar as we are willing to reinterpret "natural" as racial, rather than rational (2:42).

Franz Böhm's *Anti-Cartesianism* is a thoroughgoing polemic against universals and logic that, much like Rosenberg's own critique, sees Hegel as a traitor to the Germanic spirit: "Not because we can refute Hegel do we come across the reality he deprived us of; on the contrary, because the racial-political reality of our German life is once again present do we everywhere encounter the artificial restraints through which Hegel's universalism separated us from our own origins" (35). In contrast to Hegel, Böhm elevates positions that are "anti-rational, because anti-universal" (43).

The early twentieth-century failure to recognize and ground absolute truths was not restricted to academic philosophy. A judicial corollary to perspectival morality and power positivism is the positive law theory of justice, a theory dominant in the Weimar era. Moreover, the Weimar Constitution, as has been noted by thinkers as diverse as Carl Schmitt and Hermann Broch,[11] lacked any absolute foundation. It was a document dependent on legal positivism and a relativistic, consensus theory of truth. A two-thirds majority in parliament could change not just ordinary legislation but the most fundamental elements of the Constitution; thus minorities were susceptible to majority rule. Still worse, a two-thirds majority could make arbitrary changes, and then conclude that the Constitution could never again be changed.[12] It was not merely Article 48, which allowed for the emergency suspension of civil rights, that gave Hitler a legal map to power; the Enabling Act of 24 March 1933, based on Article 76, the clause that allowed for the Constitution's self-cancellation, guaranteed the lawful passage from Weimar to the Third Reich. Either there are normative values that transcend democratic consensus, or it is illegitimate to protect, constitutionally, any position from possible shifts in consensus. In the face of such a dilemma it should be clear that only a political and constitutional structure based on logically coherent transcendent norms can guarantee individual rights when majority opinion opposes this or when historical changes occur.[13]

We must distinguish between absolutists who make their claims blindly and irrationally and refuse to acknowledge the validity of immanent critique and those who arrive at their stances by exhibiting the self-cancellation of alternative positions.[14] Through the figure of self-cancellation we can apply *a priori* principles to shed light on complex political and judicial issues. In conjunction with the project of German Idealism could be seen increased reflection on the philosophy of right, the creation of a coherent university system, the abolition of torture, arguments against the death penalty, and the development of new freedoms.[15] Within a postmodernist framework, on the other hand, we cannot ground our arguments against injustice; particular interests are no longer subordinate to *a priori* truths, and justice is reduced to historical convention (or law) and personal preference (or power).

It is important to recognize what is normative and what is not,[16] so that truth can be both eternal and dynamic, rigid and flexible.[17] Contingency and flux do exist, but if these categories themselves become absolute, then, by a simple process of self-reflection, they, too, should be viewed as contingent, as not absolute. That we have moved too far away from what is universal and noncontingent is one of Bloom's claims, a claim that I am willing to take seriously, especially as the need for universal action on behalf of international peace and on behalf of the environment becomes ever more severe. More reflection on universal, and not just particular, issues strikes me as a need, a need that, if we wait too long, will no longer exist. Not all normative thinkers ground their norms, and not all thoughts need be normative; neither of the above statements, however, is an argument against the need for coherent norms where norms are necessary.[18]

Notes

[1]Cf. Hovey 45 and Schlesinger.

[2]Cf. Moglen 62.

[3]Cf. Schultz 66.

[4]"Natural" right, a term Bloom inherited from his predecessors, is a misnomer. Cf. Hegel 10:311-12.

[5]Among other sources, see Gorbachev's elevation of universal interests over even class interests in his *Perestroika*, esp. 144-49.

[6]According to Dannhauser, the book has been compared to *Mein Kampf* (24).

[7]Schlesinger associates normative thinking, rather than relativism, with the violation of human rights. Even philosophers who argue against relativism, such as Jacobs, often suggest that "the historical record is with the relativist" (76) and thus are unaware of an intimate philosophical and historical connection between relativism and National Socialism.

[8]The translations of Rosenberg stem from Ann Blackler and Mark Roche. Vivian Bird's recent translation of Rosenberg's *Myth* is unreliable; moreover, it omits selected passages. The remaining translations are my own.

[9]See Hegel 5:44. For why the assertion is well-grounded see Wandschneider's insightful essay.

[10]If Rauschning is to be believed, not only other philosophers, but Hitler himself shared Rosenberg's relativism. Rauschning reports Hitler as saying: "There is no truth, neither in a moral nor a scientific sense. The thought of a free and presuppositionless science could only have surfaced in the age of liberalism. It is absurd" (210).

[11]For further analysis see Hösle and Vitzthum.

[12]The Basic Law of the Federal Republic of Germany avoids this self-canceling structure with its declaration that the elimination of articles 1 and 20 is inadmissible. See Art. 79, par. 3. The one weakness in the German Constitution's guarantee of rights is that it is nowhere stated, even if it is perhaps implied, that Art. 79, par. 3 may not be changed.

[13]It is a widespread view in contemporary society that "the notion of democracy cannot be grounded in some ahistorical, transcendent notion of truth" (Giroux 28). My argument— an argument I share with Martin Luther King, Jr., among others—is that without any transcendent or stable concept of truth, democracy cannot guarantee minority rights and so runs the risk of passing over into totalitarianism.

[14]Bloom uses the figure of self-cancellation himself on occasion (see, for example, 36, 204, and 214), but most of his norms are asserted, rather than grounded.

[15]The resistance movement against Hitler was in part informed by the categories of transcendental idealism. One thinks, for example, of Adam von Trott zu Solz, a member of the Stauffenberg circle, whose dissertation of 1932 explored international justice from

the perspective of Hegel's *Philosophy of Right*, or Hans Scholl and Kurt Huber, central figures in the resistance group known as "The White Rose." The former was a careful reader of Plato, the latter a consequent Kantian. See Scholl 16 and Gollwitzer 159-61.

[16]I would recognize three levels of norms. First, some positions, such as the arbitrary advantage of the more powerful, evidenced, for example, in slavery, are categorically wrong; they are self-contradictory (see Roche). The establishment of norms against injustice follows from reason. Second, some norms, though not absolutely valid, are compatible with reason and can be viewed as necessary under specific historical conditions. For example, it is necessary that laws limiting the consumption of water be introduced in a society that has a restricted supply of usable water. Third, some norms cannot be deduced from reason or historical conditions; the norms are decisionistic. It does not matter what the norm is, merely that there be a norm, for example, whether one drives on the right or the left. Either is appropriate, but in a particular culture it must be one or the other. Cf. Hegel 7:34-46.

[17]One must distinguish between systematic and material truth, between those positions that are valid *a priori* and those that change through time. On this distinction see Hösle's *Wahrheit und Geschichte*.

[18]Short passages from this essay will also appear in my book *Gottfried Benn's Static Poetry: Aesthetic and Intellectual-Historical Interpretations* (Chapel Hill, N.C. and London: University of North Carolina Press, 1991). This material is used here with the gracious permission of the University of North Carolina Press.

Works Cited

Bloom, Allan. *The Closing of the American Mind: How Higher Education Has Failed Democracy and Impoverished the Souls of Today's Students*. New York: Simon, 1987.

Böhm, Franz. *Anti-Cartesianismus: Deutsche Philosophie im Widerstand*. Leipzig: Meiner, 1938.

Dannhauser, Werner J. "Allan Bloom and the Critics." *Essays on* The Closing of the American Mind. Ed. Robert L. Stone. (Chicago: Chicago Review P, 1989) 22-27.

Giroux, Henry A. *Schooling and the Struggle for Public Life: Critical Pedagogy in the Modern Age*. Minneapolis: U of Minnesota P, 1988.

Gollwitzer, Helmut, Käthe Kuhn, and Reinhold Schneider, ed. *Dying We Live: The Final Messages and Records of the Resistance*. Trans. Reinhard C. Kuhn. New York: Pantheon, 1956.

Gorbachev, Mikhail. *Perestroika: New Thinking for Our Country and the World*. New York: Harper and Row, 1987.

Hegel, G.W.F. *Werke in zwanzig Bänden*. Ed. Eva Moldenhauer and Karl Markus Michel. Frankfurt: Suhrkamp, 1970.

Hösle, Vittorio. "Carl Schmitts Kritik an der Selbstaufhebung einer wertneutralen Verfassung in 'Legalität und Legitimität.' " *Deutsche Vierteljahrsschrift für Literaturwissenschaft und Geistesgeschichte* 61 (1987): 1-34.

―――. *Wahrheit und Geschichte: Studien zur Struktur der Philosophiegeschichte unter paradigmatischer Analyse der Entwicklung von Parmenides bis Platon*. Elea 1. Stuttgart-Bad Cannstatt: Frommann-Holzboog, 1984.

140   Beyond Cheering and Bashing

Hovey, Kenneth Alan. "The Great Books versus America: Reassessing *The Closing of the American Mind.*" *Profession 88.* Ed. Phyllis Franklin. (New York: MLA, 1988) 40-45.

Jacobs, Jonathon. "Relativism, rationality and repression." *Journal of Value Inquiry* 23 (1989): 69-77.

King, Martin Luther, Jr. "Letter from Birmingham City Jail." *Non-Violence in America: A Documentary History.* Ed. Staughton Lynd. (New York: Bobbs-Merrill, 1966) 461-81.

Krieck, Ernst. *Völkisch=politische Anthropologie.* 3 vols. 2nd ed. Leipzig: Armanen=Verlag, 1938.

Moglen, Helene. "Allan Bloom and E. D. Hirsch: Educational Reform as Tragedy and Farce." *Profession 88.* Ed. Phyllis Franklin. (New York: MLA, 1988) 59-64.

Rauschning, Hermann. *Gespräche mit Hitler.* New York: Europa, 1940.

Roche, Mark W. "Plato and the Structures of Injustice." *Inquiries into Values: The Inaugural Session of the International Society for Value Inquiry.* Ed. Sander H. Lee. Problems in Contemporary Philosophy 11. (Lewiston, N.Y.: Mellen, 1988) 279-90.

Rosenberg, Alfred. *The Myth of the Twentieth Century: An Evaluation of the Spiritual-Intellectual Confrontations of our Age.* Trans. Vivian Bird. Torrance, CA: Noontide, 1982.

———. *Der Mythus des 20. Jahrhunderts: Eine Wertung der seelisch-geistigen Gestaltenkämpfe unserer Zeit.* Munich: Hoheneichen, 1943.

Schlesinger, Arthur, Jr. "The Opening of the American Mind." *The New York Times Book Review.* 23 July 1989: 1, 26-27.

Scholl, Inge. *The White Rose.* Trans. Arthur R. Schultz. Middletown, Conn.: Wesleyan UP, 1970.

Schultz, James A. "Stick to the Facts: Educational Politics, Academic Freedom, and the MLA." *Profession 88.* Ed. Phyllis Franklin. (New York: MLA, 1988) 65-69.

Trott zu Solz, Adam von. *Hegels Staatstheorie und das Internationale Recht.* Ed. Hans Rothfels. 2nd ed. Göttingen: Vandenhoeck, 1967.

Vitzthum, Wolfgang Graf. "Brochs demokratie- und völkerbundtheoretische Schriften." *Hermann Broch.* Ed. Paul Michael Lützeler. Suhrkamp Taschenbuch 2065. (Frankfurt: Suhrkamp, 1986) 289-307.

Wandschneider, Dieter. "Die Absolutheit des Logischen und das Sein der Natur. Systematische Uberlegungen zum absolut-idealistischen Ansatz Hegels." *Zeitschrift für philosophische Forschung* 39 (1985): 331-51.

Allan Bloom and the Limits of Reason

William Thickstun

Allan Bloom's *The Closing of the American Mind* has both deepened and broadened our current national debates on higher education. By proposing that the problems involved have philosophical roots, and require philosophical solutions, Bloom has contributed to an awareness that educational reform in any direction must involve more than mere tinkering with programs or calendars. At the same time, by reaching a wide audience he has helped to identify and prepare a large constituency for serious discussion of educational issues. The success of Bloom's book identifies an extraordinary popular hunger for talk about what Bloom calls "the important questions," questions which are increasingly missing from the undergraduate curriculum.

The important questions remain what they have been since Plato's time: How should one live? What is the best kind of life? What work are we called to do? How can we best make political and social arrangements for living together with each other? What are our responsibilities as stewards of the natural world? What is the right attitude about death? All students still come to college with these questions. But they seem to ask them with less frequency and insistency than my generation did in the sixties and seventies. Bloom misses this shift in blurring the entire post-sixties period together; twenty years ago, students were more likely to think they had time and leisure to engage the important issues. Students today have become more willing to waste their powers in getting and spending, perhaps because faculty too often validate their assumptions about the unimportance of learning by focusing on abstruse academic specialties that seem unrelated to the real questions of life. We should instead encourage them to ask those questions, and to see that the same questions resonate throughout the intellectual traditions that we are passing on to them.

Such is at any rate my reading of Bloom's argument at its best; beneath his elitist and sexist rhetoric I see a clear vision of what is often missing in undergraduate education today. Bloom's radical conservatism, however, has undermined his credibility among precisely those liberal intellectuals who ought to be receptive to his most serious claims. The reactionary rhetoric is not essential to what is most valuable in Bloom's argument; I think it arises because he has misidentified the enemy, even misidentified his own position. The students who rose up against the university in 1969 were asking the same questions Bloom cares about. As he himself observes, most of those who found their way into his courses felt no need to rebel because they had discovered a mode of inquiry that engaged those questions directly. Cornell's capitulation to irrational student pressure was not in itself a failure, but merely an admission that the university's ostensible commitment to liberal education had already failed in some profound way. The failure that Bloom points to ultimately lies not in our having abandoned the claims of reason in 1969, but in having invested too heavily in the power of reason to begin with.

As Bloom is aware, history offers two possible sources of knowledge beyond that provided directly by our senses: reason and revelation. These two claims for extended knowledge are associated with philosophy and science on the one hand, religion and poetry on the other. Subjects organized rationally are systematic and progressive; subjects organized religiously are canonical, earlier work being granted priority or at least parity with more recent achievements. Paradoxically, the central portions of philosophy itself are organized canonically, around certain key philosophers and texts, because to describe the first principles of science you need a mode of discussion founded in some medium beyond the one at issue. Conversely, the most central activities in theological and literary study are the reasoned criticism, evaluation and interpretation of texts to consider their claims to wisdom and determine standards for their inclusion in or exclusion from the canon.

Plato illustrates that these paradoxes reside at the heart of all human knowledge by embodying his philosophy in literary form while simultaneously defining a philosophic standard for literature. In *The Republic*, Socrates and his interlocutors banish poetry from the best regime—all of poetry, that is, except the parts that are "hymns to gods or celebration of good men" (607a)—because it imitates the bad as well as the good and fosters the indulgence of self-pitying emotion even in the best men. But the founders of this city in speech are themselves so "charmed" by Homer and the other poets that they will remain open to counter-arguments:

All the same, let it be said that, if poetry directed to pleasure and imitation have any argument to give showing that they should be in a city with good laws, we should be delighted to receive them back from exile... And surely we would also give its protectors, those who aren't poets but lovers of poetry, occasion to speak an argument...on its behalf, showing that it's not only pleasant but also beneficial to regimes and human life... For surely we shall gain if it should turn out to be not only pleasant but also beneficial. (607c-d)

In banishing poetry from the philosophic realm while inviting it to argue its way back in, Plato gave a new turn to what Socrates already refers to here as "the old quarrel between philosophy and poetry" (607b). Philosophy had once been the suitor in Greek life and thought, arguing for admission to the minds and the cities of men dominated by poetry and myths. It was Socrates who was compelled to make an apology, a defense, for the claims of philosophy. But the ultimate success of Socrates and Plato created a revolution in this relationship; in modern times poetry has become the suitor, arguing in apologies and defenses for its place in a Western civilization dominated by philosophy and science.

In this context, Allan Bloom's position seems revealingly misconceived. He clearly thinks he is a rationalist, a political scientist, but he actually belongs to the poetic party without knowing it. He believes that education should be canonical, centered on reading great books and training one's own mind by contact with received wisdom. When education involves questioning and evaluating those texts as well as learning from them, it allows the exercise of reason, though it is not clear that Bloom approves of exposing most students to even this much practical philosophy. But the great books approach itself is always initially literary, religious, authoritative. It says "here is what we have always known, laid out by the great minds who first grasped it; here is wisdom on how to live." It is suggestive to look at Bloom's bibliography and realize that he has published translations, a book on Shakespeare, a famous article on Swift, but almost no work that we would call philosophy or science. He is not concerned with progressive rational knowledge; he believes that Plato and Shakespeare have more to offer students than any contemporary scientist or philosopher. As a literary critic, I must say as Marlow said of Lord Jim (and with some of the same complex ambivalence) that Bloom is clearly "one of us."

Ironically, however, while Bloom has been pursuing literary study under the guise of philosophic rationalism, the field of literary study has found itself in the midst of a rationalist revolution like that which occurred in the social sciences at the turn of the century. Natural science has been so effective in its core subjects that its perceived methodology has gradually overturned canonical models in discipline after discipline. Until the early nineteenth century all subjects were organized canonically, and until perhaps twenty years ago literary critics remained what Plato calls "lovers of poetry" as distinct from philosophers, or "lovers of wisdom." Critics saw their task as scrutinizing literary texts to support the argument that literature is "not only pleasant but also beneficial to regimes and human life." Since the Enlightenment dismissal of theology, literary study had in fact become the most serious intellectual alternative to systematic rational knowledge. Lovers of poetry were the loyal opposition in the philosophic world; they engaged the debate on the terms that Plato had laid down, attempting to make rational claims for the non-rational elements in literary imagination. But as this formulation suggests, and as Plato was surely aware, the philosophical context makes the whole project of traditional criticism rationally self-contradictory from the beginning. As a result, practitioners of literary studies, particularly in America, have become increasingly disenchanted with their position outside the mainstream of rational thought.

Broadly speaking, contemporary literary theory is concerned with moving the study of literature away from texts and towards ideas and systems; we are to study not *Lear* and *Middlemarch* but theories of reading and arguments about language. The best conventional literary criticism always embodied a creative tension between the writer's reading of the text and his argument about the text: the responsibilities of sensitive reading test and shape the argument even as the argument organizes and inspirits the reading. The goal of such criticism is met when the reading and the argument emerge as complementary equals, illuminating each other. In contrast, contemporary theory proposes a model for literary study analogous to the relationship between physics and nature, in which theory emerges as the real subject and texts are demoted to the status of mere evidence cited in defense of theoretical positions. (An early and influential formulation of this model appears in Frye, 11). This scientific model is most conspicuous in early structuralist theories, where the goal is to discover, define and catalog the various semiotic conventions—tropes, plots, narrative structures and other phenomena—which make literary meaning possible (see, for example, Todorov). Many theorists admit to scientific leanings; Jonathan Culler, one of the most influential sponsors of literary theory in America, prefers the French expression *les sciences humaines* to the English *humanities*, in which he sees a "futile attempt to distinguish the humanities from the social sciences" (20). One of the frequently cited attractions of the scientific model is that if literary study becomes a properly progressive discipline, it will no longer be necessary to read arguments more than five or ten years old. Allan Bloom, on the other hand, working under the rubric of "political science," often gives the impression that most writers since Plato and Aristotle are too modern for his tastes.

The attempt to apply scientific methodology to literary study rapidly runs aground, however, on the central paradox of all human knowledge: just as canonical judgments can only be assessed rationally, rational foundations can only be established canonically. This old paradox finds new expression in the deconstructive philosophy of Jacques Derrida, who attacks the "logocentrism" of all Western thought, observing that it is grounded in an irreducible "metaphysics of presence" which resides outside the domain of logos (speech and reason) itself (*Grammatology* 12, *Writing and Difference* 278-281). The Derridean critique of logocentrism is rationally unassailable, in the obvious sense that you can't use reason to prove the validity of reason. For those who will admit only rational evidence in defense of meaning the matter ends here, and truth claims become impossible. All written and spoken discourse becomes either game and play (in the comic view), part of a continuous dynamic of shifting power relations (in the tragic), or both of these at once. Comic skepticism leads to the punning, puckish pyrotechnics of deconstructive writing; tragic skepticism leads to an ethic of aggressive academic professionalism, an openly expressed imperialism in taking over existing institutions. Old-school scholars have been generally unable to resist these developments because they have attempted to rest their defense on rational claims alone, opening themselves up to charges of naivete and ignorance, leaving themselves vulnerable to the extremely powerful critical arguments which Derridean skepticism makes available. Bloom's response is typical of even more offhand dismissals; he characterizes deconstruction as a mere "fad" (379), apparently failing to perceive that Derrida justifies the relativist position he deplores, and completely undermines his own implicit claims to ground the search for truth in reason.

Derrida can be challenged only from ground outside the realm of logocentric discourse—in other words, only from a position taken ultimately on faith. To thoroughgoing skeptics who find such challenges the ultimate in ignorance and naivete, no response is possible, except the observation that all moral agendas (for example the advancement of minorities and women, the elimination of colonial oppression, and so on) are inevitably precluded by the skeptical position. If the play of linguistic difference permits no truth claims at all—if all meaning is relative—then might makes right, and only failure in the exercise of power condemns a Hitler or a Stalin (for example, their failure to manipulate discourse sufficiently well to ensure their historical valorization). To those who follow the Derridean argument yet find such conclusions intolerable, some form of openly-embraced, non-rational faith becomes necessary as the complement and ground of reason. Well-chosen premises can perhaps later be validated, *a posteriori*, by pragmatic success, as when Newton and Liebniz decided simply to assume that instantaneous rates of change were possible, and so invented calculus. But no one can begin to build a rational structure without taking an initial leap of faith.

Derridean philosophy, parodying the presumed rationality of pure science, sees this reliance on faith as a fatal flaw in all knowledge, but it is not a flaw at all. True knowledge requires both reason and revelation, neither of which is sufficient in itself. Numerous writers of the past two centuries—Wordsworth, Thoreau, George Eliot, Virginia Woolf, Wallace Stevens among others—have worked to detach revelation from its association with conventional religion, realizing that a humanistic interdependency of reason and revelation is the only possible escape from the nihilistic dilemma. They were trying, as T. S. Eliot observed of Joyce, to make the modern world possible for art, but they were no less engaged in making the modern world possible for scientific thought. The marriage of Mr. and Mrs. Ramsay in Woolf's *To the Lighthouse* offers a paradigm for the marriage of reason and revelation, either perspective alone being inadequate; without the aid of his wife's access to other sources of knowledge, Mr. Ramsay's reason (influenced by the earlier skepticism of Hume and Berkeley) cannot even convince him that the world is real. Because they need not defend their truth claims rationally, literature and poetry continue to create—just as they did in Plato's time—the metaphysical ground upon which reason builds, the structure of faith in the possibility of meaning which reason cannot make alone. Literary study emerges, in this view, not as a minor branch of philosophy, but as the study of the principal human activity (now that religion is widely disbelieved) which complements philosophy and makes it possible.

Most opponents of deconstructive skepticism resist this line of thinking because they are caught, consciously or unconsciously, in the same positivistic attitude toward truth that gives rise to the Derridean critique in the first place. Once successfully born in the attack on medieval religious faith, modernism adopted extravagant claims for the autonomous power of reason, which inevitably culminate in the attacks of Nietzsche, Heidegger and Derrida on the philosophic faith in reason itself. Our age has peculiar difficulty in understanding that reason is only a tool, a way of building and ordering knowledge, and that all knowledge ultimately has to stand on something outside reason—some premise, some assumption, some ground, some starting point, as we can see most conveniently in the five postulates of Euclidean geometry. Because faith and reason are both essential parts of knowledge, the trick in generating new knowledge is to identify those points previously taken on faith that can be dispensed with or replaced without undermining the possibility of knowledge itself. By forcing us to acknowledge openly the necessity for faith, Derrida provides the useful service of all radical skeptics in clearing the air of wishful thinking.

Allan Bloom, in contrast, illustrates the equally revealing problem with all counter-arguments to nihilism that fail to acknowledge their ultimate grounding in faith: once reason speciously claims autonomy, it can no longer recognize the importance of confining its unproven premises in the narrowest possible way (a point which Euclid, for example, understood clearly). Through an impressively broad survey of the philosophic tradition, Bloom traces the unfolding of modernism's central insight—that any attempt to apply reason to the study of its own foundations leads to nihilism, despair at the possibliity of meaning. But having brought us to this point, Bloom refuses to acknowledge that reason alone is not enough. Even Plato himself clearly understood the necessity for grounding reason outside of reason, relying on love, analogy and myth at the foundations of his philosophic system. In the *Symposium*, for example, Socrates talks at length about philosophic eros, the intellectual love upon which logic and reason are founded; such love mediates in the mind's apprehension of the highest good and beauty, which are inaccessible to reason alone (202a-212c). In attempting to escape the trap of nihilism without admitting the need for revealed knowledge, Bloom can only fall back on blind reactionary prejudices to take the place of faith. The result is a form of discourse in which unconfined belief overruns all bounds, and mere prejudice can seem to claim rational foundations.

The most serious of Bloom's prejudices, and the one that has cost him the most goodwill among serious readers, is his assumption that sexual hierarchy is natural rather than conventional. He simply contends that "the women's movement is not founded on nature" (100) and proceeds without further argument to outline what he sees as its ill consequences. Nature is not defined here, though Bloom later implies sympathy with an Aristotelian view that "nature is the fullness of its own kind that each of the beings strives to attain" (181). The argument for sexual hierarchy appeals to this pre-Enlightenment, teleological notion of natural purpose, implying that because of biological differences, women are of a fundamentally different "kind" than men, and must therefore be naturally dedicated to different ends. Modern science, however, is firmly committed to the integrity of *homo sapiens* as one species possessing homologous reproductive organs differentiated solely for sexual function, and to an evolution of means rather than a teleology of ends as the primary determinant of natural phenomena. Oddly enough, Bloom does not accept similar teleological arguments for racial hierarchy; he contends that "racial justice is an imperative of our theory and historical practice" (334), and never attacks the civil rights movement as he attacks feminism. He offers only one possible explanation for this difference, in arguing that feminism poses a more serious challenge to the great books: racism "just did not play a role in the classic literature" (mainly, of course, because non-whites are excluded altogether from the texts he cares about), whereas "*all* literature up to today is sexist" (65). He fails to perceive that feminism's critical evaluation of literature in the name of justice is far less radical than Plato's banishment and censorship of literature in the name of justice. The feminist argument is, however, like Plato's, a philosophical one, whereas Bloom's argument is religiously canonical, implying that the textual tradition ought to be immune to criticism merely because it is traditional.

Such arguments are classic illustrations of the pre-rational judgement, or prejudice, in defense of one's own traditions and one's own way which Socrates and Plato sought to have us overcome. They illustrate excess of faith to precisely the same degree that the deconstructive argument illustrates excess of skepticism. Martha Nussbaum identifies this problem as "the tension between Bloom's official allegiance to Socrates and the more dogmatic and religious conception of philosophy to which he is drawn" (21). The only complicating factor, which

Nussbaum does not consider, is that for Plato and Socrates tradition rested almost exclusively on revelation, whereas today our traditions also include the classic philosophic texts themselves. On the one hand, therefore, it becomes clear that reason cannot reject tradition as single-mindedly as it did in ancient times, and some degree of Bloom's reverence for the writing and thinking of the past is not misplaced. On the other hand, reason cannot simply reject criticism of tradition, or it ceases to be reasonable. The old myths have not been banished, as Socrates advocated in the *Republic*, but have merely been supplemented and modified by reason; even those completely overturned frequently remain with us, as when we speak of the sun rising and setting. Feminism's critique of the traditional canon derives directly from Socratic practice, and fills the same purpose in seeking out ideas previously taken on faith which need to be challenged in the name of truth and justice. The philosophic and literary canon will survive feminism's critique just as Homer survived Plato's, but the influence of its hidden assumptions on our daily practice will be better revealed and neutralized.

Bloom's sexism points the way toward the elitism which is his second major prejudice, and which has caused him similar problems of credibility. Because Bloom acknowledges the rightness of feminism's case according to those arguments of modern philosophy which underlie the basic principles of our political order (128), his anti-feminism ultimately implies a profound dissatisfaction with those founding principles of our regime which he elsewhere seems to praise. In fact, Bloom nowhere attempts to reconcile his apparent enthusiasm for the liberal democracy of the American founding with his larger argument that the modern rationalism it derives from leads inevitably to nihilism and relativism. He shares this ambivalence about democracy with Plato, who sees it as in some ways the "fairest" regime, because its freedom and diversity allow the *practice* of philosophy, and in other ways the least attractive regime, because its ignorant mob leadership most obviously precludes the *rule* of philosophy (*Republic* 557c-569c). Locke and the American founders thought otherwise, and believed that rational democratic structures could be designed to channel individual interests into a common good. If it is impossible, as Socrates and his interlocuters agree, "that a multitude be philosophic" (492a), it is at least conceivable that a majority can learn enough respect for reason to consider its claims. The broad goal of education in a democratic society is thus to help citizens become as receptive to rational debate as possible, trusting for the results of that debate to Milton's conviction that so long as "Truth be in the field" she cannot be put to the worse by falsehood (*Areopagitica* 746). Any departure from this broad educational goal must be viewed with deep suspicion, whether it comes from a right-leaning elitism that defines most people as incapable of reason, or a left-leaning skepticism that denies truth's presence in the field of discourse.

Bloom's aristocratic bias is suggested by his failure to make clear the democratic argument for focusing on students in "the twenty or thirty best universities" (22), a focus which, in the absence of that argument, has brought him widespread criticism. Ideas first discussed and transmitted in the best universities filter out to other colleges and universities via graduate programs, from those institutions into the public schools through the training of teachers, and from the public schools into the unquestioned philosophic assumptions of the population at large. What is merely thought in one generation is often lived in the next. Because the power of teaching radiates outward, the social stakes of philosophic debate at intellectual centers are high. As Bloom understands, this process has been largely responsible for the spread of religious skepticism, scientific confidence, and philosophic relativism; he points in particular to the broadly disseminated influence of John Dewey's scientific pragmatism (56, 195). For a more recent example one can observe the gradual spread, still in progress, of literary theory outward from a few universities—Yale, Johns Hopkins, Cornell—until virtually all literature departments in the country now engage in some degree of theoretical training and discussion. Literary theory, despite its usual alliance with egalitarian politics, could not have dispersed its influence so rapidly from the margins of our educational system. In practice, contemporary theory initially creates an elitism more powerful and subtle than Bloom's, by employing an arcane and abstruse language whose decoding is confined to a small circle of knowers.

It is difficult to judge how our current intellectual debates will influence the next generation of Americans. Academia is sharply divided today between those who believe that truth is possible and those who do not. Allan Bloom stands firmly on the side of truth, but for all his learning he makes the standard error of the right in suggesting that what we need to do is return to a mythic golden age when truth was simpler, when men and women lived in clear social hierarchies which defined their places in a "natural" order and made them easily identifiable as "types" (a favorite Bloomian expression) rather than as individuals. In opposition to such reactionary views, however, we all too often find only the standard contemporary error of the left, which is to assume that truth is impossible. This assumption is no less a matter of faith, of course, than its opposite; believing that truth is impossible is just another form of believing that truth is simple. What we desperately need is thinkers willing to embrace the possibility of truth without bringing along the baggage of radical conservatism. Only a willingness to suspend disbelief at the outset of inquiry can establish the perspective that truth is complex, subtle, elusive, perhaps never fully knowable, but ultimately possible.

Such rigorous naivete is directly responsible for the success of natural science in modern times. The physicist Stephen Hawking suggests that "general relativity is only an incomplete theory: it cannot tell us how the universe started off, because it predicts that all physical theories, including itself, break down at the beginning of the universe" (50-51). This prediction is identical to the deconstructive argument that all theories, including itself, contain the sources of their own unravelling. All rational theories break down at the source, the ground, the origin; this breakdown is part of what proves a theory to be rational and not mystical. Thoughtful natural scientists understand that while each successive scientific theory may rest on fewer unproven premises, may press further toward discovering the ideal truth of things, it will always be possible for a later scientist to come along and construct a more nearly "true" explanation, because the foundations of reason are themselves not rational. Hawking's friend the mathematician Roger Penrose has recently suggested a revolutionary notion in the science of mind: that quantum phenomena, as opposed to mere chemical reactions, may be involved in the more complex activities of the human brain.

As Bloom reminds us (177), the Cartesian problem of how mind is grounded in body has never been solved by science. As long as we do not yet even know whether to look for the answers to the first questions in chemistry or quantum physics, how is it possible to speak of a human science? Natural science can tell us what the universe was like within four seconds of its creation, but still contributes almost nothing to our understanding of how the human mind comes to grasp such knowledge. We have created the social sciences as stopgaps because we need answers to the important questions about human nature immediately, not when science gets around to providing them in the fullness of time. But social science often betrays our hopes because it substitutes a long series of unacknowledged premises for a true natural science of mind.

Literature, in contrast to social science, provides a serious alternative to the scientific tradition engaging important human issues. The real issue in contemporary education is that rational science is still very far from being able to solve all problems. Science is the art of asking answerable questions; literature is the art of asking important ones, whether they are answerable or not. We face innumerable moral and ethical problems in the modern world, many of them resulting from the success of progressive science itself, yet about which science has nothing to say. Science can tell us how to make a baby in a test tube, but not whether we ought to do so; how to prolong life, but not how to accept death; how to destroy the world, but not how to avoid destroying it. Our real enemy is the assumption that a positivistic science is the only valid mode of intellectual inquiry, and that where it fails the only possibility is despair at the possibility of meaning. Traditional literary study, of which Bloom is a distinguished (if unconscious) exponent, proposes that subjective answers to important questions are as necessary as objective answers to answerable ones. Or, as Plato puts it, the ideal city, though not attainable in practice, can at least become "a pattern...laid up for the man who wants to see and found a city within himself... For he would mind the things of this city alone, and no other" (*Republic* 592b). The study of great ideas and great books provides what Milton calls "a Paradise within" (*PL* 12:587), a vision of possibility that can serve as a guide to living right.

Because literature rests on the openly non-rational, it offers more direct access than social science to potential wisdom on the questions that natural science leaves answered. But in order to best achieve its goal, literary teaching must retain its canonical structure. As Bloom acknowledges (344), the "great books" method of teaching raises serious questions: who evaluates and selects them? According to what standards? But problems of a similar sort arise in systematic organization: who designs the structure? According to what standards? In the social sciences, whole fields often seem to consist solely of debates on these questions. It is often objected that in canonical fields, no independent structure even exists to determine what questions to ask about the texts; but it can equally be objected that in progressive fields, no authority exists to define a field of data that appropriately tests the structure. These paradoxes trace back to the indeterminate nature of all human knowledge. In literary study, arguments about the canon attempt, however inadequately, to define standards of judgment through vigorous debate. Recent discussions about opening up the literary canon to the neglected works of women and minorities are almost certain to strengthen the canon, since the resistance of both sides in the debate to the claims of the other will help to ensure that the works to be added, and those retained, will both be the best that their supporters can put forward. The debate rests on two premises: openness, in engaging new challenges to canonical tradition; and faith, in the possibility that some abstract standard of judgement exists which we can approximate.

Bloom is right to attack the sunny optimism of American relativism, which moves beyond nihilism to the odd notion that if one truth is impossible, all claims to truth must be equal. But in his misconception of his own position and his failure to grasp the limits of reason, he closes his mind to the special claims of the literature he loves. As a result, we risk dismissing the problem he identifies. The real danger in American education today is the gradual disappearance of traditional literary study, because it is the last discipline which offers a serious canonical study of books and authors. Literature has remained one of the few fields where large numbers of students are confronted with real texts and important questions; the triumph of systematic theory, as in the social sciences, would leave us with even fewer minds trained to engage the moral and ethical issues that matter most.

Works Cited

Bloom, Allan. *The Closing of the American Mind: How Higher Education Has Failed Democracy and Impoverished the Souls of Today's Students.* New York: Simon, 1987.

Culler, Jonathan. *The Pursuit of Signs: Semiotics, Literature, Deconstruction.* Ithaca: Cornell UP, 1981.

Derrida, Jacques. *Of Grammatology.* Trans. Gayatri Chakravorty Spivak. Baltimore: Johns Hopkins UP, 1976.

——— *Writing and Difference.* Trans. Alan Bass. Chicago: Chicago UP, 1978.

Eliot, T. S. "*Ulysses*, Order and Myth." *Dial* (1923). Rpt. *James Joyce: Two Decades of Criticism.* Ed. Seon Givens. New York: Vanguard, 1948.

Frye, Northrop. *Anatomy of Criticism: Four Essays.* Princeton: Princeton UP, 1957.

Hawking, Stephen W. *A Brief History of Time: From the Big Bang to Black Holes.* New York: Bantam, 1988.

Milton, John. *Complete Poems and Major Prose.* Ed. Merritt Y. Hughes. New York: Odyssey, 1957.

Nussbaum, Martha. "Undemocratic Vistas." *New York Review of Books* 34 (1987): 20-6.

Penrose, Roger. *The Emperor's New Mind: Concerning Computers, Minds, and the Laws of Physics.* New York: Oxford UP, 1989.

Plato. *The Republic.* Trans. Allan Bloom. New York: Basic, 1968.

——— *The Symposium.* Trans. Walter Hamilton. New York: Penguin, 1951.

Todorov, Tzvetan. "Structural Analysis of Narrative." *Novel* 3:1 (1969): 70-76.

Woolf, Virginia. *To the Lighthouse.* New York: Harcourt, 1927.

Allan Bloom and Gerald Graff:
On Mimesis as Freedom

Lorraine Clark

The most successful tyranny is not the one that uses force to assure uniformity but the one that removes the awareness of other possibilities, that makes it seem inconceivable that other ways are viable, that removes the sense that *there is an outside.*
—Allan Bloom, *The Closing of the American Mind*

Allan Bloom's assessment of the brave new world of humanities education has been anticipated in narrower measure within the field of literary studies by Gerald Graff's *Literature Against Itself.*[1] Graff's diagnosis of the crisis facing the literary institution—and to a lesser extent, his proposed solution—bears some uncanny resemblances to Bloom's, and this similarity is surely significant. For that two theorists from nearly opposite ends of the political spectrum should arrive at a virtually unanimous diagnosis suggests that the diagnosis may well be correct, even true, heretical as it has become to invoke such terms. Further, it suggests that the issue at stake here is—or ought to be—something beyond politics or at least political differences, equally heretical as it has become to suggest such a possibility. Graff in particular argues cogently that much of this crisis stems from a naively sophisticated "politics of anti-realism" that is deeply mistaken, and that a de-politicizing of the crisis is paradoxically essential to restoring real intellectual and political vigor to the humanities.

Fundamentally, Bloom and Graff argue that the humanities have brought a crisis upon themselves by abolishing the mimetic theory and hence the truth claims of literature; and both propose reinstating the mimetic theory as the solution. But their appeals to the restored ideals of nature, reality, truth, objectivity, and reason entailed by mimetic theory are assumed to be inherently politically repressive, inherently theological, naively objectivist, and worst of all, inherently ahistorical. Such appeals to a restored objectivity have led many to attack Graff and especially Bloom as naive reactionaries; yet such attacks either dogmatically reject mimesis outright as self-evidently "disproven" by anti-mimetic theories, or uncritically assume that the content or objectivity of literature can and should somehow be "reconstituted" on postmodern grounds as a kind of "relatively objective objectivity." Bloom and Graff correctly see that such a reconciliation of mimetic theory with the contemporary attacks upon it is neither possible nor desirable; yet their "returns" to mimesis are neither oblivious to those attacks nor simply reactionary. The sophistication of their shared strategy is to see that the only way to reinstate the content or objectivity of literature

151

is not to try to reconcile it with the contemporary relativism that claims to dissolve it, but to sharpen the opposition between the two, a sharpening that will restore the vitality of *both* mimetic and anti-mimetic theories. Together, their accounts provide a powerful critique of the fallacies underlying most contemporary resistance to mimetic theories of literature, a critique that both see as vital to restoring real debate within the humanities.

The root of the crisis as Bloom and Graff agree in defining it is that mimetic theory has been abolished as "tyrannical" by the "cultural vanguard;" and they agree in rejecting, by precisely *inverting*, this definition of tyranny. As both point out, mimetic theories are held to be inherently repressive on the uncritically romantic grounds that any accountability to something "outside"—call it God, nature, truth, reality—is a restriction on true freedom, which (as Milton's Satan insists) is by definition unaccountable to anything. The current doctrine of the humanities is thus merely deconstructionist doctrine writ large: "Nothing outside the text" has become simply "nothing outside"—no truth outside the text to which it can refer or be held accountable; no text outside interpretations to which they can refer or be held accountable; no reason outside the realm of mere opinion or prejudice; no criterion of value outside the whims of contemporary society to which that society can be held accountable. By uncritically embracing this romantic doctrine, the humanities renounce their own truth claims and hence their potentially *corrective* function. Ironically, this liberation thus enslaves them to their own powerlessness, an inconsequentiality they attempt to celebrate (again like Milton's Satan) by asserting what Graff calls "the power of powerlessness"[2]—that they are "all there is," again, because "there is nothing outside." The fictionality of the texts they teach need not disqualify them from serious consideration, for reality is only fictional too; life, after all, is literature.

Emancipation from mimesis thus supposedly liberates humanists in two ways: it liberates them from dogmatic absolutism, accountability to a tyrannical truth; and it liberates them from the naive realism and objectivism assumed to characterize the unsophisticated contemporary society outside the university, whose children can in turn be liberated from their parents' naivete by coming to college. But Bloom and Graff argue that far from being liberated, the humanities are enslaved not only by their own romantically mind-forged manacles, but by the very society they think they oppose. For their romantic idea of freedom— their pervasive relativism—does not oppose but merely reflects the values of contemporary society. Where Bloom sees this relativism as symptomatic of the potential dangers or "blindnesses" of democracy, Graff locates its cause in consumer capitalist society, "for liberation from traditional constraints is an essential condition for the expansion of consumption."[3] Nothing serves consumerism, Graff argues, like the conviction of the ephemerality or fictionality of all reality. Bent on dissolving the tyrannical absolutism assumed to characterize both the academy and contemporary society, the cultural vanguard thus "ignores the disappearance of the paternalistic repressions it seeks to dissolve";[4] attacks on such alleged monoliths as the reference theory of language, the mimetic theory of literature, and the bourgeois humanist tradition ignore the manifest truth that those monoliths have already dissolved under the pressures of contemporary democratic (Bloom) or capitalist (Graff) society. The vanguard is thus engaged in shadow-boxing of a most peculiar sort: convinced of its profound romantic "alienation" from the alleged values of contemporary society, the alienation that is the very source of its revisionary power, it prepares for (or engages in) the revolution. But its alienation like its power is illusory, for by its own admission "there is nothing outside"—not even itself.

If for the cultural vanguard tyranny is "something outside" and liberation from tyranny is "nothing outside," for Bloom and Graff, then, precisely the reverse is true: tyranny is "nothing outside" and liberation can only come from reinstating "something outside": the real otherness or objectivity that has been dissolved (or declared to be dissolved) by anti-mimetic theory. And while their notions of a reconstituted objectivity (especially Bloom's) may yet meet with considerable resistance, one suspects that their diagnosis is already acknowledged implicitly if not explicitly by many. Having spent generations (charted by both Bloom and Graff)[5] systematically divesting literature of its content, humanists are now frantically scrambling to reinvest it, with "politics," "history," "sexuality," and "ethics" (or "values").

It is critical to see that in thus indicting contemporary relativism, neither Bloom nor Graff seeks to abolish it for absolutism, but rather to restore the debate between the two—again, the sense that there is "something outside" relativism, a vital alternative. Both declare unequivocally that it is not relativism they oppose but the *dogmatism* with which it is held and taught. Everyone "is free to write as if 'everybody knows' that mimesis is a dead issue," Graff remarks[6] (a remark that holds equally true for anything smacking of essentialism, absolutism, or objectivity); no one is free to write as if it is not.

By restoring debates that have been so dogmatically precluded, Bloom and Graff above all want to restore real choices—which is to say, not merely relative choices but absolute choices that by definition have real consequences—into a world that denies the possibility of such choices and celebrates the inconsequentiality of choice. In this respect they make a familiar philosophical move, responding, like Kierkegaard and Nietzsche to the dissolution of choice effected by the Hegelian system (both-and), by trying to reinstate the notion of exclusive or "tragic" choices (either/or). Yet the very familiarity of this philosophical move may be what makes us most skeptical of their success: for can Gerald Graff and Allan Bloom succeed where Kierkegaard and Nietzsche did not? Bloom admires the spirit of Nietzsche's enterprise and laments its failure;[7] and Graff's tracing of contemporary theory as a recapitulation of romantic thought suggests the possibility that his reaction against it, like Kierkegaard's against romanticism, will not reverse that line of thought but merely continue it.[8] The very notion of a reason, objectivity, and power of choice as willfully *reconstituted* out of a prior dissolution suggests an inherent fragility and tenuousness that may be their undoing. As Bloom himself cogently argues, "value-positing" is no solution to "value-relativism"[9]—which means that if his and Graff's "reason," "nature," and "objectivity" are merely reconstituted or posited they will fail on their own terms to provide the objective ground for values that they claim to reinstate.

On the other hand, so engrained is our skepticism that any attempted return to ideas of reason and objectivity that ignores the romantic, modern, and postmodern attacks on such concepts will be dismissed as naively reactionary and presumed insufficient even by those most sympathetic to the enterprise. To be convincing, any return must show full theoretical awareness of the sustained attacks that have been made against it. This is where Graff might appear to be more successful than Bloom; for despite Graff's return to an objective text he rejects any return to "literature itself," insisting that "no text is an island" but must be understood within a thickly-textured historical, sociological, philosophical, and linguistic context.[10] This seems directly at odds with Bloom's call for a return to "the good old Great Books approach," which means "reading certain generally recognized classic texts, just reading them, letting them dictate what the questions are and the method of approaching them—not forcing them into categories we make up, not treating them as historical products, but trying to read them as their authors wished them to be read."[11] But a closer look reveals, I think, otherwise.

Bloom's allegedly ahistorical essentialism, objectivism, and universalism lies in his claim that there is an essential human nature to whose permanent problems "great literature" addresses itself: the "great questions" or "tragic choices" of "reason-revelation, freedom-necessity, democracy-aristocracy, good-evil, body-soul, self-other, city-man, eternity-time, being-nothing"[12] (this by no means exhausts the list, but probably covers most of the central questions as they appear in other guises). It is these tensions or problems that are permanent, he claims, not their proposed solutions, which have been very different for different authors, times, and places. More accurately, the choices for one alternative or the other have been made differently by different authors in different (and sometimes the same) times and places, for Bloom insists that there neither can nor should be any "solutions" that harmonize or reconcile these exclusive choices. By declaring that history has simply taken us "beyond" such choices, contemporary relativism denies that the choices any longer exist. But Bloom argues that it is sheer dogmatism to declare these choices unavailable on the grounds of a pervasive historicism which asserts first of all that there is no essential human nature, only a radically historicized one, and secondly that history has rendered these choices irrelevant to contemporary life. Everyone is free to speak as if God is dead, necessity rules, democracy is clearly superior to aristocracy, we are beyond good and evil, there is only the body, etc.; no one is free to speak as though these are not foregone conclusions but open to rational debate.

To the charge that he is an essentialist, Bloom would readily acknowledge that this is so. But he would simply deny the implication that this self-evidently disqualifies his position from serious consideration. Only on historicist grounds, grounds that are not self-evidently true (and indeed disqualify themselves from such a possibility) does his essentialism disqualify his arguments; but those grounds are quite simply not the only grounds as historicism assumes. There is something outside itself.

Bloom would also reject a second implication of the essentialist charge: that essentialism is inherently dogmatic, imposing an unchanging, monolithic truth on human nature. For while the questions may be permanent, he would insist again that they can never be answered. The permanence of the questions or conflicts is indeed what guarantees the continuing vitality of human life; for if the questions could be resolved the struggles that constitute life would cease. (Here again we can see how Bloom shares his definition of life with Kierkegaard and Nietzsche, who similarly insist that without continual struggle the life of the spirit effectively stops.)[13] Curiously, relativism itself claims to engage in the ceaseless, vital striving that is "life"; but Bloom, like Kierkegaard, sees that such striving is illusory. For as Kierkegaard so correctly saw, to relativize choices is to reconcile them, whether in the "positive unity" of Hegelian mediation or in the "negative unity" of nihilism.

A third implication of the essentialist charge is that essentialism is inherently ahistorical. Again, such a charge results from relativism's refusal (or inability) to see anything outside itself, for it assumes that the only way to be historical is to be historicist. Bloom could legitimately argue that his analysis of the permanent questions or conflicts is in fact truer to history than historicism can ever be, for his claim to "truth" and "knowledge" allows him the possibility of access to historical fact as historicism's premises do not. It allows him, in other words, to make truth claims for his historical knowledge, truth claims relinquished by historicism as self-deluded. Only the conviction that one can get at the truth of, say, the seventeenth century, Bloom would argue, allows for the theoretical and practical possibility that one can understand the seventeenth century as it understood itself; to deny as historicism does that such access is possible virtually guarantees its failure. True, we may never know with absolute certainty whether we "really do" understand an age as it understood itself; but neither will we ever know with complete certainty that we do not. And why dogmatically foreclose the very possibility of doing so? Further, by denying not only that we can know, for example, how the ancients, Hobbes, Locke, Rousseau, and Nietzsche understood "freedom," but also that there may be an absolute or essential or true definition of freedom, historicism forfeits any grounds for evaluating or choosing among those definitions, rendering them mere curiosities of only passing interest, mere twilight "history" without any living force. And while this may not appear to have significant philosophical consequences (for philosophy perhaps inhabits a twilight world), in the realm of politics the consequences can be very serious indeed—for as Bloom points out, such historicism leaves itself without any basis for arguing on the grounds of human freedom that one political regime is better than another.[14] Once again, it abdicates any corrective function.

Far from being ahistorical, then, Bloom's essentialism is arguably what allows for the truest, living sense of history. His claim that the problem of human freedom is a permanent one is what allows (and motivates) us to trace the different attempts to solve that problem, giving us the principle of continuity essential to any perception of difference. (And would anyone deny that the problem of human freedom is a permanent one?) His insistence on keeping open the possibility that history is an object whose truth or objectivity can be known allows us the possibility again of understanding true otherness or difference, the reality of an age as it understood itself. And his essentialist insistence on an absolute ideal of freedom—however necessarily "empty" that ideal must remain, a utopian ideal—independent of its different definitions throughout history is what keeps those definitions alive despite their historical distance. For they do not lose their reality or vitality as a function of historical distance (the further away in time, the less available they are as viable options for contemporary life), but according to their distance from this ideal of human freedom. This is why, for example, Bloom can argue for Enlightenment ideas of reason and human freedom as "the best"; they have not become relics of a dead past, rendered automatically unavailable by the inevitable march of history, but kept alive as real options in a living present by their proximity to a universal ideal.

Bloom's allegedly ahistorical essentialism may be more of a practical than a theoretical problem, for in theory his essentialism, though anti-historicist, is not ahistorical. But in practice it seems to mean reading "great books" in isolation from their historical context, a context assumed to be either irrelevant (since as purveyors of "the permanent questions" books are not mere products of history), somehow mystically inherent in the text, or already in place in the students' minds. These are Graff's objections to any return to "literature itself" as a workable solution to the crisis. The historical context is never irrelevant to a given text, he argues; and while it may be true that all texts, as historical documents, do imply or contain their own contexts, one cannot assume that the students are sufficiently knowledgeable to recognize those implied contexts. For to recognize them requires prior "outside" knowledge of those contexts, a knowledge Graff argues is mistakenly assumed to have been conveyed by a coherent "humanist tradition" that no longer exists—if indeed it ever did. The "great humanist myth" assumes that one can freely teach texts "in themselves" divorced from one another and from their contexts because it assumes that somehow all these isolated experiences in a student's curriculum add up to a coherent whole. But they do not, for there is no "great tradition" uniting the student's educational experiences; and Graff urges as a result that all teachers do their utmost to contextualize historically the books they teach.[15]

One wonders whether Bloom would really disagree; for while it is probably true that the real context Bloom wants to invoke for his texts is not historical but the context of the permanent questions, his own understanding of texts is clearly deeply (and intentionally) historical and contextual. He does not want to regard texts as historically determined or as *merely* products of their times; but one has only to read his highly historical account of the changes in the American intellectual and political scene—his history of American ideas—in *Closing* to see that history, politics, and even sociology are deeply implicated in his understanding of ideas. This evolutionary tracing of ideas is itself another way of providing historical context, one that Graff argues we must return to as well (despite the supposed dissolution of such evolutionary ideas of history and the acknowledged danger of reductive historical generalizations).[16] And Bloom acknowledges that while he used to think that "nature" or "the primary natural experience" of "the book" was all—that books did in a sense simply "teach themselves"—he no longer believes this to be sufficient.[17]

The "nature" to which literature refers, then, is for Bloom essentially "human nature," defined partly in terms of its permanent problems, tensions, or conflicts. And these conflicts are permanent precisely because by definition they can never be resolved, despite the "peculiarly modern" desire for universal solutions—the very desire Bloom argues impels relativism to solve the problem of choice by declaring the inconsequentiality of choice.[18] In this emphasis on conflict as the real content of literature, Bloom again shares to some extent Graff's definition of that content or "reality." For Graff similarly defines the study of literature as the study of conflicts, although it is less clear that he would regard these conflicts, however irreconcilable, as permanent problems of human nature. The conflicts for Graff are largely institutional conflicts inscribed within the history of institutions: conflicts over what should be included in the canon, over critical approaches to texts—all of which he argues should be taught as part of the "context" for understanding a given text.[19] This may make Graff sound more self-referential (more interested in his approach or method than in "the text itself") than he really is, however; for by "conflict" he also means the specific conflict(s) to which a given text addresses itself. Understanding Hawthorne's "The Artist of the Beautiful," for instance, means knowing something about the conflict between theories of "aesthetic transcendence" and the "American philistinism" to which the story responds. And while this conflict is a historically specific one, part of America's cultural history, Graff remarks that it illuminates "still-present conflicts in American culture,"[20] ongoing conflicts that perhaps have no solutions.[21]

If Graff is somewhat equivocal about whether the conflicts to which literature "refers" are permanent conflicts of human nature, he is less equivocal in sharing Bloom's insistence that concepts like "justice," "oppression," and "equality" can be *true*—that is, that they are not always "mere party slogans and rationalizations" for abuses of power. To argue that such terms are inherently ideological attacks the very possibility of political discourse, which Graff argues depends on the possibility of stable meanings grounded not merely in shared conventions but in "a real world" outside of language. Political demystification of language means to free terms from "misuse" "by attaching them to the appropriate referents, not to dissolve the very notion that language can have referents."[22] Graff also unequivocally shares Bloom's claim for a universal human nature whose essence is "reason," insisting on the return to reason entailed by his return to an objective text and to an objective reality to which that text refers. Like Bloom, Graff holds it as a self-evident truth that we do have reason— to consider this, like the social nature of man, to be one of the "unrefusable facts" of our experience.[23] And while relativism again denies the existence of such self-evident truths or facts, it cannot escape the embarrassment of holding its own denial as self-evidently true without any rationale for making such a claim. When it does however sometimes acknowledge rationality as a common human attribute it refuses to grant it superiority over other faculties as what is most fundamentally or essentially human. The Freudian "unmasking" of reason as "grounded" in a deeper irrationality or subconscious is assumed to disqualify its pretensions to mastery; yet this is a version of what Graff calls "the genetic fallacy," which confounds a thing's identity with its origin or ground.[24] As Bloom points out, the presence of lower as well as higher faculties can also be understood as evidence that the lower can aspire to the higher—that one can be "educated" to one's fullest potential, the passions' self-fulfillment in reason's mastery.[25] Again, such rational "mastery" is assumed to be inherently tyrannical and self-deluded, a Urizenic fiction to be exposed as such and overthrown.

For Bloom and Graff, again, it is not so much this romantic denigration of reason as its *ubiquity* that is staggering. The uncritically romantic assertion that reason is inherently repressive, politically conservative, and tyrannical (the latter terms synonymous) seems oblivious to the possibility of other ideas of reason "outside" its own: to the opposing arguments (so powerfully made by

Milton for instance as well as by Enlightenment thinkers) that reason is "the essential freedom that justifies the other freedoms;"[26] that a hierarchy of the faculties may be more liberating than their equality; that reason need not be narrowly (and romantically) conceived as coldly mechanistic, technological, and lifeless, but has been conceived (by classical, Renaissance, and Enlightenment thinkers) as "moral and evaluative *and* objective."[27] What cultural radicalism attacks, in other words, is not necessarily reason itself but a caricature set up to facilitate its demolition. Further, as Graff points out, the attacks on reason confound reason with the uses to which it is put: indicting reason instead of some particular *abuses* of reason throws out the baby along with the bath, attacking not only the particular "tyranny" at issue but "the rationale of principled *resistance* to tyranny."[28] Nor is reason necessarily naively objectivist as cultural radicalism dogmatically assumes. Science has demonstrated that the ideal of observational neutrality—reason's self-proclaimed objective stance—is impossible, runs the argument; therefore it is pointless to attempt to adopt such a stance. Yet as Graff argues, one need not be naively objectivist to acknowledge that while *complete* observational neutrality may be impossible, it is nonetheless relatively approachable as an ideal, and can be improved with training or education. To assume that either complete observational neutrality must be demonstrably possible or it must be abandoned altogether as an ideal is a curiously absolutist claim for relativism to make.[29]

To assume that it is necessarily theological or utopian, a kind of "transcendental mysticism" to lay claim to the possibility of "something outside"—either an objective reason outside mere opinion or an objective reality outside interpretation—is for Graff and Bloom similarly mistaken. Graff in particular has virtually no interest in theology; and while Bloom acknowledges the power of its competing claims, "philosophy" and hence a non-theological "reason" have for him the strongest claims to truth. The universalism of reason as the highest human faculty is for Bloom precisely what frees us from the potential dogmatism and authority of religion—for the authority of a "natural" human reason is what all men potentially share and what potentially guarantees their freedom.[30]

My summary of these arguments is necessarily sketchy. But it is important to see that the single greatest corrective force of Bloom's and Graff's arguments for a restored ideal of objectivity is quite simply their insistence that objectivity *need not* be associated with all the qualities that have blocked its acceptance. Objectivity is not "inherently" *anything*. It is not inherently ahistorical, tyrannical, reactionary, conservative, naive, utopian, or theological. It can be appropriated by anyone and put to any use whatsoever, and in this freedom lies its extraordinary potency as an instrument for change. That the humanities have so resolutely, dogmatically banished it from their utopia as inherently invested with everything "nobody would want to be associated with if he could help it," as Graff puts it,[31] is what has guaranteed their own powerlessness, denying them any real corrective—including self-corrective—force.

The romantic through postmodern attack on all forms of objectivity is simply that: romantic, a narrow "programmatic moralism" (Graff) that naively equates "something— *anything*—outside" with tyranny, "mimetic representation with conformism."[32] Objectivity cannot be "reconstituted" on postmodern grounds, as Bloom and Graff correctly see, in a vain (and ultimately misguided) attempt to reconcile mimetic with anti-mimetic theory. But it can be freed from all that has falsely "tainted" it and thus precluded its consideration as a real alternative. This is why Bloom and Graff are not theoretically naive in their strategic insistence that a return to objectivity is the only way to restore real vitality and debate— that the only solution is not to try to reconcile but to restore the debate between absolutism *reconceived as a vital alternative* and relativism, between an uncompromised objectivity and the relativism that claims to have dissolved it. The desire to reconcile mimetic with anti-mimetic theory, objectivity with perspectivism, absolutism with relativism by somehow "reconstituting" mimesis, objectivity, and absolutism on relativistic grounds is itself symptomatic of the problem, and is deeply mistaken. In the guise of an embrace, it is yet another, disguised manifestation of the tyranny that declares "there is nothing outside."

Gerald Graff and Allan Bloom may be politically worlds apart (of this I have no certain knowledge). But if so, that in itself is testimony to the objectivity of their respective critiques and to their shared insistence that mimetic and anti-mimetic theories, while never "apolitical" because always susceptible to political use, are not inherently identifiable with any particular political position. And whatever their politics, both are genuine cultural radicals in issuing the challenge of radically redefining the task of the humanities as precisely the opposite of what it is uncritically assumed to be. The task as they redefine it is not to liberate students from the tyranny of a monolithic tradition, but to liberate them from the "triviality of a 'freedom' without content or direction."[33] The task is to point out that relativism does not have a monopoly on freedom.

Notes

[1]Gerald Graff *Literature Against Itself* (Chicago, 1979).
[2]Graff, 90.
[3]Graff, 92.
[4]Graff, 95.
[5]Graff, 13-101 and 129-180; Allan Bloom, *The Closing of the American Mind* (New York, 1987), 65-67 and 313-380.
[6]Graff, 4.
[7]Bloom, 197-207; 228.
[8]Graff, 31-62.
[9]Bloom, 141-144.
[10]Graff, *Professing Literature: An Institutional History* (Chicago, 1987), 10.
[11]Bloom, 344.
[12]Bloom, 227-229.
[13]Bloom, 198, 228; see also 170-171, where Bloom points out that antiquity also "treated the fundamental tensions as permanent."
[14]Bloom, 40.
[15]Graff, *Professing*, 1-15.
[16]Graff, *Literature*, 124.
[17]Bloom, 51.
[18]Bloom, 170-171.
[19]Graff, *Professing*, 14-15.

[20]Graff, "The University and the Prevention of Culture," in *Criticism in the University*, ed. Graff and Reginald Gibbons (Northwestern, 1985), 79.

[21]Graff's most recent work which focuses on "teaching the conflicts" more decisively defines the fundamentally historical (and historicized) nature of the conflicts he means, in opposition to Bloom's focus on the permanent questions or conflicts which great literature addresses or is "about." Graff's new, pronounced emphasis on the institutional, social, and historical nature of the conflicts he would have us "teach" marks a sharp turn away from his early defense of reference theories of language and literature, and aligns him (I would argue) more with the anti-referential theorists he earlier attacked. We might ask which position is more "open": the one which declares that teaching literature should mean teaching the historicized interpretive conflicts through which literature is and has been "constituted" (Graff's current position), or the one which declares that teaching literature should mean teaching not only historicized conflicts but the permanent conflicts which literature is "about" (Bloom's position). The latter would seem to accommodate both kinds of conflict as Graff's position does not.

[22]Graff, *Literature*, 90.

[23]Graff, 202.

[24]Graff, 198-199.

[25]Bloom, 232, 292.

[26]Bloom, 39.

[27]Graff, *Literature*, 28.

[28]Graff, 85.

[29]Graff, 86-87.

[30]See especially Bloom's discussion of Weber and the conflict between reason and revelation, 194-216; also 253: "The essence of philosophy is the abandonment of all authority in favor of the individual human reason."

[31]Graff, *Literature*, 24.

[32]Graff, 23.

[33]Graff, 214.

Response

Gerald Graff

You are right, I think, to see *Literature Against Itself* anticipating some of the arguments of *The Closing of the American Mind*, though you recognized that I was coming from the political Left not the Right (I can't emphasize that too strongly). I feel I *have* changed my position since writing that book. In fact, it was probably the stream of polemics by Bloom and other Right-wing ideologues in the 80s that did more than anything to convince me of the bankruptcy of my former arguments, especially of making relativism the scapegoat for all of today's problems.

Relativism may be a genuine philosophical problem, but it is obvious that recent conservative attacks on it—and defenses of reason and objectivity—are disguised attacks on democratic debate and on overtly politicized forms of culture. In any case, reading Bloom and his cohorts forced me to rethink the notion that all the evils of the modern world can be reduced to the loss of faith in philosophical realism and objectivity. What Bloom et. al. call relativism looks merely like a degree of conflict that goes beyond the narrow restrictions they would keep on discussions of literature, culture, and the humanities—restrictions that for them would rule feminist, Marxist, and other political questions out of order.

It was also Bloom's and other diatribes, ostensibly on behalf of disinterested reason but in fact blatantly and virulently ideological, that made me more sympathetic to the theorists I had attacked in *Literature Against Itself* who insist on the inescapability of politics and ideology. It's not that I've stopped believing in truth, but I now think it's a mistake to suppose that, as you put it, if concepts like truth, justice, oppression, and equality, are *"inherently* ideological," then "the very possibility of political discourse" is done for. All ideas and language *are* "inherently ideological," in the sense that they necessarily have social consequences. That is all the term "ideological" means, or needs to mean to give bite to the current post-structuralist insistence that no theory or discursive practice is politically innocent. When one says a certain text or concept is "ideological," one says that it has certain social consequences, which may be progressive or regressive (or in some cases both), quite apart from its truth or falsity.

In fact, the claim that everything is ideological in this sense would be a truism or a barren tautology were it not that people like Bloom deny it or evade its implications, as when they attack canon-busting professors for "politicizing" literary study while they themselves grossly politicize literary study without acknowledging the fact. (A good case in point is NEH Head Lynne V. Cheney's

161

hypocritical assertion of the transcendent nature of literary values while she pushes the Reagan-Bush campaign to move the country back to "traditional values.")

For this reason, I am now skeptical toward the kind of claims I made in *Literature Against Itself* for value-free neutrality, a concept which seems defensible only in an abstract realm divorced from any context. I started to become skeptical when critics on the Right invoked my defense of value-free neutrality in order to debunk post-structuralist theory—a good example of non-neutrality posing as neutrality. "Two plus two equals four" may be a value-free proposition (in that it is consistent with different and conflicting value-systems), but once it is used in social practice (as it necessarily is) it acquires a performative function that is not value-free—as when one says, "The truth of that is as clear as 2 + 2 = 4."

Along the same lines, I now think that to say that concepts are always ideological is not, as you put it, to attack "the very possibility of political discourse," again unless you wrongly assume that the fact that a concept functions ideologically compromises its truth or validity. Statements like "X percentage of Y group is on welfare" function ideologically in pernicious or progressive ways without necessarily being untrue.

It is true that some theorists write as if the ideological (or discursively constituted) nature of concepts compromises the possibility of their truth, and this reasoning does entail a self-defeating relativism. But I now think that the predominant effect of these recent arguments—certainly the most interesting tendency—is not relativism but social constructionism. In *Literature Against Itself*, most of which was written in the early and mid-70s, I was too quick to conflate post-structuralism with 1960s counter-cultural irrationalism. It now seems to me a reductive overstatement to talk, as I did and you do, of "the humanities" having "so resolutely, dogmatically banished" objectivity from their utopia as inherently authoritarian. It's just not that simple.

Objectivity has not been "banished" so much as "problematized," "contextualized," treated as a mode of thought that has been historically and socially constructed with profoundly different consequences for different social groups. To historicize, politicize, or contextualize any form of culture is certainly to "relativize" it in the sense of pointing out that how we describe that form of culture is necessarily *relative* to the contexts in which it operates. But this is not relativism if by that word one means a skeptical know-nothingism. The important contributions to knowledge that have been made and inspired by thinkers like Derrida and Foucault should be sufficient to explode the charge that these thinkers are promoting mere relativism.

But then, I suspect that the real fear underlying the charge is not that these thinkers don't believe in truth but that they may be telling the truth. In this respect, it is Bloom and his friends who are the know-nothings trying to prevent troubling questions from being asked.

You are right to stress that "objectivity is not 'inherently' *anything*," that is, that it has no one *specific* political valence outside the variable contexts in which the concept functions. This point now seems to me the most useful (and still pertinent) part of the argument of *Literature Against Itself*, that we should not be so confident that we know which theories and critical methods are "oppositional" or "complicitous" without a more contextual analysis of how they function in specific social situations such as that of consumer capitalism. What I failed to see was the extent to which this very point was being made by deconstructionists and other post-structuralists theorists of indeterminacy.

The much-maligned theory that meanings are indeterminate, undecidable, or problematic is in fact a way of making the very point you make about the limited specificity of ideological classifications—that no text or meaning has its political effect in itself, apart from overdetermined contexts. Derrida makes this point very clearly in the Afterword to the Northwestern University Press edition of *Limited Inc.*, which I recently edited. (Working with Derrida on *Limited Inc.*, by the way, convinced me that my understanding of deconstruction had been sloppy and inadequate.) The point that we can't move *a priori* from "X is political" to "X has the following political effects, subversive or repressive, or whatever" is made over and over by post-structuralists, including cultural materialists like Jonathan Dollimore and Alan Sinfield, for example (see the collection they edited, *Political Shakespeare*), and pragmatists like Stanley Fish and Walter Benn Michaels (see Fish's recent *Doing What Comes Naturally*).

But what about what I in 1979 rather portentously called "the triviality of a 'freedom' without content or direction"? I guess that freedom doesn't any longer seem so "trivial" to me now that Bloom and his cronies are so eager to prescribe what its "content and direction" will be.

Contributors

Susan Bourgeois has a Ph.D. in English from Miami University with a speciality in eighteenth-century British literature. She teaches Literature by Women at the University of Missouri at Kansas City and is Coordinator of Academic Support Services at Penn Valley Community College. She has written a study of sensibility in eighteenth-century novels, *Nervous Juyces and the Feeling Heart*, and is resuming work on a study of the critical principles of Margaret Anderson and *The Little Review*.

William K. Buckley is Associate Professor of English and Director of Freshman Writing in the English Department at Indiana University, Northwest.

Frank Caucci was educated in Québec, Ontario (B.A. Spanish; M.A. Comparative Literature—Carleton University), and France (Doctorate, Comparative Literature—University of Paris). He has taught French and Comparative Literature at McGill (Montréal) and Acadia (Nova Scotia) Universities. He has been teaching French and Canadian Studies at Indiana University Northwest since 1986. He has published articles on 19th and 20th century French, European, and Canadian authors, particularly in the area of influence and reception.

Lorraine Clark received her B.A. and M.A. from the University of Toronto, and her Ph.D. from the University of Virginia. She has taught English literature at the University of British Columbia, the University of Virginia, Mount Holyoke College, and is currently an assistant professor at Trent University in Peterborough, Ontario, Canada. Her book *Blake, Kierkegaard, and the Spectre of Dialectic* is forthcoming from Cambridge University Press in fall 1991.

Gerald Graff is the author of *Literature Against Itself* (1979) and *Progressive Literature: An Institutional History* (1987). He has taught since 1966 at Northwestern University and in 1991 will become George M. Pullman Professor of English and Education at the University of Chicago.

Bonnie Hain is an Assistant Professor of English at Southeastern Louisiana University in Hammond, Louisiana. Her teaching and research efforts are focused primarily on rhetoric, literary theory, and 18th century studies.

Kenneth Hovey attended tiny utopian Deep Springs College in 1962-1965, then transferred to Cornell University where he lived at Telluride House and graduated in 1967. He received his doctorate in English at the University of Virginia in 1982 and is currently associate professor at the University of Texas at San Antonio. He has published chiefly on seventeenth-century British and antebellum American literature in such journals as *Renaissance Quarterly, American Quarterly, Studies in Philology,* and *PMLA*, and in various anthologies, including the canon-revising *Heath Anthology of American Literature*.

164

Margaret C. Jones is an assistant professor at Central Washington State University. She has also taught at the Polytechnic University, New York, at Goucher College, and at the University of Alexandria, Egypt. Her articles and short fiction have appeared in the *Contemporary Review*, the *Minnesota Review*, and the *Christian Science Monitor*. Her book *Prophets in Babylon*, a study of California novelists in the 1930s, will be published in August 1992 by the Peter Lang Press. Jones is currently completing a book on women contributors to *The Masses* (provisionally titled "Heretics and Hellraisers.")

Christopher Lasch teaches history at the University of Rochester. His most recent book is *The True and Only Heaven: Progress and its Critics*.

Patricia Lorimer Lundberg is Assistant Professor of English at Indiana University Northwest, teaches British Literature and writing. Her publications include articles on feminism and Bakhtin's dialogics in *Reader: Essays in Reader-Oriented Theory, Criticism, and Pedagogy*, on feminized dialogics in Charlotte Bronte's novels in *Journal of Narrative Technique*, on *Middlemarch* in *Studies in the Novel*, on *Troilus and Criseyde* in *Illinois Medieval Association Proceedings*, on *Beowulf* in *Ball State University Forum*, and on Mary St. Leger Kingsley Harrison ("Lucas Malet") in *British Women Writers' Critical Reference Guide*. She is writing books on Gendered Reading Communities and Lucas Malet, the Lost Kingsley.

John Peacock teaches literature and philosophy at the Maryland Institute College of Art in Baltimore and at the Corcoran School of Art in Washington, D.C. A past Mellon and Fulbright fellow, he has published essays on film, photography, literature and culture in a number of magazines and has contributed poetry and short fiction to a small press anthology, *Fourteen by Four*, ed. Ann Fessler (Baltimore: Dophin Street Press, 1989).

Mark W. Roche received a BA in the History of Ideas from Williams College in 1978, an MA in Philosophy from the University of Tübingen in 1980, and a PhD in German Literature from Princeton University in 1984. The author of *Gottfried Benn's Static Poetry: Aesthetic and Intellectual—Historical Interpretations* (1991) and *Dynamic Stillness: Philosophical Conceptions of Ruhe in Schiller, Hölderlin, Büchner, and Heine* (1987), he has also published on Plato, Lessing, Büchner, Nietzsche, Schnitzler, Heinrich Mann, Thomas Mann, Broch, Hitchcock, transcendental pragmatics, and literature pedagogy. He is currently Chair of the Department of German at Ohio State University.

John K. Roth is the Pitzer Professor of Philosophy at Claremont McKenna College, where he has taught since 1966. His most recent books include *American Ground, The Questions of Philosophy, Ethics*, and *Memory Offended*. In 1988 Roth was named National Professor of the Year by the Council for Advancement and Support of Education and the Carnegie Foundation for the Advancement of Teaching.

James Seaton is Professor of English at Michigan State University. He has discussed *The Closing of the American Mind* in essays such as "Cultural Conservatism, Political Radicalism," *Journal of American Culture* 12:3 (Fall, 1989) and "The Reopening of the American Mind," *South Carolina Review* 22:2 (Spring, 1990). The author of *A Reading of Vergil's Georgics*, he is completing a book entitled *Cultural Conservatism, Political Radicalism*.

Peter Siedlecki who received his Ph.D. from SUNY Buffalo, is professor of English at Daemen College in Amherst, NY, where he has taught since 1965. He has also taught in the Attica State Correctional Facility since 1975 and has held Fulbright Senior Lectureships in Poland (1982-84) and in the German Democratic Republic (1988-89). His poetry has been published in numerous little magazines, and articles on Melville, Hawthorne, John Fiske, and the Poetry of Gerald Stern have appeared in Literary Journals.

Milton R. Stern is Dean Emeritus of University Extension at the University of California at Berkeley. He was Dean from 1971, and before that had been an administrator and associate professor of English and education at New York University and the University of Michigan. He is presently a Visiting Fellow at the Institute for Governmental Studies at Berkeley and Faculty Associate at the Center for Studies in Higher Education. In 1989 he was a Visiting Fellow at Rewley House, Oxford. He has lectured at Oxford, Edinburgh, and many other British universities. Dean Stern began his teaching career in France. He is *Chevalier dans l'Ordre des Palmes Académiques*, and holds an L.H.D. (honorary) from the Johns Hopkins University.

William Thickstun received his BA from Middlebury College, his MA and PhD in English from Cornell University. He has taught at Cornell, Mount Holyoke and Hamilton, and is the author of *Visionary Closure in the Modern Novel* (New York: St. Martin's, 1988). From 1986 to the present he has worked part-time in database consulting, programming and training with Abend Associates, Inc. His essay on Allan Bloom is part of a continuing project on literary theory and liberal education, one which has been fostered by the juxtaposition of simultaneous careers in academia, business and parenthood. He lives in Clinton, New York, with his wife Margaret and son John.

Daniel Zins is an Associate Professor in the Liberal Arts Department of the Atlanta College of Art. He is working on a book, *Exploding the Canon: Rethinking the English Department in an Age of Mass Death.*